How the Good News came to Reading

The Story of Christianity in Our Town

How the Good News came to Reading

The Story of Christianity in Our Town

John Dearing

Also by the author:
The Church that would not Die
Some Hymn Writers connected with Reading
Beautiful the Landscape
In Grateful Memory
Sent from Reading
(As Editor) *The Reading Book of Days*

Published by Sherman Press
27, Sherman Road, Reading RG1 2PJ
email: john@jbdearing.co.uk

ISBN 978-1-7399388-1-9

Copyright: © John Dearing, 2025

.

Contents

	Author's Note	vii
1	The Story up to the Norman Conquest	1
2	The Founding of Reading Abbey	9
3	Reading's Ancient Parish Churches – St Mary, St Laurence and St Giles	27
4	The Greyfriars in Reading	35
5	The End of the Middle Ages	43
6	Reading and the Reformation	51
7	William Laud and the Civil War period	67
8	Stirrings of Dissent	77
9	Restoration to Revival	91
10	Reading's Great Awakening	99
11	William Talbot and Jonathan Britain	115
12	John Wesley in Reading	127
13	Charles Simeon and the Great Societies	145
14	Education, Education, Education	159
15	The Roman Catholic Revival	171
16	A Tale of Two Chapels – and a Church	179
17	Religion in Reading 1851	193
18	Dissent post-1800	205
19	Reading's Second Coming	221
20	Bishops for Reading	231
21	Building for an Expanding Town – the Case of St Luke's	251
22	The Twentieth Century and After	263
Appendix One	Bishops with Jurisdiction over Reading	273
Appendix Two	Dissenting Places of Worship Registered within Reading 1728-1849	281

Appendix Three	Provision of Church Services in Reading in the late 19th Century	283

Bibliography	289
Index	297

List of illustrations

4th century Baptismal tank from Caversham	3
Leominster Priory in Herefordshire	14
The Abbey Hospitium	21
Norman Font in St Peter's, Caversham	32
Cartoon of Memorial to John Eynon	49
21st century Reading Friends in traditional Quaker costume	87
Title-page of John Cennick's Sermon	102
Memorial tablet to William Bromley Cadogan	113
John Wesley, founder of Methodism	138
Charles Simeon, born in Reading	144
Statue of Dr Richard Valpy	158
James Sherman, Minister of Castle Street Chapel	182
Caversham Hill Chapel	183
Holy Trinity, the former proprietary chapel	188
The restored Greyfriars church	189
Gravestone of Seymour Henry Soole	191
Broad Street Chapel, 19th Century	210
George Ibberson Tubbs	240
St Luke's Church, Erleigh Road	257
Interior of St Agnes, Silver Street	262
John Page, Greyfriars, 1947-68	268

Author's Note

This book is based on a series of articles that appeared in the Newsletter of St Mary's, Castle Street, Reading, between January 2011 and December 2012. At about the time that the series was completed, I was informed that an occasional attender at the chapel, a Roman Catholic named John and/ or William Kelly, had suggested it would make a good book.

The thought took root in my brain cells but I was not able to do very much towards realising the thought until I had completed the book that I was then writing, entitled *Sent from Reading*, covering just one aspect of the town's Christian history in some depth. On finishing that work, I felt that there might indeed be a place for a more general volume chronicling the progress of Christendom in the place I have made my home for the last 40 plus years. And this is it, thanks in many ways to the now late John William.

Thanks are also due to Mr Malcolm Summers for reading the manuscript and making a number of useful suggestions, not least enlightening me as to the correct conversion factor from perches to metres! Also for technical assistance.

I have expanded the original version considerably, including the incorporation of older material that was relevant to the theme and new material that had come to my attention, mainly through the excellent publications of the Berkshire Record Society. In addition, it should be noted that the story was originally written for the edification of a particular species of Christians, Anglicans faithful to the Reformed Catholic formularies of the Church of England. I am myself a convinced Evangelical Anglican and, since no historian, especially a rank amateur such as myself, can be wholly impartial, I am sure this point of view will be apparent to the reader. I have, however, also endeavoured to give fair coverage of other forms of Christianity across a broad spectrum from Roman Catholicism to the more exotic versions of Protestantism that followed after the Reformation. Having been brought up as an Anglo-Catholic with parents educated respectively at a Roman Catholic convent and a Methodist Boarding-School who in later life came to fullness of faith at a Baptist Church, I think I can claim a certain breadth of religious experience!

And there, so to speak, I rest my case.

1 The Story up to the Norman Conquest

The origins of Reading itself are a little obscure and so it is scarcely surprising that the same must be said of the gospel in Reading. We need, in the first instance, to ask what we mean by Reading - the small town between the Thames and the Kennet that existed in the Middle Ages, or the present borough that has taken in Caversham, Emmer Green, Tilehurst and parts of Earley, or the even wider conurbation that includes such outlying areas as Woodley, Lower Earley, Purley and Shinfield. As this is intended as an easily readable narrative rather than a strictly scholarly investigation (not that the two are necessarily incompatible) it is likely that it will be seen to vary in its geographical scope. This perhaps justifies the author in starting his story well outside the current boundaries!

In Roman times, the town of Calleva Atrebatum (later known as Silchester), near what is now the Hampshire/Berkshire border and nine miles to the south-west of Reading, was the major centre of population in this region. Possible evidence of Christianity has been found at Silchester, at one time dated to the fourth century. First discovered in 1892 and re-excavated in 1961, the remains of a church-shaped building are located in Insula IV southeast of the forum. The building comprises a nave, aisles, embryonic transepts, an apse and a vestibule, all of which suggest a church. However, the latest scholarly opinion, as outlined by Professor Mike Fulford, dates the building to the third rather than the fourth century, that is before the adoption of Christianity as the religion of the Roman Empire in 313. This does not necessarily rule out its being of Christian origin but the jury, as they say, is still out, and perhaps likely to stay out.

Such scattered settlements as existed in and around the later town of Reading were in all likelihood administered from Silchester. Even more to the point perhaps, gravel-extractions at Deans Farm beside the Thames in Lower Caversham in 1988 revealed in the base of a Roman well the existence of a lead vessel, decorated with the Christian *Chi-Rho* (XP) symbol. This has been identified as part of a portable Roman baptismal font, and dated to 360. The font, referred to technically as a 'liturgical tank,' is on display in Reading Museum, where it is classified as 'Museum object number REDMG: 1988.41.1.' It is regarded as the earliest firm piece of evidence for Christianity in the middle Thames Valley. As described on the museum's website, the find consisted of a 'well base… formed of four stout timbers and… a group of Roman objects from the 4th century AD, including broken pottery, glass, horse trappings, a scythe, an iron spearhead, broken tiles, two wooden buckets and a large piece of crumpled lead.'

These suggested the existence of a Roman villa in the locality. 'On closer examination the crumpled lead panel was found to be the side of an early Christian font' comprising 'two strips of lead welded together to form the side of a circular tank, originally fixed to a now missing circular base.' The sides each contained four rectangular panels with a saltire cross and, in addition, one of the panels contained the 'Chi-Rho' symbol, representing Christ and familiar to visitors to the catacombs of Rome.

4th century Baptismal tank from Caversham.
Copyright Reading Museum (Reading Borough Council).
All rights reserved.

According to Luke Over, the tank is one of 16 that have been found in Britain, six of which are decorated with Christian symbols such as the Chi-Rho. Over also surmises that the Caversham tank might have been dismantled and thrust down the well in 361 when the Emperor Julian the Apostate (361-3), nephew of the first professing Christian emperor, Constantine, briefly restored the old pagan religion.

At that time the Thames Valley was part of the province of Roman Britain called Britannia Prima centred on Corinium (Cirencester) to the west and a presbyter[1] from Corinium is believed to have participated at the Council of

---

[1] Derived from the Greek *presbuteros*, this word denotes 'elder' rather than the other English word also derived from the Greek, 'priest.' The confusion between the Old Testament style sacrificing priest (Greek, *hieros*) and the elder who presides at the Lord's Table has been the cause of much of the controversy between Roman Catholicism and Protestantism.

Arles in 314 AD, effectively representing Thames Valley Christians. This Council, although not one of the universally recognised 'ecumenical' councils, was summoned by Constantine shortly after his conversion and is considered important as condemning the Donatist[2] heresy[3] and pronouncing on such matters as the date of Easter, non-residence of clergy and condemnation of gladiatorial combats.

By this time the Roman Empire was beginning to crumble at least in the west and Constantine moved his seat of government to Byzantium (Constantinople) in 330. The last Roman legions left Britain in 410 AD although Roman influence remained and historians differ considerably in their interpretation of the records of the next two centuries during which, on the traditional view, the Romano-British and the Anglo-Saxons vied for mastery in what is now England with the latter finally prevailing.

The traditional view requires the re-conversion of the country to Christianity but in reality it seems likely that

---

[2] Donatists originated in North Africa and taught among other things that sinless perfection was necessary, in particular in Christian priests, without which they could not effectually administer the sacraments.

[3] Heresy is perhaps a somewhat overworked word and can sometimes be misused for comparatively minor infringements of doctrine. It is most appropriately employed in relation to those sects that depart from the teachings of the three 'catholic' creeds – Apostles', Nicene and Athanasian (or *Quicunque Vult*) – that set out the teaching of the church throughout the ages on the doctrines of the Trinity (Father, Son and Holy Spirit) and the Incarnation and dual nature (God and Man) of the Lord Jesus Christ.

pockets of Romano-British civilization continued and with them the Christian faith. As regards our own region, the next date we can be reasonably certain of is 634[4] when one Birinus, possibly a Frank, was sent by Pope Honorius the First (628-35), in the words of Bede, to 'sow the seed of the holy faith in the inner parts of the dominions of the English, where no other teachers had been before him.' His original sights had been set on neighbouring Mercia, where the warlike pagan king, Penda, held sway but Birinus stayed in Wessex and became in effect the apostle of the Thames Valley. He established his seat at Dorchester-on-Thames – some 17 miles from Reading - and now the seat of one of the area (suffragan) bishops within the Oxford Diocese.

The somewhat sparse accounts of his ministry have him landing at either Portchester or Southampton and passing through Silchester on his route northward, in which case we may assume that he also passed near the site of Reading. One recent historian of the period, Martin Henig, argues that Birinus may have been a Romano-Briton and that he was given his seat at Dorchester because there was already a pre-Saxon Christian community there. Traditionally, however, once more according to Bede, when 'he first entered the nation of the Gewissae' [West Saxons] he found 'all there most confirmed pagans' and 'thought it better to preach the word of God there, than to proceed further to seek for others to preach to.' In 1963, a church dedicated to St Birinus was opened in Calcot, just outside Reading's present boundaries, although the church

---

[4] The conversion of Anglo-Saxon England traditionally begins with the mission of Augustine to Kent in 597 but thereafter progress westwards and northwards was slow.

building was recycled to non-Anglican use early in the 21st Century.[5]

As the apostle of Wessex, Birinus has been associated with the foundation of many churches in the region, including St Mary's in Reading. This, however, is considered to be very unlikely. There seems no reason, though, to doubt that St Mary's is in terms of its origins, if not its present fabric, the oldest church in the borough. Another, more credible, tradition places its foundation in 979, when Elfrida (or Aelfthryth), widow of King Edgar the Peaceful and mother of the reigning monarch, Ethelred II (the *Unrede*, meaning ill-advised), is said to have founded a nunnery in Reading as penance for her part in the murder of her stepson, King Edward the Martyr, at Corfe Castle.[6] No traces of this structure have, however, been found and if it did exist it is possible that it was destroyed by the marauding Danes when they hit Reading in 1006. If the story is true[7] there would be some incongruity in the Queen's actions for Elfrida is believed to have been in league with a group of powerful ealdormen, headed by Aelfhere of Mercia, who had been opposed to Edgar's policy of giving land away to the monasteries. They feared that Edward would continue it,

---

[5] The parish is now known as Parish of Tilehurst: St Catherine and Calcot: St Birinus. The former parish church of St Birinus is now used by The Gate (formerly Reading Community Church) and known as 'The Gate: Empress Road'.

[6] A play entitled *The Penance of Elfrida* by a writer from Corfe is stated in Alan Wykes' documentary film *All Change Reading* to have been performed in commemoration of the thousandth anniversary of these events in 1979.

[7] It is lent some credibility by the discovery of silver coins dated to the ninth century in the churchyard.

whereas it was felt that the younger and more pliable Ethelred might be persuaded to their way of thinking.[8]

Whatever may be the truth of the connections between St Mary's and Birinus and/ or Elfrida, Dr Cecil Slade considers that, although the familiar English parochial structure in Berkshire was very slow to develop, encompassing the three centuries from 634, it is 'probable that the area of Reading had one of the mother churches, for it was about the right size and was possibly already held by the king.' It is considered likely that this mother church or 'minster'[9] covered a wide area encompassing Tilehurst, Purley, Pangbourne and Theale. It is interesting to note that in the current 'post-Christian' phase of the church's history, the wheel is almost turning full circle, as the autonomous parish is replaced by combined benefices, team ministries and minster-style arrangements.

The Danes finally achieved their ambition of conquering England in 1016 when Canute became King. Dr Slade relates another legend about Reading dating from this period; since it is supposed to illustrate the people of Reading's lack of piety, it may well contain a grain of truth!

---

[8] Historians seem to differ as regards the extent of Elfrida's involvement in the plot. Frank Stenton, Professor of History at Reading, in *Anglo-Saxon England,* for instance, is inclined to discount it altogether. All seem to agree, however, that Edward was a rather unpleasant teenager, given to violent tantrums, hardly the stuff of the sainthood later conferred upon him!

[9] Originally the minster church was associated with a monastic foundation – indeed the very word is supposed to be a corruption of the Latin *monasterium.* In the case of Reading, this might lend some credibility to the tradition of a convent founded in the late 10th century. See also Gerald Bray, *History of Christianity in Britain and Ireland*, Apollos, 2021.

'The story goes that Tovi [or Tofig, Canute's standard-bearer] had acquired the holy cross which had been found some years before at Montacute in Somerset, and wanted to found a religious house worthy of it. All manner of sites were suggested, but the efforts of neither oxen nor men could move the cart which was carrying the cross. Among the sites proposed was his favoured domicile of Reading, and he tearfully implored Christ to let that be the place, promising to give the vill and all around to those serving the holy cross. But it was no good, and it was not until the name of Waltham was mentioned[10] that cart and oxen set off at speed. So the future great abbey of Waltham Holy Cross was founded and Reading was not to have an abbey for nearly another hundred years.' That event came about indirectly as a result of the next conquest of England in 1066 by the Normans.

The reader with an eye looking forward to later events might notice a certain aptness in the story of the oxen bolting away from Reading. Seven hundred or more years later, as recounted in Chapter 12, an itinerant evangelist would compare the people of the town to a herd of stupid oxen!

---

[10] Since it seems that Tofig was well-acquainted with Waltham, as the owner of a hunting lodge there, he may well have mentioned it himself!

2   The Founding of Reading Abbey

It was certainly true when I was at school and I am sure it is so for many readers of this book: the best known date in English history is 1066, the year of the Battle of Senlac (i.e. Hastings) and the start of the Norman Conquest. There is even visible evidence of it in Reading, for the Museum houses a splendid Victorian copy of the Bayeux Tapestry celebrating the exploits of William the Conqueror. However, Norman influence did not begin with William's victory. Edward the Confessor (1042-66), son of Ethelred II, had a Norman mother, Emma, and had lived in exile in Normandy for 25 years (1015-40). His decision to rebuild the abbey church at Westminster 'on a grand scale' may well have been influenced by what he saw in Northern France. Edward also probably began the process of 'putting Reading on the map' by granting borough status to what had hitherto been little more than a village. Even so at the time of the Conquest it was still a fairly insignificant town, compared with Wallingford or Abingdon, with only a few hundred inhabitants. It was a Norman king and another abbey that advanced Reading's cause further.

William I's fourth son, Henry I ruled from 1100 to 1135 and for the first 20 years of his long reign showed no exceptional signs of piety. However, the death by drowning of his only son, William, in the disaster of the 'White Ship' in November 1120 distressed him greatly and led him to brood upon the condition of his soul. The loss of the royal heir by drowning, with the disappearance of his mortal remains, was seen as a sign of God's judgement; such chroniclers as Henry of Huntingdon were not slow to locate the root cause of that judgement in the dissolute lifestyle of the young prince and his companions. By this time, too, the truths of the gospel had been largely mislaid by the church in England as elsewhere and, in Cecil Slade's words,[11] 'founding and endowing of abbeys was a widespread practice at this time, for not only was it an act of piety but founder's rights included solemn burial there, and prayers and masses[12] for the founder's soul.'

Reading was possibly chosen because the King owned the land and it was also conveniently close to the royal castles at London and Windsor. From the viewpoint of the builders the site could not have been better situated: beside the River Kennet, where a new wharf was probably constructed for unloading the Caen stone and other materials used in the construction of the abbey. For the contemporary chronicler, William of Malmesbury, however, the King chose the location with the traveller in mind: [he] 'built this monastery between the rivers Kennet and Thames, in a spot calculated for the reception of almost all who might have occasion to travel to the more populous cities of England.'[13]

Reading Abbey was designed to accommodate at least 100 monks of the Cluniac Order, which observed a reformed version of the Benedictine Rule, originally enacted by St Benedict in the sixth century. The Cluniacs took their name from the mother house at Cluny in

---

[11] In *The Town of Reading and its Abbey*.

[12] According to classic Protestant teaching salvation is dependent on justifying faith, granted by divine grace prior to death; prayers for the dead are, therefore, futile.

[13] Quoted by Hurry from the *Gesta Regum Anglorum*, first published in 1125.

Burgundy, which had been established in 910. The first Cluniac house in England was a priory, founded at Lewes around 1080 and the first monks to arrive in Reading on 18th June 1121 came from there and also from the mother house with Peter from Cluny serving as Prior. This event is described thus in the Annals of Reading Abbey:

> Peter the prior, and seven brethren with him were sent to England by Abbot Pons of Cluny at the request of King Henry and, joined by several brethren from the monastery of St. Pancras,[14] began the observance of the Cluniac order in the monastery newly founded by the king on the 14th kalend of July [i.e., 18th June].[15]

Of the distinctive ethos of Cluniac monasticism, Lionel Butler and Chris Given-Wilson write in *Mediaeval Monasteries of Great Britain*: '[it] was distinguished by its overriding emphasis on the liturgy. The time given to the singing of the Office, the number of daily psalms and prayers, the elaborate ceremonies and the intercessions and masses and public almsgivings by the monks were increased far beyond what was usual elsewhere... Cluny gave up all educational, intellectual and artistic pursuits for the sake of its liturgy.' A less complimentary description of life at Cluny is given by Christopher Tyerman: 'a sort of

---

[14] The Lewes priory was dedicated to St Pancras of Rome, a fourth century boy-martyr.

[15] In the Roman system of time-keeping, the Kalends are the first day of each month and so the 14th kalend here signifies a period two weeks before the commencement of July.

eternal choir practice.'[16] Today Cluny is perhaps best known to 'the man in the pew' for the familiar hymns derived from John Mason Neale's translation of a long satirical poem of 3,000 lines, *De Contemptu Mundi*, by Bernard de Cluny, who was a monk there in the mid-12th century; these include 'Jerusalem the Golden' and 'Brief life is here our portion'.

It is believed that Henry I was especially drawn to the grandeur and ceremony of the worship at Cluny and may also have been influenced by the fact that his long-widowed sister, Adela, Countess of Blois, had become a Cluniac nun the previous year.[17] William of Malmesbury was clearly impressed by the spirituality and lifestyle of the monks of Reading Abbey, for the passage quoted above continues: [there] 'he placed monks of the Cluniac Order, who are at this day a noble pattern of holiness, and an example of unwearied and delightful hospitality.'

The priories came under the direct jurisdiction of the mother house but within a few years Reading, perhaps because of its sheer size[18] and royal influence, obtained its independence as an abbey in its own right. For many years

---

[16] In *Who's Who in Early Mediaeval England* in relation to St Anselm's decision to join the mainstream Benedictine Abbey of Bec rather than Cluny.

[17] Henry's devotion to Cluny backfired in 1127 when he imposed a Cluniac abbot on the abbey of Peterborough against the wishes of the monks there. The appointment was unsuccessful and the King's appointee, Henry of Poitou, returned to France, effectively driven out by the monks.

[18] At 470 ft in length (143 metres), Reading's abbey church was only 50 ft (15 metres) shorter than Cluny, then said to be the longest Christian church in existence. It was eventually surpassed by St Peter's, Rome.

it was in fact the only Cluniac abbey in England, the rest being priories, and eventually it became affiliated to the main Benedictine Order. Abbots from the first two centuries are listed below:

Hugh de Boves, of Amiens	1123–1130
Anscher	1130–1135
Edward	1136–1154
Reginald	1154–1158
Roger	1158–1165
William I	1165–1173
Joseph	1173–1186
Hugh II of Anjou	1186–1199
Elias	1199–1213
Simon	1213–1226
Adam of Lathbury	1226–1238
Richard I of Chichester[19]	1238–1262
Richard II of Reading alias Banaster	1262–1269
Robert of Burgate	1269–1290

In 1123 Reading Abbey received not only its independence but its own dependency when the manor of Leominster in Herefordshire was granted to it. A former monastic foundation at Leominster which had fallen into disuse was then revived as a daughter-priory to Reading and the two institutions remained closely allied up until their dissolution under Henry VIII. There was also a coincidental resemblance between the 'pre-history' of the two sites, for, as allegedly at Reading, the pre-Conquest

---

[19] Not to be confused with St. Richard de Wych, Bishop of Chichester from 1244 to 1253 and sometimes referred to as Richard of Chichester.

convent[20] had been a nunnery and there were also links with Edward the Martyr and his stepmother. In other respects the sites are complementary for, whereas at Reading substantial ruins of the domestic buildings of the Abbey survive but relatively little of the abbey church apart from the South Transept, Leominster Priory's living quarters are largely lost but the priory church survives, including much of the original Norman architecture on a similar ground plan to that of Reading. It is thus well worth a visit to Leominster in order to get an idea of just what we have lost.[21]

Leominster Priory in Herefordshire, a daughter-house to Reading Abbey.

---

[20] Although the term 'convent' is most often used at the present day to refer to a community of nuns it was originally gender-neutral.
[21] This the author did in January 2022.

Henry I endowed the abbey not only with lands but also with an important relic that was to make it a popular place of pilgrimage during the Middle Ages. This was the supposed hand of Saint James the Apostle, the first of the Twelve to die a martyr's death, circa 43 AD, under King Herod Agrippa.[22] It was originally brought to England from Germany in 1126 by the King's daughter, Matilda, following the death of her husband, Henry V, the Holy Roman Emperor, and given to the Abbey but it was removed by the Bishop of Winchester after King Henry's death. The bishop was a Cluniac called Henry of Blois, who just happened to be the brother of King Stephen, Henry's successor and deadly enemy of his rival for the crown, the Empress Matilda. Not surprisingly, therefore, one of the first acts of her son, Henry II (1154-89), on his accession was to restore the hand to the abbey in 1155!

Twenty-eight miracles were ascribed to the hand's powers in a writing of circa 1200, which is included in the late Brian Kemp's 2018-published miscellany of Reading abbey records. These accounts show that the hand benefited not only the inhabitants of Reading and its environs but people from as far afield as Essex, Suffolk and Herefordshire who sought the aid of its miraculous powers. In many cases these powers were transmitted through drinking the 'water of Saint James' in which the reliquary containing the hand had been dipped. Here is one of the shorter of these records, in which, appropriately perhaps, a monk of Reading receives healing for a withered hand:

---

[22] See *Acts of the Apostles*, Chapter 12, verses 1-2.

The hand of a certain monk of Reading named John had withered and had for the most part lost its power of movement. He could neither raise his hand nor keep hold of anything he might grasp. Coming therefore to the remedy which had been tried by many people, he bathed his hand with water of Saint James and immediately, on that very day, his hand acquired its original movement and its habitual agility which he longed for.

Such was the potency ascribed to the hand that King John, who seems to have enjoyed cordial relations with the monks of Reading, if with few other of his subjects, took it with him to Les Andelys on the River Seine in Normandy in 1200 so that the King of France could swear an oath on it to keep the peace; if the reader recalls the story of William the Conqueror requiring Harold to swear allegiance to him[23] as Edward the Confessor's successor, he will know the importance ascribed to such swearing on relics in the Middle Ages. Thus the Annals:

> To Andelys was brought the hand of Saint James with many relics of the saints, on which Philip, King of France, swore an oath solemnly and willingly before the magnates of both kingdoms, promising that he would keep peace with the king of the English all the days of his life, without evil intent.

Alas, it appears that Philip kept his promise no more faithfully than did Harold back in 1066!

---

[23] Chapter Five Scene One according to Reading Museum's useful synopsis of the Bayeux Tapestry.

With post-Reformation eyes we may be inclined to regard the hand as a fake[24] but there is no reason to doubt the sincere, if perhaps misguided, piety which surrounded the cult at this time. Later in the Middle Ages, as the corruption of the church intensified, it was not unknown for relics to be forged by the monasteries as a means of 'feathering their nests.'[25] The hand itself was hidden by the monks in an iron chest at the Dissolution to be rediscovered by workmen in 1796. It eventually found its way into the possession of Saint Peter's RC church, Marlow, where it remains to this day.

It was by no means the only valuable relic held by the Abbey; there was also the alleged skull of St Philip the Apostle.[26] Altogether over 200 relics existed although a list prepared during the Dissolution contained only 23, possibly just the choicest items.

Reading's first fully-fledged abbot, Hugh, was trained at Cluny and served as Prior of Lewes before moving to Reading. Hugh was a noted theologian of the day and during his seven years at the abbey, he worked on his seven books of *Dialogi de Summo Bono*, the contents of which are

---

[24] According to Lindsay Mullaney, herself writing from a Roman Catholic viewpoint (in *Henry I and his Abbey*), radiocarbon dating at Oxford University has suggested that the hand dates from the 10th or 11th century.

[25] The example often cited is that of the 'Holy Blood' of Christ, allegedly kept in a phial at Hailes Abbey in Gloucestershire, which was admitted to be a fake by the Abbot before the Dissolution. Thomas Cromwell's Commissioners declared that it was kept topped up with duck's blood!

[26] That is the Philip who was one of the Twelve Disciples rather than Philip the Deacon, whose ministry in Samaria and Gaza is detailed in Chapter 8 of the *Acts of the Apostles*.

said to cover the attributes of God, the creation, the fall of Satan and of man, free will, the Sacraments, and eternal life. In 1130 he was consecrated Archbishop of Rouen and held that office until his death in 1164. During his archiepiscopate he paid frequent visits to England and continued to dabble in its politics. He also ministered to the dying King Henry I, who famously succumbed to a surfeit of lampreys during a visit to Rouen in 1135. Under the direction of Archbishop Hugh, the King's body was embalmed and brought back to Reading, where it was buried in the abbey church in January 1136. Dr Hurry's account of these events may be quoted:

> His body was embalmed in bulls' hides, and brought to Reading, where the obsequies were celebrated with great pomp in the Abbey Church on January 4, 1136, King Stephen, the Archbishops, Bishops and nobles of the kingdom being present at the funeral.

The Archbishop is said to have reported on the King's death to Pope Innocent II, stating that 'he confessed his sins, beat his breast, and laid aside also all animosities,' receiving the sacraments of Communion and Extreme Unction. His widow, Adeliza, 'gave 100 shillings per annum to maintain a lamp which burnt continually before the royal tomb, on which a splendid [life-sized] effigy was subsequently placed.' At time of writing, there is every hope that, once the intentions of the new owner of Reading Gaol have been clarified, the Royal Founder's final resting-place will be rediscovered.

Anscher (also called Aucherius) had like his predecessor served as Prior of Lewes before moving to Reading; he began an important part of the abbey's work by founding a leper hospital dedicated to St Mary Magdalene in 1134, located on the site of the present Assize Courts. It lasted until 1413 when it was closed 'because no lepers are forthcoming'.

Royal visits continued with Adeliza making a further visitation on the first anniversary of the King's death. In 1140 and 1141 respectively the abbey received King Stephen and his cousin and rival for the throne, the Empress Matilda. Among the rank and file of the monks during these early years was, it is believed, one Robert de Sigello, who was later Lord Chancellor (Keeper of the Great Seal) from 1133-35 and from 1141 till his death ten years later Bishop of London. He received the latter appointment from the Empress during the brief period when she had the upper hand in the Civil War, as recorded by Florence of Worcester (evidently a fan of Matilda):

> Her first care was to take measures for the good of God's holy church, according to the advice of good men. She therefore gave the bishopric of London to a monk of Reading, a venerable man, Robert by name, who accepted it in the presence and by the command of his reverend abbot, Edward.

When the advantage was regained by the King, Robert was captured by the time-serving Geoffrey de Mandeville, and obliged to pay a ransom before he could resume his episcopal duties.

In 1156 Reading saw another royal burial, that of Henry II's eldest son, William, aged three. In 1163 the monks of Reading Abbey tended the wounds of Henry de Essex, after he had been assumed dead following a fight by single combat with Roger de Montfort on Fry's Island in the Thames by Caversham Bridge. Henry recovered and spent the last seven years of his life in Reading as a Benedictine monk. Abbot Roger's rule also saw the abbey church finally consecrated[27] on Sunday 19th April 1164 by the Archbishop of Canterbury, Thomas Becket, in the presence of King Henry II, grandson of the founding monarch. In the words of the Annals: 'Dedication of the church of Reading by St Thomas, archbishop of Canterbury and martyr, on the 13th kalend of May (i.e. 19th April).' The consecration took place at a time when relations between Henry and his Archbishop and former friend were reaching that state of outright hostility that would eventually lead to Becket's murder in 1170.

Roger's successor, William I, also called the Templar, later became Archbishop of Bordeaux from 1173 to 1187. William also has the unusual distinction of appearing in a historical novel, *Devil's Brood* (2008), by Sharon Kay Penman, set against the conflict between Henry II, his wife Eleanor of Aquitaine, and their four sons.

Hugh of Anjou, another former Prior of Lewes, is best known for building the hospitium (guest house) for visitors to the Abbey. This is one of the few portions of the abbey to survive at least in part, albeit from a rebuilding in 1438.[28]

Originally it could house 400 guests. Hugh was described as a 'very religious man of very upright life.' At Reading he 'ruled the monastery with vigour..., in many

---

[27] Rather curiously the 'timeline' presented to visitors to Reading's 'Abbey Quarter' states that the abbey was 'officially opened' almost as if Becket pulled a cord to reveal all. Surely we have not become such a secular nation that we do not understand what 'consecrated' means?

[28] Not to mention a further drastic 'restoration' in 1892 when it was converted to use by the new University College.

ways enlarged the buildings and expanded the worship and income, and in several ways improved the state of the house.' In 1191 he was granted the right by Pope Clement III to wear the regalia of a leading abbot, comprising episcopal mitre and ring, dalmatic, tunic, gloves and sandals.[29] When he left in 1199 it was to become Hugh V, Abbot of Cluny, up to his death in 1207.

The Abbey Hospitium (or guest house) as it appears today.

---

[29] Thus Durrant and Painter in *Reading Abbey and the Abbey Quarter*. An earlier historian, Leslie Harman, in his *History of Christianity in Reading* (1952) is evidently incorrect in stating that the right to wear a mitre was 'apparently given first' to William de Sutton in 1288. According to Hurry a papal licence was granted in that year but this must have been a renewal of the previous arrangement.

Hugh's successor, Elias the chamberlain,[30] also receives rich praise in the Annals: 'of good memory, a man praiseworthy in all things, a particular lover of the house of God, who acquired [for it] magnificent ornaments…, an assiduous preserver of the peace and religion of the convent and the order.'

The next abbot, Simon, took office on 31st July 1213, only ten days after the death of Elias. The following year, he was entrusted by King John to undertake a mission to France to 'the imprisoned Earl of Salisbury.' This was William Longespee, an illegitimate half-brother of John, who is also described by Christopher Tyerman in his *Who's Who* as 'his gambling and drinking crony.' William had been captured after the battle of Bouvines in July 1214 and imprisoned by Philip II of France. He was later released in an exchange of prisoners but whether Abbot Simon's mission played any part in this process is unknown. The Annals only record the disastrous end to the adventure when the Abbot's 'ship was lost off Wissant' during the return journey 'with a large part of his gear, and six of his household servants, the rest just managing to escape.'

In 1215 Simon was one of 900 abbots from across Christendom who attended the Fourth Lateran Council (or 'universal synod' as the chronicler calls it) 'held in Rome under the presidency of Pope Innocent III.' This was the Council which among many other matters defined the

---

[30] 'The chamberlain was responsible for clothing the members of the abbey and providing tools used for every-day tasks. Shoes, capes and bedding were all supplied and their maintenance overseen by the chamberlain.'
(www.timeref.com/life/abbey4.htm)

doctrine of transubstantiation[31] in relation to the nature of the Eucharist. This teaching, as further refined by Thomas Aquinas and others, was set to become a major battleground in the Reformation and remains to this day one of the principal areas of disagreement between Roman Catholicism and Reformed Christianity. Simon's attendance at the Council resulted in his absence from the Abbey for over 16 weeks.

Among the later abbots listed above, Simon's successor, Adam of Lathbury, is notable for having previously served as Prior of Leominster; it was during his time that the Greyfriars arrived in Reading, as related in Chapter Four. Richard II was one of 25 leading abbots who were summoned to the first representative parliament held in 1265; his successor, Robert of Burgate, proved himself a less than able administrator, allowing the abbey to fall into serious debt, resulting eventually in his removal from office in 1290. He also controversially passed to the control of the Bishop of St Andrews a cell of the abbey that had been founded in 1153 on the Isle of May in the Firth of Forth for nine monks from Reading. While the transfer of control might seem a tidy and logical step, it apparently took place without the consent of the monks!

---

[31] According to this doctrine the elements of bread and wine are changed by the priestly act of consecration into the body and blood of Our Lord Jesus Christ, while retaining the appearance (accidents) of bread and wine. Luther held to a modification of this doctrine known as 'consubstantiation' but most other reformers taught that the elements were purely symbols of the body and blood of Christ and that the eucharist was essentially a memorial meal. In some cases they added a spiritual presence in the heart of the true believer.

A number of national and international events involving the church took place in Reading in the period between 1150 and 1300, mostly because of the town's royal connections and the consequent prestige of its abbey:

- In 1184, the abbey was used for a council of bishops and monks to elect a new Archbishop of Canterbury, the King being present. This resulted in the choice of Baldwin of Exeter, Bishop of Worcester, who served as primate for six years.
- The following year, Heraclius, the Patriarch of Jerusalem, visited the King in Reading and invited him to accept the kingdom of Jerusalem, an offer that allegedly moved him to tears but ultimately was graciously declined by Henry II. This was at the time that Henry was having trouble with his rebellious sons and would not have wanted to risk the security of his existing realms.
- There were two meetings in connection with the travails of King John, first in October 1206 when the Papal Legate, John of Florence, attempted to effect a reconciliation between the King and various exiled bishops.
- Then in 1213 the King met with Archbishop Stephen Langton and a later Legate, Nicholas of Tusculum, to discuss compensation to the clergy for their losses during the recent interdict. This measure, involving the excommunication of the entire population, had been imposed on England in 1208 on account of John's interference (as the Pope saw it) in the appointment of the new Archbishop.
- In 1235, the consecration of Robert Grosseteste ('Bighead') as Bishop of Lincoln and Peter or Hywel

the Friar as Bishop of St Asaph took place at Reading. One of the great scholar-bishops of the period, Grosseteste has been described as 'the real founder of the tradition of scientific thought in medieval Oxford, and in some ways, of the modern English intellectual tradition.'[32]

- In 1279, the new Archbishop, John Peckham, 'summoned all the bishops under his jurisdiction' to 'a synod at Reading.' This took place on the feast of St James, 29th July.

Finally, reverting to our theme of the founding of the abbey, it is perhaps not generally known by citizens of Reading that this subject is covered in one of the earliest English novels, *Thomas of Reading*, by Thomas Deloney, writing at the end of the 16th century, and celebrating a wealthy clothmaker named Thomas Cole. Deloney provides a description of King Henry I's visit to Reading with a somewhat fanciful explanation of the genesis of the Abbey (spelling partly modernised):

> And when his Grace came to Reading, he was entertained with great Joy and Triumph: Thomas Cole being the chief Man of Regard in all the Towne, the

---

[32] He can also be seen as one of the earliest precursors of the English Reformation; on one occasion, he memorably stated that 'to follow a pope who rebels against the will of Christ is to separate Christ from his body; and if ever a time should come when all men follow an erring pontiff, then will be the great apostasy. Then will true Christians refuse to obey, and Rome will be the cause of an unprecedented schism.' Pope Innocent IV responded as follows to these truly prophetic words: 'Who is that crazy, foolish and silly old man who has the effrontery to sit in judgement thus upon my doings?'

King honoured his House with his Princely Presence, where during the King's Abode, he and his Son and Nobles were highly feasted.

There the King beheld the great Number of People, that was by that one Man maintained in Work, whose hearty Affection and Love toward his Majesty did well appear, as well by their out-ward Countenances, as their Gifts presented unto him. But of Cole himself the King was so well persuaded, that he committed such Trust in him, and put him in great Authority in the Towne. Furthermore the King said, that for the Love which those People bore him living, that he would lay his Bones among them when he was dead. For I know not, said he, where they may be better bestowed, till the blessed Day of Resurrection, than among these my Friends, which are like to be happy Partakers of the same.

Whereupon his Majesty caused there to be builded a most goodly and famous Abbey: in which he might shew his Devotion to God, by increasing his Service, and leave Example to other his Successors to do the like. Likewise within the Towne he after builded a fair and goodly Castle, in the which he often kept his Court, which was a Place of his chief Residence during his Life, saying to the Clothiers, that seeing he found them such faithful Subjects, he would be their Neighbour, and dwell among them.

3 Reading's Ancient Parish Churches – St Mary, St Laurence and St Giles

In our first chapter we referred to the various legends concerning the foundation of St Mary's Church, in particular its supposed connection with the murder of King Edward the Martyr. Whatever may be the truth behind these stories, it seems pretty certain that the church antedated the Norman Conquest and is the unnamed church mentioned in the Domesday Book of 1086. This states that it had formerly been held by the Abbess Leveva (or Leofgifu) of King Edward (the Confessor) and was now worth three pounds a year to the Abbot of Battle, who along with the church owned 29 dwellings in the town, yielding a total rent of 28 shillings and eight pence (£1.43), as well as extensive agricultural land. Battle Abbey itself had been founded in 1070 on the site of the Battle of Hastings but was still unfinished at the time of Domesday, so that we may reasonably suppose that the income accrued from Reading helped pay for its completion. The Hastings connection remains to this day as Battle is the name of one of the ward divisions of Reading's Borough Council, comprising the area bounded by the Oxford Road, the river and the railway, formerly owned by Battle Abbey. However, St Mary's was transferred to the possession of Reading Abbey, following the latter's foundation.

It seems likely that the original St Mary's church was rebuilt under the Normans and, although the present structure dates from the 16th century and was extensively 'restored' in the 19th, architectural historians are able to detect fragments of doorways and arches dating from around 1200. However, the matter is complicated by the fact that the 1551-3 reconstruction used building material of a similar date rescued from the former Reading Abbey. Tyack and Bradley in their expansion of the original Pevsner guide to Berkshire buildings acknowledge this difficulty, referring to transitional[33] Norman work in the south arcade. This has been identified with a payment recorded for 'pyllers' from the Abbey which, however, 'have the character of ordinary parochial work of c. 1200.' The dedication of the church is, of course, to St Mary the Virgin, mother of Our Lord, one shared currently with over 2,300 others[34] in the Church of England.

Early records of incumbents are as sketchy as the history of the church. William de Lincoln is named in 1173 and Benedictus de Eboraco (York)[35] in 1180. One Gilbert is referred to as Capellanus (curate) in 1190. There is then a long gap until Nicholas de Whiteley in 1307.

Later in the 14th century, in 1371, the church was embellished by a chantry chapel known as the Colley or Colney chapel, the purpose of which well illustrates the prevailing belief in the efficacy of prayers for the dead referred to in Chapter Two: a licence was granted to 'celebrate a mass for the good estate of the king, of William

---

[33] A 12th century phase of architecture in which we can detect the transition from the typical round arches of Norman or Romanesque towards the pointed arches of the Early English phase of Gothic architecture.

[34] This makes the Virgin Mary the most popular dedicatee of CE churches, although in some cases the dedication was shared. Churches dedicated solely to the Blessed Virgin are said to number around 1,500.

[35] I tentatively suggest that Benedict may have been a monk from the abbey of York, also dedicated to St Mary.

Catour, and of Johanna his wife, so long as they shall live, and for their souls after their decease, and for the souls of Thomas de Colney and John de Colney, and the souls of the faithful…every day.'

St Giles appears to have had its origins in the 1100s, probably at first acting as a chapel-of-ease to St Mary's. Parts of the lower tower point to the existence of a Norman church, suggesting a 12th century foundation, although as with St Mary's the present building is mainly of much later date. It is mentioned in a papal charter of 1191, granting a number of churches to Reading Abbey. These included: St Giles itself, St Mary's, although this gift is also mentioned in the Abbey's foundation charter, and nearby churches in Thatcham and Bucklebury, as well as the more far-flung parish of Aston in Hertfordshire.[36] At this time the Chaplain of St Giles is recorded by name as Thomas. The next recorded clergy are around 1240, when there appears to have been a Magister (probably indicating that the Vicar was a Master of the University) named James and a Chaplain named Peter. This would suggest that by this date St Giles had become a parish church in its own right.

There is then a further gap until 1297 when the earliest surviving episcopal registers of Salisbury begin. Thereafter the following are listed up to the end of the 14th century:

---

[36] As with St Mary's, this appears to be the confirmation of a previous arrangement: according to the Victoria County History of Hertfordshire, the manor of Aston (also spelt Estone and Easton) was presented by Henry I in dower to his second wife, Adeliza, upon their marriage in 1121 and later bestowed by her on Reading Abbey when she visited it in 1136 on the first anniversary of her husband's death – see previous chapter.

Michael (1297), Walter de Holme (1326), John Crowe (1329), Peter Leverech (1334), Henry Waterstoke (1385) and John Ymmere (1388).

St Giles was a sixth century French saint in whose life story fact and fiction are somewhat interwoven. It was a popular dedication in the Middle Ages with some 160 churches of that name in England, not to mention the 'cathedral' of the now Presbyterian Church of Scotland.

St Laurence's is probably of a similar age to St Giles but retains more of its original fabric from the mid-12th century, as well as later work from the additions made around 1196 and 1220.[37] During the lifetime of the Abbey it had a close connection with it as 'chapel ante portas' (before the gates). One Richard is referred to as Vicar in 1240 in the same document that records the clergy of St Giles, and there is a substantially complete list from 1299 in the registers of the Salisbury diocese: Hugo de Dreyton (1299), Willielmus de Depeford (1307), John de Wynchedon (1324), Johannes de Longa Sutton (1325), Willielmus de Berton (1332), Willielmus de Appleford (1342), Adam Att Aumerie (1344), Walter de Harewell (1349), Johannes de Northlech, (1349), William (died 1360), Henry Lambyn (1360), Johannes Schippelake (1389), Walter Bartholomew (1397) and Johannes Serne (1397) served the parish up to the year 1400. It is

---

[37] Charles Kerry in his history of St Laurence's, dated 1883, suggests that it replaced a Saxon church with the 'not improbable' dedication to St Matthew, which occupied part of the abbey site and was thus demolished before 1121. This theory is based on there having been a fair on St Matthew's Day during the Middle Ages. Evidence of the existence of this earlier church was strengthened during archaeological excavations at the abbey site undertaken by Dr Cecil Slade in the 1970s.

remarkable that, during the 51 years that the people of St Giles evidently enjoyed the ministrations of Peter Leverech, no fewer than seven clergy served St Laurence's! St Laurence's did enjoy one lengthy incumbency in the 15th century, that of William Goldore who in 1435 exchanged his previous living as Rector of Lasham, Hants, with the recently (1434) appointed Henry Couper, and seems to have stayed at the church till his death in 1468.

St Laurence was a third century Spaniard who was martyred as a deacon in Rome in 258. Like Giles he was a popular object of devotion in these times with 245 church dedications, far outstripping Britain's native martyr, St Alban, on a mere 52!

The expansion of Reading's boundaries between 1887 and 1911 brought two other ancient churches within the borough: St Peter's, Caversham, also a Norman foundation, and St Michael's, Tilehurst, which was founded in 1189 and includes some 14th century work in its fabric; it also boasts a 15th century monumental brass.

St Peter's has a Norman marble font and fragments of Norman work in the fabric, together with more abundant evidence of the 14th and 15th centuries; like most of Reading's other mediaeval churches it underwent drastic restoration in the Victorian era.[38]

Reading's ecclesiastical stock in the Middle Ages also included St Edmund's Chapel, founded in 1204 by one Laurence Burgeys, bailiff of the town, by permission of Abbot Elias. This was located at the western end of what became Friar Street but fell into disuse in the 15th century.

---

[38] Some of this the work of Joseph Morris – see Chapter 19.

Norman font in St Peter's, Caversham

Two other mediaeval places of worship are worthy of notice, Greyfriars, which is covered in the next chapter, and the chapel of St Anne on the Bridge, which has not survived to modern times. This was one of many such bridge chapels that were erected during the Middle Ages for the use of travellers to pray for a safe journey and usually staffed by a priest or hermit who collected a 'donation' from the wayfarers. There are fine surviving examples at Derby and Wakefield, although the latter displays a restoration by George Gilbert Scott, which probably bears as much relation to the original as does his reconstruction of Reading Abbey Gateway! Additionally, it is notable that the Borough Church of Maidenhead, St

Andrew and St Mary Magdalene, also had its origin in such a chapel, though the present building, the fourth, dates only from 1965.[39]

According to extra-biblical tradition St Anne was the mother of the Blessed Virgin Mary. Some sources also indicate the existence (for good measure) of a second chapel dedicated to the Holy Spirit on the Reading side of the river. Although St Anne's was located at the Caversham end of the bridge, it probably owed its existence initially to Reading Abbey. The monks are said to have influenced the construction of the bridge as they required a thoroughfare linking Reading and Oxford. Although some authorities believe the bridge dated from the late 12th century, the earliest reference to the chapel is in May 1231 when Henry III commanded the Sheriff of Oxfordshire to visit it; two months later, perhaps as a result of this visitation, the King ordered an oak from Windsor Forest to be delivered to the Sergeant of Caversham for the construction of a ferry boat, evidently as a back-up to the bridge for 'poor people.'

Further oaks were supplied during the 1240s for the roofing of the chapel, which was described in a deed of 1314 as 'the little chapel on the great bridge.' The profits from the work of the chapel were devoted to the upkeep both of the bridge and of St Laurence's Church, the Abbey's town side church. By 1376 the ownership of the chapel had passed into the hands of Notley Abbey near Long Crendon in Buckinghamshire. Writing in 1536, John Leland recorded 'at the north end of Caversham Bridge, as

---

[39] It is also interesting to note in passing that Harold Hewitson Nash, Vicar of Caversham from 1943-62, was the son of a former Vicar of St Mary's, Maidenhead.

we came from Reading… a fair old chapel of stone on the right hand, piled in the foundation for the rage of the stream of the Thames.'

Following the Reformation and the dissolution of the Abbey, the bridge and its chapel are said to have fallen into a 'ruinous state and great Decay for default of repairs' with a great deal of buck-passing between various authorities as to the responsibility for their upkeep. The bridge chapel seems to have been demolished by 1714 but in 1924 during the construction of the present bridge parts of its foundations were discovered and some of the stones were built into the wall and altar of the new Roman Catholic church of Our Lady and St. Anne in Caversham.[40]

---

[40] This church also incorporates a shrine to the Virgin Mary, intended to revive the shrine of Our Lady of Caversham, which existed in the Middle Ages but was closed at the Dissolution in 1538. The shrine's exact location is unknown but it is believed by some to have been in the region of Dean's Farm, mentioned in Chapter 1.

4 The Greyfriars in Reading

I may be a little prejudiced, having been confirmed into membership of a church dedicated to him, but few will, I think, dispute, that one of the most attractive characters in the annals of the mediaeval church is Saint Francis of Assisi (1182-1226). After a somewhat frivolous youth Francis espoused a life of poverty and c. 1209 founded an order of brothers (friars), who became known by the colour of their habit, as the Grey Friars, distinguishing them from the Dominicans or Black Friars, who came into being about the same time. Their official name, however, was the *ordo fratrum minorum,* 'the order of lesser brothers' and they are also often referred to after their founder as Franciscans.

The Friars were distinguished from the older monastic orders by being less tied to the cloister so that they soon became an active force in the public life of the church, preaching in the cities, teaching in the universities and taking the gospel to the heathen. Francis himself famously visited the Sultan Kamil in 1218 with this end in view. Also, somewhat less attractively, they were employed in combating what passed for heresy, the Dominicans in particular being closely involved in the work of the Inquisition.[41]

The new order soon spread far and wide across Christendom so that as early as 1224 the first Franciscans reached England and established their friary at Canterbury. In 1233, within a decade of Francis' death, they arrived in

---

[41] This resulted from the establishment in 1231 of the Papal Inquisition under Pope Gregory IX.

Reading.[42] The Abbot of Reading, Adam de Lathbury, granted the friars 'land in the culture called Vastern… towards the bridge of Caversham.' The site was 33 perches in length and 23 in breadth, which in metric measurements is roughly equivalent to 166 by 116 metres. The friars somewhat unwisely undertook not to seek any other land or extension of the existing site from the abbey authorities. King Henry III, who was noted for his piety, evidently took an interest in their welfare and in 1234 allowed them to draw on the resources of Windsor Forest in the construction of their church[43] and 'before the winter of 1239, the Sheriff was instructed to purchase 52 ells[44] of russet to make tunics for the thirteen men and, in following years, wood for burning.'

St Francis was never one much given to comfort and might well have approved of the somewhat damp conditions that the friars enjoyed in an area subject to flooding in winter. However by 1282 we find John Peckham, Archbishop of Canterbury (1279-92), himself a Franciscan and briefly (1275) provincial of the order in England, addressing the Abbot of Reading[45] on their behalf, seeking permission to enlarge their house. This request was somewhat grudgingly granted by the monks, who tended to resent the growing influence of the upstart

---

[42] As well as Canterbury, 17 Franciscan houses, including those at Oxford, Nottingham, London, Stamford, Lincoln, Bristol and Gloucester are reckoned to antedate Reading; while those at Coventry, York and Ipswich were of slightly later antiquity.

[43] At this early date, it seems, most Franciscan churches were constructed from wood.

[44] Equivalent to 195 feet or just under 60 metres.

[45] Peckham had also been educated by the Cluniacs at Lewes and so no doubt 'spoke the same language' as the Abbot.

friars. The result was a new covenant whereby in the words of the *Victoria County History*:

> The abbot and convent of Reading stated that they had unanimously received as guests the Franciscan friars in the town of Reading, upon a piece of ground..... extending from the common way called New Street, the use whereof the friars should continue to have, of the grace of the abbey and convent, saving the following conditions: It should be lawful for the friars to build and dwell upon this additional plot of land (16½ perches by 16 perches) so long as they remained without property and, in accordance with their profession, observers of the deepest poverty.
>
> The friars promised, for themselves and their successors, that they would never seek any other dwelling on the land of the abbey, or extend their boundaries, and that they would never ask alms from the abbey as a due, but only out of mercy and by special grace.

Further restrictions included limitations on rights of burial of 'deceased parishioners of the monastery or of the churches appropriated to the abbey in Reading' without the agreement of the abbot 'and that they would never receive tithes or offerings or legacies due of certain knowledge or by custom to the abbey.'

New Street was the road that we now know as Friar Street so that the brothers' additional site was on higher ground and thus rather drier than the former. It was only adding a small area (83 x 80 metres) to the existing site but the friars set to work to build their church within these confines, their chief object being 'to rear a church suitable for the crowds who flocked to hear their zealous preaching.' King Edward I, following in his father's footsteps, took an interest in the project and granted 56 oaks from the forest of Windsor for the new building. The great church was finally completed in 1311[46] and thus celebrated its seventh centenary in 2011. Originally it may have been dedicated to St James, although the majority of Franciscan houses in England bore the name of the founder of the order, following his canonization in 1228. It is the oldest Franciscan church in Great Britain still in use as a place of worship, although for over three hundred years it was put to secular uses, some of them rather ignoble. The story of its restoration is told in Chapter 16.

In contrast to the Abbey, for which we have a full list of the priors and abbots from its foundation to its dissolution, the names of only five Wardens (as they were called) of the Friary have survived with some lengthy gaps in the record: 1320, Warner; 1327, Williamus de Assewell; 1492, William (possibly surnamed Wursley); 1516, John Thacham; and 1531-8, Peter Schefford, also known as Peter Lorence.

We know of Warner because he was licensed by the Bishop of Salisbury to hear confessions in the diocese in 1320. His probable successor, Williamus de Assewell became Warden on 1st August 1327. William Wursley is recorded as having been ordained to the diaconate on 19th December 1489 and it is considered likely that he is the same William who, as Warden, wrote to 'his dearly beloved in Christ, Katherine Goddarde and William, her son,' in 1492. John Thacham was the recipient of 6s. 8d (33p) by

---

[46] It is perhaps more accurate to say 'by 1311.' Malcolm Summers considers it possible that the completion date was several years earlier.

the 1516 will of one John Stanshawe who also stumped up £1 for the friars to pray for him after his passing, along with 12d (5p) for the maintenance of the light before the rood in the north chapel. Stanshawe Road behind Greyfriars church is named after his son, Robert, a groom of the King's chamber, who purchased the friary site from the King in 1540.

Although the friary remained to some extent under the shadow of the great abbey, at least two of the Reading friars distinguished themselves in scholarly circles. William Boteler (died c.1416) was Minister-Provincial of the order in England from 1408-10 and also taught at Oxford before retiring to Reading in or around 1413. He was much busied in combating the Wycliffite 'heresy' and also wrote a treatise against the translation of the Bible into English, arguing that 'reading of the Bible by unlearned folk would lead to infinite Errors, most foolish Interpretations, intolerable Abuses and grievous Scandals.' He also wrote (presumably favourably) on the subject of papal indulgences. In the previous century John Lathbury became a Doctor of Divinity at Oxford and 'wrote much which was highly esteemed in his day.' 'Greatly commended by Leland (see below) for his manifold Learning both sacred and profane,' he is said to have died at Reading in 1362 at an advanced age. We also find, recorded by his death in 1327/8 the name of William de Okam, a priest and teacher. This is not the famous William of Ockham, the man with the Razor, who was also a Franciscan friar. Presumably though, like his more renowned namesake, he may have originally hailed from Ockham, near Cobham, in Surrey.

The chronicler, Florence of Worcester, records a perhaps less worthy friar of Reading, named Robert, under the year 1275:

> One of the order of preachers at London, called Friar Robert of Reading, an excellent preacher, and deeply skilled in the Hebrew tongue, apostatized, and, being converted to Judaism, married a Jewess, was circumcised, and took the name of Haggai.[47]

He was summoned before the King who 'finding him argue in public with great boldness against the Christian law, turned him over to the Archbishop of Canterbury.'

There is a persistent tradition suggesting that the friars later built a daughter house in Castle Street and that following the dissolution this formed the site of the County Gaol, which in turn gave way to the New Chapel built in 1798, now known as St Mary's, Castle Street. This is ultimately based on a sentence in John Leland's description of Reading in his *Itinerary*, written following his visit to the town in 1542: 'On the north side of Castell-streat was a late fair house of Gray Freres.' This reference has been embroidered by a number of later historians,

---

[47] It is not clear from Florence's account whether he had been a friar at the Reading friary or merely hailed from Reading. It is also claimed by some that he was a Dominican rather than a Franciscan. Matters are complicated by the fact that a Dominican from Oxford also converted to Judaism half a century earlier and is sometimes confused with Robert of Reading. The Oxford man was executed for his apostasy in 1222 but his Reading counterpart seems to have escaped this fate, though the incident is believed to have contributed to the wave of anti-semitism that led to the expulsion of the Jews from England in 1290.

notably Thomas Tanner (1744), John Man (1816) and John Doran (1835). However, as Greyfriars historian, Malcolm Summers,[48] has pointed out it is remarkable that Leland made no reference at all to the principal Franciscan house in Friar Street and on that basis considers it more than likely 'that Leland got his street names muddled, and this led to a duplication of locations.' This argument is strengthened by the fact that there are no other known examples of the Greyfriars establishing a daughter-house or second settlement among the 60 known friaries in England and Wales.

We know quite a bit about the last Warden of the Reading Greyfriars, Peter Schefford, partly because of a long-running dispute with Lord Lisle over masses that had been said for his wife's first husband, Lord Dudley, after his execution in 1510. It is not clear whether the dispute was ever settled or remained unfinished business when the friary came under the 1536 Act for the Dissolution of the 'Lesser Monasteries' that followed King Henry VIII's UDI from papal authority. In August 1538, Thomas Cromwell's assistant, Dr John London, wrote to his master as follows (spelling modernised):

> A friend of mine, the warden of the Grey Friars in Reading [i.e. Peter Schefford], hath also desired me to be an humble suitor for him and his brethren, that they may with your lordship's favour also change their garments with their papistical manner of livings. The most part of them be very aged men, and be not of

---

[48] Writing in the *Newsletter of the History of Reading Society*, No. 55. Winter 2020/21. The present writer admits to having swallowed the erroneous tradition 'hook, line and sinker' when writing *The Church that would not Die* (1993)!

strength to go much abroad for their livings, wherefore their desire is that it might please your lordship to be a mediator unto the king's grace for them that they might during their lives enjoy their chambers and orchard, and they would assuredly pray unto almighty God long to preserve the king's grace and your lordship to his most blessed pleasure.

As the King's need of finance overrode all other considerations Schefford's special pleading was to no avail and on 13th September 1538 the Warden and 11 friars then resident signed an Act of Surrender which yielded up 'our house and place we dwell in… into the hands and disposition of our most noble sovereign Lord, the King's Majesty.' In November of the following year, Peter Schefford (here named Lorence) appears in a list of prisoners incarcerated in the Tower of London, along with another Reading friar, Giles Coventry, as alleged followers of the executed Abbot of Reading, Hugh Faringdon. Giles was released from his imprisonment in 1544 but nothing appears to be known of the fate of Peter Schefford.

5   The End of the Middle Ages

In this chapter we resume and conclude the story of Reading Abbey. In Chapter Two we listed the Abbots up to 1290 and so we may begin by recording the names of their successors:

William Sutton	1287-1305
Nicholas Quappelade	1305-1328
John Appleford	1328-1342
Henry Appleford	1342-1361
William Dombleton	1361-1368
John Sutton	1368-1378
Richard Yateley	1378-1409
Thomas Earley	1409-1430
Thomas Henley	1430-1446
John Thorne I	1446-1486
John Thorne II	1486-1519
Thomas Worcester	1519-1520
Hugh Cook Faringdon	1520-1539

While this may appear to be just a list of names it must be remembered that Abbots were men of great power and influence, not only in matters spiritual but also in the secular world. Up until the disappearance of the monasteries under Henry VIII they formed part of the Lords Spiritual in the House of Lords, along with the Bishops. Furthermore, and particularly so in Reading, the Abbot came to wield considerable weight in local affairs. In the 15th century, as the nation began to move into a post-feudal world, this sometimes led to conflict with the representatives of the laity, who were also beginning to flex their muscles through the Guild, ancestor of our present-day Borough Council and Unitary Authority.

Matters seem to have come to a head during the lengthy abbacy of John Thorne I with a series of disputes including one over the seemingly trivial matter of the Mayor's mace. During a visit to Reading in 1458 Henry VI 'gave permission for the warden of the gild to have a mace borne before him, providing "that it be not prejudicial unto our church and monastery of Reading." ' In consequence a mace was produced at a cost of 3s 4d (17p) with the warden assuming the title of Mayor. The Abbot took great exception to this innovation since, according to long-established privileges, 'only the abbot's bailiff in the borough was entitled to have two tipped staves' carried before him on formal occasions. Further instructions led to the King ordering that the 'Mayor' should be known only as 'keeper of the Guild of Reading.' Later in the century there was another dispute over repairs to the stocks but gradually matters became resolved to the extent that in 1498-9 we read of an unexpected gift of two pike, three perches and two couple of capons being presented by the Guild to 'my Lord [Abbot] of Reading' at a total cost of 9s 4d (47p) – nearly three times the price of the offending mace!

These petty skirmishings may seem a long way from the Gospel but already the light was beginning to shine in England, even in rural Berkshire, with ample evidence to suggest activity on the part of the followers of the teachings of John Wycliffe. These were known as Lollards, literally meaning 'babblers.' As early as 1396 Reading's bailiffs were 'ordered to arrest any Lollards there and to hand them over to the Bishop of Salisbury for imprisonment and correction.' However, it does not appear that any were identified at that time. In 1412, a chapman named William Mundy from nearby Wokingham was tried for public preaching of heretical doctrines before the Bishop's court at Potterne in Wiltshire and found guilty, whereas Thomas Punche from Reading itself was acquitted after a hearing at the bishop's court in Sonning.[49] Four years later in 1416 there is a reference to Lollard broadsheets being distributed in Reading. Possibly these related to the plot hatched by the prominent Lollard layman, Sir John Oldcastle, against King Henry V.[50] At the turn of the 15th century there is evidence in ecclesiastical court records of the existence of a group of eight Lollards in Reading.[51] Newbury was also an important centre of Lollard activity and the earliest Protestant Martyr in Berkshire is believed to have been Christopher Shoemaker, who was burnt at the stake in Newbury in 1518 for reading the Gospels to a follower named John Say. Thomas Quick from Reading is one of 87 Lollards from Berkshire and Buckinghamshire reported to the Bishop of Lincoln by a quisling named Robert Pope in 1521.

In 1520 began the reign of Reading's last Abbot, Hugh Cook Faringdon. As his name suggests, he almost certainly hailed from Faringdon in the north-west of Berkshire,[52]

---

[49] See Charles Kightly, *The Early Lollards*, p. 328-9, 32. Kightly has identified further Reading prosecutions in 1434, 1491 and 1508. Mundy was presumably tried at Potterne because Wokingham was then a distant enclave of the county of Wiltshire; it seems that he recanted his 'heretical' doctrines.

[50] Kightly, op cit, p. 427.

[51] See Professor Ralph Houlbrooke's contribution to the *Historical Atlas of Berkshire*, pp. 58-59.

[52] In the Vale of White Horse, which was taken into Oxfordshire in 1974.

although his family is said to have originated in Kent. Before becoming abbot he served as sub-chamberlain. The pro-Tudor chronicler, Edward Hall, describes him as 'a stubborn monk, and utterly without learning' but this seems to be an unjust description of one who sought to encourage education, working closely with the Reading School master, Leonard Coxe. Initially, Hugh was on good terms with the King and was even spoken of as 'the king's own abbot.' He supported Henry over his divorce from Catherine of Aragon on the grounds that his marriage to his deceased brother's wife was invalid, even to the extent of lending the King books to prove the point. Along with other members of Convocation he accepted Henry's assumption of supremacy within the realm of England 'so far as the law of Christ allows' but privately he still adhered to the authority of the Pope and, moreover, was suspected of aiding the northern pro-papal rebellion, known as the Pilgrimage of Grace (October 1536). As late as Sunday, 4th November, 1537, he sang the requiem and dirge for Queen Jane Seymour, and was present at her burial eight days later. The crunch came in April 1539 when an act for the suppression of the Greater Monasteries followed that of the Lesser but Hugh refused to surrender the abbey when required to do so. This show of opposition to the royal will finally resulted in his arrest by Thomas Cromwell on three charges of treasonably upholding papal supremacy.

Cromwell's henchman, Dr John London, Warden of New College, Oxford, was instrumental in the suppression of both the Franciscan friary and Reading Abbey, together with the Marian shrine in Caversham, alluded to in the previous chapter. A papist at heart,[53] London was also opposed to superstition and idolatry and took great delight in removing some of the objects of devotion from the shrine which included 'the holy knife that killed St Edward' – perhaps donated by his penitent stepmother?

During his examination, Abbot Hugh is said to have exclaimed: 'Those who made the King Supreme Head of the Church were false heretics, and cursed by God's own mouth.' On 14th November 1539, after being dragged round the town and still refusing to recant his loyalty to Rome, he was hung, drawn and quartered in the Forbury before the Abbey Gateway, together with two other recalcitrant members of the Reading clergy. These were John Eynon, formerly Vicar of St Giles from 1520 to 1533, who had also come to oppose the royal supremacy, and John Rugge, a Prebend of Chichester Cathedral who was resident in Reading. Rugge is believed to have been largely responsible for the concealment and preservation of the supposed hand of St James, held by Reading Abbey.

The last Abbot of Reading is remembered today through a church dedicated to him at Faringdon[54] and, in Reading, the Hugh Faringdon RC Comprehensive School and briefly (strange to relate) a public house, the former Jack of Both Sides having been renamed in 2010 as the Abbot Cook.[55] John Eynon is commemorated by a

---

[53] Bishop John Bale, not one of his greatest fans, described him as a 'waterer of the pope's garden.'

[54] This is the RC church of the Blessed Hugh and St. George in Marlborough Street, originally built as a Congregational Chapel in 1840 and sold to the RCs c. 1975.

[55] Alas, the name changed yet again in 2018 to 'Hope and Bear' but survives in the title of an encyclopaedic history of Reading's

memorial to him in St Giles Church, erected in the 1980s. Although, along with John Rugge, they were both beatified in 1895, they were, perhaps curiously, not counted among the 40 English Martyrs raised to sainthood by Pope Paul VI in 1970. It is said, however, that they are included in the dedication of the RC Church of the English Martyrs by Prospect Park, which opened in 1926.

Their deaths, whether regarded as martyrdom[56] or otherwise, may be taken to mark the end of the Middle Ages. In the next section we shall consider the impact of the Reformation on Reading.

---

hospitality industry published in 2021, co-written by the present writer: *Abbot Cook to Zerodegrees*.

[56] In the cases of Thomas More, Bishop John Fisher and Hugh Faringdon (and colleagues) it seems reasonable to argue that these men died for their faith and deserve the title of martyr. However, this is much less clear in relation to those who died under Elizabeth I. In 1570 the Pope foolishly issued a papal bull which effectively invited Elizabeth's subjects to do away with her and replace her with a Roman Catholic monarch. Those who sought to propagate Roman Catholicism in England were thereafter regarded as traitors and executed for treason.

Cartoon of the memorial to John Eynon
in St Giles' Church. Sculptor: David John

6   Reading and the Reformation

In the last chapter, we mentioned the earliest Protestant Martyr in Berkshire, Christopher Shoemaker, who was burnt at the stake in Newbury in 1518 during the rule of Henry VIII and of whom John Foxe in his famous *Book of Martyrs* gives the following, tantalisingly brief account: 'During this year, one Christopher, a shoemaker, was burnt alive at Newbury, in Berkshire, for denying those popish articles[57] which we have already mentioned. This man had gotten some books in English, which were sufficient to render him obnoxious to the Romish clergy.' As we have noted above, it seems likely that he was one of the Lollards who are known to have been active in Newbury and Reading at this time.

Reading subsequently played a 'bit part' in the careers of two of the early martyrs to the Reformation cause who were active during the remainder of the reign of King Henry, as well as claiming its part in the Marian Persecutions through Julins Palmer.

---

[57] The reference appears to be to the act of 1401 concerning which Foxe writes: 'The followers of Wickliffe, then called Lollards, were become extremely numerous, and the clergy were so vexed to see them increase whatever power or influence they might have to molest them in an underhand manner, they had no authority by law to put them to death. However, the clergy embraced the favourable opportunity, and prevailed upon the king to suffer a bill to be brought into parliament, by which all Lollards who remained obstinate, should be delivered over to the secular power, and burnt as heretics. This act was the first in Britain for the burning of people for their religious sentiments; it passed in the year 1401, and was soon after put into execution.'

Before looking at these men we must, however, understand that the Reformation had various distinct phases, or it could be said that there was not one English Reformation but three: Henrician, Edwardian and Elizabethan. Henry's chief concern was the resolution of his problems over his marriage to Catherine of Aragon and desire for a male heir. The Henrician Reformation (1534-47) solved this problem by removing the authority of the Pope but for the most part Henry remained faithful to foundational Roman Catholic doctrines such as transubstantiation and the place of good works in salvation. The principal reforming influence from the continent during this phase was the humanist, Erasmus, and reformation was largely confined to the correction of abuses such as indulgences. During this period, nevertheless, Henry's Archbishop, Thomas Cranmer, moved gradually towards a more fully reformed position on doctrinal issues and there is inconclusive evidence that during the King's final illness he brought the dying Henry to an understanding of justification by faith, a doctrine also espoused by his sixth and last wife, Katherine Parr.[58]

During the Edwardian Reformation (1547-53) Cranmer had a fairly free rein to move the Church of England in a Protestant direction and himself developed a more mature reformed position under the influence of such continental reformers as Martin Bucer and Peter Martyr, who were welcomed to these shores as advisors. If Cranmer's first

---

[58] Katherine's faith is expressed in her treatise, *Lamentation of a Sinner*. This is incorporated in a life of Queen Katherine by Don Matzat, *Katherine Parr: Opportunist, Queen Reformer*, (Amberley, 2020). An excellent fictional account of this period can be found in C. J. Sansom's novel, *Lamentation* (Headstone, 2014).

Prayer Book of 1549 was perhaps more Lutheran in doctrine by that of 1552 the Church of England's doctrines had moved closer to those of the Swiss reformers centred on Zurich (Zwingli/Bullinger) and Geneva (Calvin), particularly in regard to eucharistic doctrine.

Following the part-reversion to papal authority under Mary I (1553-58), the Elizabethan Reformation is best understood under its usual name, the Elizabethan Settlement. This attempted to create a comprehensive church, so that for instance in the Holy Communion service of the 1559 prayer book the words of administration from the 1549 book were combined with those of 1552, arguably permitting a Lutheran/ Catholic understanding of the real presence of Christ in the Eucharist, as well as the more Zwinglian position of the Second Prayer Book. However, the church's official confessional statement, the 39 Articles of Religion, which reached its final form under Elizabeth, is closer to the Swiss reformed position in these matters.

The first of the martyrs with Reading connections was Thomas Garrett (1500-40), who is also sometimes referred to as Thomas Gerrard. Garrett was a student of Oxford who graduated as B.A. in 1518, later becoming a D.D. at the other place. He became known as a bookseller, distributing Lutheran literature among the scholarly fraternity and also in the late 1520s helping in the distribution of Tyndale's translation of the New Testament. Among his customers was Prior John Sherbourne of Reading, who is said to have bought some sixty books from him and ended up in the Tower as a result. Garrett's activities brought him to the attention of the authorities and the Bishop of Lincoln, John Longland, described him as 'a very subtyll, crafty, soleyn and untrue man.' However, at this stage Garrett obtained the patronage of Cardinal Wolsey and thus escaped punishment. By the mid-1530s as the mood-swings of Tudor England began to favour the reformed party we find him acting as Chaplain to both Hugh Latimer, Bishop of Worcester and to Thomas Cranmer himself. In 1540 the King's mood swung back in the opposite direction and in common with two other leading reformers, Robert Barnes and William Jerome, Garrett was burnt at the stake at Smithfield for heresy on 30th July 1540.

If Garrett's connection with Reading is a little tenuous, the same cannot be said of John Frith (1503-33). Frith was a man of Kent and like a later and greater evangelist, George Whitefield, the son of an innkeeper. At school in Sevenoaks he was taught by Stephen Gardiner, a man who was initially sympathetic to reform but who later as Bishop of Winchester became known for his bitter opposition to Protestantism. Frith differed from Garrett in that his earlier studies were at Cambridge where he was involved with the group of reformers who met at the White Horse Inn. He moved to Oxford in 1525 and subsequently worked with Garrett in the distribution of reformed literature. As a result in 1528 he came under suspicion of heresy and, having been imprisoned in Cardinal Wolsey's fish cellar for possessing forbidden books, escaped to the continent where he joined Tyndale.

Frith returned to England in 1531 and here his story is taken up by Brian Raynor in his study, *John Frith: Scholar and Martyr*, largely quoting Foxe:

> Frith went to Reading to get in touch with Prior Sherbourne....a known Lutheran. Foxe wrote that Frith 'came over for the exhibition of the Prior of

Reading, and had the Prior over with him.' It is not clear what this means — whether he came to offer support, financial or otherwise, or whether he came to seek it. Apparently he lost touch with the Prior; all Foxe says is "that he was taken for a vagabond and brought to examination: where the simple man which could not craftily enough cover himself, was set in the stocks." ' Brian Raynor considers with some justification that Foxe here gives rather an inadequate picture of Frith's courage and intelligence.

Foxe's account continues: 'After he had sitten a long time, and was almost pined with hunger, and would not, for all that, declare what he was, at the last he desired that the schoolmaster of the town might be brought to him, who at that time was one Leonard Cox, a man very well learned. As soon as he came unto him, Frith, by and by, began in the Latin tongue to bewail his captivity.

'The schoolmaster, by and by, being overcome with his eloquence, did not only take pity and compassion upon him, but also began to love and embrace such an excellent wit and disposition unlooked for, especially in such a state and misery. Afterwards, conferring more together upon many things, as touching the universities, schools, and tongues, they fell from the Latin into the Greek, wherein Frith did so inflame the love of that schoolmaster towards him, that he brought him into a marvellous admiration, especially when the schoolmaster heard him so promptly by heart rehearse Homer's verses out of his first book of the *Iliad*; whereupon the schoolmaster went with all speed unto the magistrates, grievously complaining of the injury which they did show unto so excellent and innocent a young man.

'Thus Frith, through the help of the schoolmaster, was freely dismissed out of the stocks, and set at liberty without punishment. Albeit this his safety continued not long, through the great hatred and deadly pursuit of Sir Thomas More, who, at that time being chancellor of England, persecuted him both by land and sea, besetting all the ways and havens, yea, and promising great rewards, if any man could bring him any news or tidings of him.'[59]

Ultimately 'justice' caught up with John Frith and he endured the fires of Smithfield on July 4th 1533. Bearing in mind the gradual nature of the English Reformation referred to above, it is worth noting that in his magisterial *History of Christianity in Britain and Ireland*, Gerald Bray questions whether Frith's beliefs, along with those of Bilney, who suffered two years earlier, could be described as genuinely Protestant: '[Frith's] crime was that he questioned the necessity of believing in Purgatory and in transubstantiation rather than in any overt denial of them. To Frith these things were *adiophora*, matters 'indifferent,' which a Christian was free to believe or not… Frith thought for himself and went his own way, and that seems to have been his real 'heresy'.' This argument does perhaps beg the question, When is a Protestant not a Protestant?

---

[59] Thomas More owes much of his contemporary reputation to the play by Robert Bolt, *A Man for All Seasons* (1960) and the later film version, starring Paul Scofield. Whilst undoubtedly he had many attractive characteristics, More was an implacable enemy of the reformed faith, an aspect of his character largely ignored by Bolt.

Even Luther, whose 95 theses kicked off the Protestant Reformation scarcely moved to a fully 'Lutheran' position immediately, and, as indicated above, his theology of the Eucharist falls somewhat short of the more fully reformed position associated with the Swiss reformers.

The schoolmaster mentioned in the above account, Leonard Coxe (1490-1547), was also a significant figure in Reformation/ Renaissance history as a pioneer educationist and friend of Erasmus. Born in Thame, Oxfordshire, he studied at Cambridge and then overseas at Paris and Tübingen. His works on education included *On Teaching the Young* based on his experiences in Poland and Slovakia before his return to England. He was appointed Master of Reading Free School by Hugh Faringdon in 1530, dedicating another work, *The History of Rhetoric* to the Abbot. He somehow survived the ructions following the dissolution of the abbey and execution of Abbot Hugh, being reappointed to the newly constituted Free Grammar school by Henry VIII in 1541 with an annual salary of £10 plus rent free house. It has been argued that Coxe at least challenges the famous Dr Valpy for recognition as the greatest of Reading School's heads.

Mild though the Henrician Reformation was in terms of doctrine, there were those who opposed it including the Holy Maid of Kent, Elizabeth Barton. One of her supporters was a Franciscan friar named Richard Risby,[60] who had been born in Reading in the parish of St Laurence in 1489 but later became a Grey Friar at Canterbury. As a

---

[60] I am obliged to Steven Rolling for spotting this Reading connection and drawing it to my attention.

result he was hanged at Tyburn in 1534 along with the Holy Maid and assorted friars, monks and secular clergy.[61]

Leonard Coxe forms a link with our final 'hero,' Julins (or Julius) Palmer, who was appointed to the headship of the school in 1555 after a turbulent period during which three others had held the position in succession to Coxe. Palmer originated from Coventry, where his father was an upholsterer and served as Mayor, and was educated at Magdalen College, Oxford. At this time he was still strongly papist in his views, which seem to have contributed to his expulsion from the college shortly before Edward VI's death in 1553. Having swum against the tide under the young king, he began to espouse Protestantism under his Romanist successor.

His association with Reading was all too brief for his new faith led to his trial for heresy on 10th July 1556 and his subsequent martyrdom at the stake in Newbury. We may allow John Foxe to tell the tale of his arrest, which occurred when he returned to Reading after first fleeing the town:

> Thus then was this silly young man, for the safeguard of his life, forced to depart upon the sudden from Reading, leaving behind him in the hands of his enemies his stuff, and one quarter's stipend; and so he took his journey toward Eynsham, where his mother then dwelt, hoping to obtain at her hands certain legacies due to him by his father's last will, which he should have received certain years before; and taking his journey by Oxford, he requested certain of his

---

[61] 'Secular' here refers to clergy who are not subject to monastic rule.

friends to accompany him thither. His mother, understanding his state and errand by Master Shipper and his brother, (whom he had sent before to entreat for him,) as soon as she beheld him on his knees, asking her blessing as he had been accustomed to do: 'Thou shalt,' said she, 'have Christ's curse and mine, wheresoever thou go.' He pausing a little, as one amazed at so heavy a greeting, at length said, 'O mother! your own curse you may give me, which God knoweth I never deserved; but God's curse you cannot give me, for hath already blessed me.' 'Nay,' saith she, 'thou wentest from God's blessing into the warm sun, when thou wast banished for a heretic out of that worshipful house in Oxford; and now, for the like knavery, art driven out of Reading too.' …..

Thus poor Palmer, being destitute of worldly friendship, and cruelly repelled of her whom he took to have been his surest friend, wist not which way to turn his face…..

Afterward as he went alone, musing and pondering of matters, it came in his head (as he writeth in an epistle to one of his friends) to leave his appointed journey, and to return closely to Reading, trusting there, by the help of friends, to receive his quarter's stipend, and convey his stuff to the custody of some trusty body. To Reading he cometh, and taketh up his lodging at the Cardinal's Hat [in Minster Street near the present site of Heelas' store], desiring his hostess instantly to assign him a close chamber, where he might be alone from all resort of company. He came not so closely, but that this viperous generation had knowledge thereof: wherefore without delay they laid their heads together, and consulted what way they might most safely proceed against him, to bring their old cankered malice to pass. And soon it was concluded, that one Master Hampton, (which then bare two faces in one hood, and under the colour of a brother played the part of a dissembling hypocrite,) should resort to him under the pretence of friendship, to feel and fish out the cause of his repair to Reading.

Palmer, as he was a simple man, and without all wrinkles of cloaked collusion, opened to him his whole intent. But Hampton earnestly persuaded him to the contrary, declaring what danger might ensue if this were attempted. Against his counsel Palmer replied very much, and as they waxed hot in talk Hampton flung away in a fury, and said, as he had fished, so should he fowl, for him. Palmer not yet suspecting such pretended and devised mischief as by this crooked and pestiferous generation was now in brewing against him, called for his supper, and went quietly to bed: but quietly he could not long rest there. For within short space after, the officers and their retinue came rushing in with lanterns and bills, requiring him in the king and queen's name to make ready himself, and quietly to depart with them. So this silly young man, perceiving that he was thus Judasly betrayed without opening his lips, was led away as a lamb to the slaughter, and was committed to ward; whom the keeper, as a ravening wolf greedy of his prey, brought down into a vile, stinking, and blind dungeon, prepared for thieves and murderers. And there he left him for a time, hanging by the hands and feet in a pair of stocks, so high, that well near no part of his body touched the ground.

In this cave or dungeon he remained about ten days under the tyranny of this unmerciful keeper.

The account of Palmer's trial at Newbury is too long to quote fully here but this short extract shows that the grounds for his conviction for heresy, as in the case of so many of the reformers, were his views on the nature and efficacy of the sacraments and in particular the issue of transubstantiation of the elements of bread and wine in the Holy Communion:

> *Parson* of Englefield[62]: What seest thou yonder?
> *Palmer*: A canopy of silk, broidered with gold.
> *Parson:* Yea, but what is within it?
> *Palmer*: A piece of bread in a clout,[63] I trow.
> *Parson:* Thou art as froward a heretic as ever I talked withal. ….
> *Parson:* Do you not believe that they which receive the holy sacrament of the altar, do truly eat Christ's natural body?
> *Palmer*: If the sacrament of the Lord's supper be ministered as Christ did ordain it, the faithful receivers do indeed spiritually and truly eat and drink in it Christ's very natural body and blood.

One of those burnt at the stake with Palmer was Thomas Askin, otherwise known as Roberts, who is believed to have also been arrested in Reading. A number of others escaped the flames but suffered imprisonment including one John Bolton who after his release joined the English community in Geneva.

The fruits of the Reformation in Reading are not always clear. There is evidence to suggest that the three ancient parishes differed in the speed with which they responded

---

[62] Clement Burdett, Rector of Englefield 1542-60.
[63] Here used in the archaic sense of 'cloth'.

to change. When in 1538 parish churches were instructed to possess a copy of the Bible in English, St Laurence's complied within months at a cost of 9s. (45p), whereas St Giles, perhaps still under the influence of the Blessed John Eynon,[64] does not seem to have followed suit until 1546. The St Laurence's Churchwardens' Accounts for 1549 also suggest quick compliance with the new dispensation, referring to expenses for psalter books of the new service (two for 6d. and six for 10d.) and another book of the new service (evidently the 1549 Prayer Book), costing 4s. 8d (23p). The church was also quick off the mark in 1553 with the purchase of two copies of the new service book (the revised BCP of 1552) at a cost of 7s 8d (38p). At the same time, as Joan Dils points out, the large sum given in paschal money at the first Easter mass back under Mary in 1554, can reasonably be read as showing enthusiasm among the parishioners for the return of the old regime.

Joan Dils has also demonstrated how protestant convictions can be read into some of the wills written by leading citizens. Under the old order it was common for the person making a will to 'include a request for the

---

[64] It is also notable that the rectory and advowson (right of appointment) of St Giles was held by Sir Francis Englefield, a noted recusant. Intriguingly, a prominent layman of St Giles' parish during the period covered by the Henrician and Edwardian reformations and the Marian reaction bore the unusual name of Sabaoth Dudelsall. A resident of London Street, he was Churchwarden in 1534 and 1535 and died c. 1558. Although there is nothing to suggest that Sabaoth himself expressed strong views for or against the religious changes of the times, his given name would at a later period have indicated puritan inclinations, leading one to question whether his parents were perhaps sympathisers with the Lollards.

intercession of the Virgin Mary and the saints to secure his hope of salvation.' In 1554, however, although England was by now back under Roman governance, Thomas Kent of Southcote 'entrusted his soul to God, "that through and by the merits of Christ his passion it shall be saved." ' By the 1580s when the Elizabethan Settlement was well-entrenched such phraseology had become common. Joan Dils particularly mentions Edward Butler, a prominent citizen who had served as Reading's Mayor in 1554, 1559, 1575 and 1581. When he came to write his will in 1584, the year of his death, 'he wanted to make it quite clear that the good work he was doing in leaving money to help the poor was not done with any expectation that this would help towards his salvation but rather "because it will relieve them." ' In Butler's case this profession would seem to have been sincere, though doubtless for others it was a formality.

The financial implications of the 'regime change' for the parish can be seen in the expenses recorded in St Laurence's Churchwardens' Accounts for 1559-60 (spelling modernised), interspersed among such typical everyday 'parish pump' matters as mending the gutters:

Item paid for the Bible and Communion book	12s.
Item paid for the writing the Injunctions to the visitors' servant	2s.
Item paid to Thackham for four psalter books	6s.
Item for a book of the Homilies	14d.
Item for three psalm books in metre and an Injunction	2s. 10d.

Item for the seat of the communion table and the board and the nails and the workmanship	14d.
Item for dressing the high altar and the wall beneath and the boards where the altars stood.	2s. 8d.

The injunctions referred to ordered inter alia the replacement of altars by holy tables and the removal of shrines and images. The consequences of this are seen in the last two items, both significantly undertaken before an anticipated episcopal visitation by the Bishop of Salisbury, John Jewel.[65] Thomas Thackham was Vicar of St Laurence's under Edward V[66] and also Master of Reading School; at the time of his brief ministry in 1559 he was once again Master of the School but not, it would appear, vicar of the parish; he is described by historians of the school as a sinister figure who contributed towards the betrayal and death of his successor as Master, Julins Palmer.

Despite the evident intention of undoing the changes made in the previous reign, the Elizabethan Settlement did not please everyone, leading to the rise of the widely misunderstood Puritan movement. The man in the street probably regards puritanism as a matter of pulling long faces and adopting a prudish attitude to moral issues but essentially the first Puritans sought purity of doctrine and a desire to remove from the life of the Church of England those rites and ceremonies and practices that in their eyes

---

[65] See Chapter 20.
[66] He was deprived under Mary but this seems to have been due to his married status rather than any strong adherence to the Protestant cause.

represented a compromise with Romish doctrine, for instance kneeling to receive the elements in the Communion service and the wearing of surplices by the clergy.

In Reading, Edward Butler (see above) is thought to have had Puritan sympathies, along with Thomas Aldworth (1520-77, Mayor in 1551, 1557, 1561 and 1571 and MP for Reading during 1558-9) and the influential local landowner, Sir Francis Knollys (1514-96). The latter's son-in-law, Robert Dudley, Earl of Leicester, who was High Steward of Reading from 1566-88, is also said to have supported the Puritan cause. Among the clergy, George Baron, curate of St Laurence's in the 1560s, reportedly celebrated Communion without wearing a surplice, while later in the century, William Burton, Vicar of St Giles from 1592 to 1612, is described as a 'militant Puritan' who 'was repeatedly at loggerheads with his churchwardens and other parishioners.'[67] These issues would assume greater prominence in the following century, contributing to the rise of dissent.

---

[67] See Ralph Houlbrooke and Margaret Connolly, Puritanism and Religious Conformity 1559-1641, in *Historical Atlas of Berkshire*, pp. 68-9. For a detailed broader study of the relationship between protestant conformity and the ultimately nonconformist puritan movement see Judith Maltby, *Prayer Book and People in Elizabethan and Early Stuart England*, Cambridge, 1998.

7   William Laud and the Civil War period

In terms of attainment to high office, few would deny the honour of being Reading's most distinguished churchman to William Laud. Archbishop of Canterbury from 1633 until his beheading on Tower Hill on 10th January 1645, Laud had been born in Reading, the only son of a clothier, in 1573. His public life was largely lived out away from the town of his birth, as successively Bishop of St David's from 1621, Bath and Wells from 1626, London from 1628 and finally Primate. We cannot, however, ignore such a figure and his physical absence did not prevent Laud from influencing events in his native town.

Laud received his early education at Reading School where his schoolmaster, John Smith,[68] evidently having noticed both his shortness of stature and his academic promise, is said to have told him: 'When you are a little great man, remember Reading School.' From there he proceeded in 1589 to St John's College, Oxford. This college had been founded 34 years earlier by another Reading man, Sir Thomas White (1492-1567), Master of the Merchant Taylors, who had endowed two scholarships for boys from Reading School at the new foundation. Laud was to spend most of his next 26 years at the College, as successively scholar, fellow and ultimately President.

During his time at Oxford one of his close friends was Sir Francis Windebank (1582-1646), who came up to St John's in 1599 and was later to serve Charles I as Secretary of State. Laud was a frequent visitor to Windebank's home

---

[68] Smith was Headmaster from 1569 to 1583 and later served as Vicar of St Laurence's, Reading.

at Haines Hill, near Reading (between Hurst and Shurlock Row).

It was not until he achieved national fame via his translation to Canterbury that Laud excited much attention back in Reading. However, a local man and Puritan sympathiser named Lodovick Bowyer made up for it by publishing a libel on the new Archbishop to the effect that Laud was confined to his house under an armed guard for treasonable connections with the Bishop of Rome (the Pope). Bowyer was made to pay for his errors with a range of punishments doled out by the infamous Star Chamber including a fine of £3,000 and hard labour in perpetuity. He was also made to stand in the pillory at Reading and elsewhere with a paper declaring his offence and having his ears nailed. Here is the judgement dated 17th December 1633, instructing the Reading authorities to carry out the sentence of the court (spelling modernised):

> These are to require you that upon sight hereof you receive from the hands of the Warden of the Fleet, the body of Lodovick Bowyer, and to cause him on Saturday next, being the one and twentieth of this instant December, to be set in the pillory in the Town and Borough of Reading, in the time of the Market there, with his ears nailed to the said pillory, and a paper on his head, declaring the nature of his offence, and to cause him to read his submission and acknowledgment there, according to the direction of the decree of this Court, the last term, made at the suite of his Majesty's Attorney-General, plaintiff. And that done, to deliver him again to the custody of the Warden of the Fleet, or his servants from whom you receive him.

Quite where Bowyer, sometimes identified as a 'peasant,' was expected to find the sum of £3,000 is not clear; such absurdly impossible sentences were not untypical, it seems, of the Star Chamber court under Charles I.[69] As for the libel, it was ill-founded: although Laud was a High Churchman, Arminian[70] in doctrine and strongly opposed to Puritanism and Calvinism, he had in fact refused the secret offer of a Cardinal's hat in return for declaring his allegiance to the Pope.[71]

Shortly after his elevation to Canterbury Laud did indeed remember Reading School by leaning on the Corporation to accept his nominee, William Page, as schoolmaster and raising what had apparently hitherto

---

[69] It was abolished by Parliament in 1640.

[70] Arminians based their doctrine on the teachings of the Dutchman, Jacobus Arminius, who denied certain tenets of the prevailing Calvinist orthodoxy, over such matters as irresistible grace and the final perseverance of the elect, affirmed by Calvin but denied by Arminius. Although English churchmen attended the Synod of Dort of 1619, which largely upheld Calvinism against the innovations of Arminius, the teachings of the latter took increasing hold on the English Church, in particular during the post-Restoration period. The controversy between these two major schools of thought flared up during the Evangelical Revival with the Wesleys representing the Arminian party and Whitefield, Toplady and others upholding the teachings of John Calvin.

[71] However, the perception of papist sympathies persisted among his opponents and the charges on which he was committed to the Tower of London in 1641 included: 'That he hath *traiterously* endeavoured to reconcile us to the church of Rome; and to that end hath employed a Jesuit, a papist, and hath wrought with the pope's agents in several points.'

been a very measly stipend for this post. Unfortunately Page's leadership of the school was undistinguished, as he proved unable to discipline the boys in his charge; as a protégé of Laud, he was dismissed when Parliament gained the upper hand in the Civil War.

The Archbishop also instructed his Vicar-General, Sir Nathaniel Brent (1573-1652), who undertook the metropolitan visitation on his behalf in 1634, to look closely into the spiritual health of Reading. In the same year, he disclosed to his diary an intention 'to do the town of Reading good for their poor, which may be compassed by God's blessing upon me, though my wealth be small.' He determined 'to settle a hospital of land in Reading of £100 in a new way' but it was not until March 1640 that he had sufficient wealth to acquire from Sir John Blagrave lands in Bray with an annual value of £200. These he conveyed to the Corporation with instructions that the rents should be used two years out of three to provide £120 to apprentice twelve poor boys, ten from Reading and one each from Bray and Wokingham (his father's birthplace).[72] In the third year the same sum was to be spent on marriage-portions for poor girls, five from Reading and one from Wokingham. In addition, the Vicar

---

[72] The selection of the lucky recipients of this largesse is recorded in the Borough minutes for Wednesday 17th November 1641: 'At this day was the election of 10 poor Boys born in Reading, one poor boy born in Wokingham, and one poor boy born in Bray, to be bound Apprentices by directions of the Lord Archbishop's of Canterbury his Grace's appointment, and were nominated and agreed to be bound to such masters as the Mayor and Aldermen can find to take them with 10 pounds apiece of the said Lord Archbishop's charitable gift freely given to that intent and purpose.'

of St Laurence was to receive £50 a year and the Master of Reading School £20.

The previous December (1639) the Archbishop was called upon by the Privy Council to 'trouble-shoot' over problems that had arisen in Reading in the administration of John Kendrick's charity. Apart from the funding of the Oracle workhouse, Kendrick had also instructed that a stock of money should be used to provide loans to poor clothiers to enable them to further their trade. However, with the decline of the cloth trade in Reading the richer merchants had borrowed copious amounts from the stock in order to squeeze the poorer tradesmen out of business. As himself the son of a clothier Laud naturally took an interest and his solution was for the stock to be invested in land, with the rents used both for the original purpose of providing loans in limited amounts to the small traders and at the same time to fund apprenticeships and marriage portions, as in his own charity.

Without Laud's intervention the terms of Kendrick's will were such that the benefits of the charity would have been transferred to Christ's Hospital. Laud thus deserved the thanks of the town for this and also for his part in securing a new charter for Reading in 1638. He was determined to use his new popularity to advantage. In the prevailing political climate, he doubtless needed all the support in Parliament he could get and therefore wrote to the Mayor and Corporation, requesting the right to nominate a burgess to represent the town. His choice was Edward Herbert (1591-1658), Solicitor-General in 1640[73] and a cousin of the poet, George Herbert. Herbert did not prove popular with the Corporation but was, nevertheless,

---

[73] Subsequently (1641-5) Attorney-General.

elected as Laud's nominee. However, he was also elected for Old Sarum, later one of the notorious 'rotten boroughs,' and chose to represent that constituency rather than Reading. The Short Parliament of 1640 was followed by the Long Parliament but for this Laud declined to nominate a candidate, on the grounds that he did not wish to implicate Reading in his growing unpopularity in the rest of the country.

History tends to judge William Laud as a failure both as a politician and ultimately as a prince of the Church. However, the people of his native town had reason to be grateful for the concern he showed to them during his primacy and their descendants in the 20th century finally gave visible expression to that gratitude by naming a new road after him. In addition, in 2016 Reading School remembered its 'little great man' by naming a new house after him, Laud House.

The Civil War that resulted from the policies pursued by Laud and his royal master impacted on Reading, which initially found itself in parliamentary hands but was occupied by the royalists from November 1642 until April of the following year. The town then fell back into the hands of the King's enemies after a ten-day siege. It reverted to the King in September 1643 but in May 1644 parliamentary forces captured it once more and thereafter held it for the duration of the conflict.

The war was not, of course, primarily about religious issues although it resulted in the suppression of the existing Church of England hierarchy and its replacement by a presbyterian form of government. There was also a brief period of toleration which saw some of the first stirrings of dissent in the town, not to mention signs of heresy. One of the odder characters to emerge from this melting-pot was John Pordage (1607-81), who was born in London and educated at Pembroke College, Cambridge. Pordage was influenced by the writings of the German mystic, Jacob Boehme; the titles of his own writings are likewise suggestive of an interest in mysticism and the occult. These include *Truth Appearing through the Clouds of Undeserved Scandal* and *Innocence Appearing through the Dark Mists of Pretended Guilt*. He also claimed medical expertise, having functioned as a battlefield surgeon during the early part of the Civil War. 'Doctor' Pordage then served briefly as Curate of St Laurence's in the mid-1640s, being paid £25 'out of the late Archbishop [Laud]'s gift, for his pains in officiating the cure in St Laurence parish church the last half-year.'

Around this time Pordage's interest in astrology began to arouse criticism. His ministry at St Laurence's also coincided with a period when Parliamentary forces occupied Reading with the church used as billets for their troops. For whatever reason he found it advisable to leave Reading and take up the rectory of Bradfield, presented to that living by the Oxford scholar, Elias Ashmole, who shared his taste for the occult. It is probable that this appointment is referred to obliquely in a sermon preached by one of Pordage's successors at St Laurence's, Simon Ford,[74] which is quoted by John Man[75] as illustrating the 'fanaticism' that characterised religion in the Reading of the 1650s:

> In this little town of Reading, I am verily persuaded, if Augustine's and Epiphanius' catalogue of heresies

---

[74] Dr Simon Ford (1619-99) was Vicar of St Laurence's from 1651 to 1659 when he moved to All Saints, Northampton.
[75] In *The Stranger in Reading*.

were lost, and all other modern and ancient records of that kind, yet it would be no hard matter to restore them with considerable enlargements from this place. They love Anabaptism, Familism, Socinianism, Pelagianism, Ranting, and what not; and that the Devil was served in heterodox assemblies as frequently as God in their's; and that one of the most eminent church livings in the county was possessed by a blasphemer; one, in whose house he believed, as some then present could testify, that the Devil was as visibly familiar as one of the family.

Pordage evaded a charge of heresy in 1651 but three years later again found himself in trouble, having been summoned to appear before the 'Commissioners for Berkshire for the ejection of scandalous and insufficient ministers', which met at the Bear Inn on 8th December and duly ejected Pordage from his benefice as being 'ignorant and very insufficient for the work of the ministry'.[76]

One of the assistants to the Commissioners was the Vicar of St Mary's, Christopher Fowler (1610-78), who subsequently engaged in controversy with Pordage with a work entitled *Daemonium Meridianum* or *Satan at Noon*, accusing him of popery and mysticism and describing his doctrines as a 'spit in the face of Jesus Christ'. Pordage responded by attacking Fowler's 'fierce and bitter spirit,' following which his opponent went on the rampage, savaging not only Pordage but everybody else he regarded as heterodox, including the Quakers and Anabaptists. In

---

[76] It seems apt to observe that the Quasi Non-Governmental Organisation or 'Quango' was a notable feature of life during the Commonwealth period.

1656 he and Ford collaborated on an attack on the former sect, *A Sober Answer to an Angry Epistle*,[77] though at the Restoration the two men went their separate ways.

Unlike Ford who subsequently espoused the royalist cause and was happy to conform following the Restoration, Fowler became a leader of dissent in the town of Reading but that is a story that we will leave to the next episode. Pordage by contrast was restored to his Bradfield living at the Restoration of Charles II!

---

[77] The 'angry epistle' had been penned by a Quaker resident in Bristol named Thomas Speed.

8   Stirrings of Dissent

The restoration of King Charles II in 1660 was proclaimed in Reading on 10th May in the market-place 'with great solemnitie and rejoicing' and thereafter the Corporation tucked into a festive meal at a cost of £1 (around £80 to 90 in today's money). Doubtless, after the chaos following Cromwell's death, the people of Reading were generally pleased at the return of the monarchy but some were soon to find that, despite royal promises to the contrary, their freedoms were to be restricted. This applied not least to the Mayor for 1661-2, Samuel Jemmatt, who was removed from office as a dissenter.

Traditional members of the Church of England rightly have a high regard for the 1662 *Book of Common Prayer* as one of the foundation stones[78] of historic and reformed Anglican Christianity. However, 1662 was not all good news. Many Puritans were unhappy about the restoration of the Prayer Book[79] and found themselves unable to comply with the Act of Uniformity, which dictated that only those services authorised in the book should be used. Up to 2,000 ministers were as a result ejected from the Church of England; the exact number has been disputed by scholars and some are of the opinion that the real

---

[78] It is enshrined in canon law as one of the formularies of the Church of England, along with the *Thirty-Nine Articles of Religion* and the *Ordinal* (Canons A2, 3 and 4).

[79] During the Civil War and Commonwealth the Book of Common Prayer had been replaced by a *Directory of Public Worship* which provided guidance to ministers without requiring strict forms of liturgy. As a result extempore prayer became the norm.

number was nearer 1,000. A consequence of this disruption was that the Church moved in a high-and-dry - and in some cases broad-and-long - direction, while nonconformity, lacking the disciplined framework afforded by the preservation of the episcopate, has had a very mixed history. Many of the Independent and Presbyterian churches formed in the wake of 1662 drifted into Unitarianism in the course of the next 100 years.

Three individuals can be seen as representing the early history of nonconformity in Reading. The first of these is Christopher Fowler, of whom we learnt a little in the previous chapter. Born in Marlborough, Wiltshire, around 1610, Fowler studied at Magdalen College and later St Edmund ('Teddy') Hall, Oxford, taking his BA in 1632 and MA in 1634. He was strongly influenced by John Prideaux, Regius Professor of Divinity from 1615-41 and a strong Calvinist, and thus came to a reformed and puritan position in the theological spectrum of the times. During the 1640s and 50s Fowler held a variety of appointments, many of them concurrently, including the livings of Woodhey near Newbury in Berkshire, St Mary's, Reading and St Margaret's, Lothbury in the City of London, together with a fellowship of Eton College. He first appeared in Reading accompanying the parliamentary forces in 1644, when he supplanted the royalist Thomas Bunbury at St Mary's. As we have seen he was especially active during the 1650s, combating John Pordage's eccentric writings and also at the same time wrote against the Quaker doctrines that were then starting to infiltrate the area. Manfred Brod suggests that his opposition to the Quakers was inflamed, if not caused, by their behaviour in 'harassing the ministers in their own churches and heckling them in their pulpits.'

Fowler accepted the restoration of the monarchy but was evidently regarded with suspicion for he was deprived of his Eton fellowship and ultimately in 1662 was ejected from St Mary's. The Broad Street Congregational Chapel (now Waterstone's bookshop) dates its origins from 1662 and it is believed that for a while after his ejection Fowler held 'conventicles'[80] in his own house, 'which were numerously attended'. The new Mayor, George Thorne (1662-3), a strongly pro-Establishment man, complained that because of Fowler's meetings 'the audiences in the Churches are made very thin… The schismatics scorn persuasion and defy powers.'

It is scarcely surprising then that for a while Fowler found himself imprisoned in Windsor Castle! He later moved to London, ministering in Kennington and Southwark, where he died in January 1678; a warrant was out for his arrest as an illegal preacher at the time of his death. An attempt had been made to obtain a preaching licence for him that would permit him to resume his private ministry in Reading but the borough's Justice of the Peace, Sir William Armorer, an implacable opponent of dissent, described him as 'author of most of the evil in the town' whose return would 'set them all by the ears.' Armorer was a member of the royal court whose services were imposed on the people of Reading, maybe on account of their tendency to dissent. As a result of Armorer's opposition, the application, submitted curiously

---

[80] This term was defined in the Conventicle Act of 1664 as 'any religious meeting other than of the Church of England where there are five persons or more assembled together (other than those of the same household).' The act was largely ineffective and repealed as part of the settlement on 1689.

by Colonel Thomas Blood, who is better known for his attempt to steal the Crown Jewels, was refused.[81]

The chronicler of the ejected ministers, Edmund Calamy, quotes from Fowler's funeral sermon by Mr Cooper[82] giving him the character 'of an able, holy, faithful, indefatigable Servant of Christ; who approv'd himself by painful Studies, by patient Sufferings, by continual Prayer and Preaching. He was quick in Apprehension, solid in his Notions, clear in his Conceptions, sound in the Faith, strong and demonstrative in Arguing, mighty in Convincing, and zealous for the Truth against all Errours. He had a singular gift in Chronology, not for curious Speculation or Ostentation, but as a Key to know the Signs of the Times, and the fulfilling of Prophesies relating to the Kingdom of Christ and Antichrist,[83] the Exaltation of the One, and the Ruine of the other; wherein he was not rash or peremptory, but rather but sober, walking by Line and Rule, etc.'

The independent cause in Reading was continued by Thomas Juice, another ejected minister, who had had the cure of St Nicholas, Worcester,[84] described by Calamy as 'a sober, grave, serious, peaceable, blameless, able minister: Yet Living Pastor of a Congregation at Redding in Berk.' Also according to Calamy, 'he lost £100 per annum by his

---

[81] Despite his reputation as an adventurer, Blood was also a Presbyterian.

[82] This was the Rev William Cooper, who was a contemporary of Fowler and who had been ejected from St Olave's, Southwark, in 1662.

[83] This would have been understood to refer to the Pope.

[84] Rebuilt in 1750, this church is now a Slug and Lettuce pub-restaurant.

ejection. Afterwards, for a livelihood for himself, his wife and three children, he taught a little school till the Corporation Act took place, when he was forced to abscond. He was afterwards pastor of a congregation at Reading in Berks, and there he died.' Eventually, as the restrictions on dissenters were gradually eased, the Independents began meeting on the Broad Street site and Thomas Juice continued to minister there, probably until 1706. In 1690 the congregation is put at 'four or five hundred hearers, ye people considerably rich.'

The best known Baptist connected with 16th century Reading is clearly John Bunyan but the Baptist movement in the town antedated the start of Bunyan's preaching ministry in the mid-1650s. It is believed to have come into existence through the presence of soldiers in the town during the Civil War. There is certainly evidence of a well-established church by 1652 and the following year we find the combative Christopher Fowler inveighing publicly against the local Anabaptists. Mr B R White has identified the church founded by 1652 as Particular Baptists who held to the Calvinistic view that Christ died only for the elect (limited atonement), whereas another gathering, dated from 1656, later described themselves in their Trust Deed of 1692 as 'The Congregation of Baptists in Reading who hold the Universal Love of God to all Men in sending his Son into the World, for the Redemption of all mankind,' thus identifying themselves as General Baptists. Records of this group survive from 1660.

In 1656 also, John Sturgion, a member of Cromwell's lifeguard and a Baptist who held 'Fifth Monarchy' views, visited Reading and attracted large crowds. The Fifth Monarchists, who expected that certain prophecies of the

Book of Daniel[85] would be fulfilled in the year 1666, appealed to the exiled King, Charles II, for toleration in the face of persecution by Cromwell. However, this did not prevent six of them, John Coombes, John and Thomas Jones, Robert Keate, John Peck and Richard Steed, from being incarcerated in Reading Gaol in July 1661. They seem to have been released under an amnesty marking the King's coronation the following April.

When restrictions were eased in 1672, Jeremiah Ives, author in 1655 of a treatise entitled *Infants-Baptism Disproved and Believers Baptism Proved*, obtained a general licence to preach in Reading, while Daniel Roberts was licensed to preach in his own house; the house of one Mary Kenton was also licensed for worship. Otherwise the early history of the Baptists in Reading is somewhat vague, especially compared with other nearby centres such as Abingdon. At this time the Baptists met at a house in Pinkneys Lane, backing onto the Holybrook. This enabled them to throw a plank bridge across the stream to effect their escape if threatened with exposure as a result of the activities of Sir William Armorer and those of his ilk. John Rance was named as pastor from 1678 to 1695 and Southwark-based Benjamin Keach,[86] well-known for his early attempts at

---

[85] The 'Fifth Monarchy' was to be the Kingdom of God, which would follow the four kingdoms or monarchies outlined in the prophecy of Daniel (Babylon, Persia, Greece and Rome). Although the events of 1666, notably the Great Fire of London, were seen by some Fifth Monarchists as vindicating their beliefs, the culmination in the return of the Lord Jesus Christ, ushering in His kingdom, did not, of course, take place.

[86] This represents the traditional interpretation, based on the histories of Ernest Payne (*Baptists of Berkshire*, 1951) and C. A.

vernacular hymnody, is said to have visited Reading from time to time to preside at the Lord's Supper, along with Edward Stennett from Wallingford.

Undoubtedly the most famous visitor to the town was, however, Bunyan, who like Keach and Ives came to preach to the local congregation. He is said to have travelled through the town disguised as a waggoner to avoid recognition and arrest but on one occasion it is believed that the disguise slipped and he was briefly imprisoned, probably in the old County Gaol in Castle Street, on the site of which St Mary's Episcopal Chapel now stands. He made his last visit in August 1688 in order to reconcile a father, who belonged to the Reading church, with his erring son, who lived in Bedford and whose name was Mark Welham:

> ...it so falling out, that a young gentleman, a neighbour of Mr Bunyan, happening into the displeasure of his father, and being much troubled in mind on that account, as also that he had heard his father purposed to disinherit him, or otherwise deprive him of what he had to leave, he pitched upon Mr Bunyan as a fit man to make way for his submission, and prepare his father's mind to receive him; and he, as willing to do

---

Davis (*History of the Baptist Church in Reading*, 1891). B. R. White, writing in the *Baptist Quarterly*, 1968, argued persuasively that up until 1695 there were both General and Particular Baptist meetings in Reading. According to White the identification with Keach, by this time a Particular Baptist, is based on references in the church accounts c. 1682 to one Brother Ketch. He considers that a more likely identification would be with Henry or Joseph Keetch of Soulbury, near the modern city of Milton Keynes, Bucks.

any good office as it could be requested, as readily undertook it; and so, riding to Reading, in Berkshire, he then and there used such pressing arguments and reasons against anger and passion, as also for love and reconciliation, that the father was mollified, and his bowels yearned towards his returning son.[87]

Mission accomplished, Bunyan preached to the congregation in a boat-house beside the Kennet, presumably the house in Pinkneys Lane referred to above. He then rode back to London the following day through driving rain in order to be able to fulfil a preaching engagement in Whitechapel. This he was able to do but the soaking of the day before brought on the fever from which he died ten days later on 31st August 1688. Reading, therefore, has the honour to be the scene of Bunyan's last-but-one sermon.

In 1692 a feltmaker named James Roberts gifted to the congregation of General Baptists a new meeting-house; James' father, Daniel, had been one of its founder-members. In the later 1690s this congregation united with the Particular Baptists under the pastorate of Mark Key. This new and more permanent place of worship was located in Church Street, near St Giles' Church.

The final group of Reading dissenters to emerge from the religious ferment of these times was the Society of Friends, or Quakers. As we have seen they were withstood by Independents such as Fowler and Bunyan is also known to have opposed them. There is a rather telling story of Bunyan being visited while in prison (Bedford rather than Reading) by a Quaker who addressed him thus: 'Friend

---

[87] Quoted from the *Continuation of Mr Bunyan's Life*, appended to *Grace Abounding* in 1692.

Bunyan, the Lord hath sent me to seek for thee; I have been through several counties in search of thee; and now, I am glad I have found thee.' To which Bunyan responded wittily, if a little cruelly: 'Friend, thou speakest not truth in saying the Lord hath sent thee to seek me, for the Lord well knows I have been in this jail for some years; and if He had sent thee, He would have sent thee here directly.'[88]

The Quaker movement spread from the north of England to London and the southern counties during 1654 and two natives of Westmoreland and North Lancashire, Thomas Salthouse (1630-91) and Miles Halhead, are credited with making the first foray into Reading early in 1655. This was during an extensive tour of the south-west in the course of which they both landed up in Exeter Gaol. Since I have Salthouse blood in my veins through my Lancastrian mother, I rather like to think that Thomas may have been a distant forbear of mine, though my ardently Anglo-Catholic grandfather might have thought differently![89]

By 1659 Reading had become the main Quaker centre in Berkshire. Early meetings were held in the home of Thomas Curtis (died 1712), a wealthy woollen-draper of the town, who had been 'convinced' at Bristol; this home may have been the George Inn which was owned by Curtis

---

[88] This anecdote is related in a Memoir of Bunyan introducing a Frederick Warne edition of *The Pilgrim's Progress* c. 1900. I have not been able to locate its original source.

[89] Thomas Salthouse remained in the south-west and coincidentally later became a member of the Quaker meeting in Bristol, where my branch of the Salthouses settled in the 1930s and where I was born during the following decade. My mother's sister spent the last year of her life in a rest home in Bristol connected with the Quakers.

during the later 17th century. An early convert was Joseph Coale, who died in gaol on 26th April 1670, one of three Reading Quakers who perished following the Restoration of the Stuarts in 1660. According to Quaker historian, Chris Skidmore,[90] Coale came from Mortimer, a village a few miles to the south of Reading. He 'had been one of the first to become a Quaker in Reading, in 1655 when he was about 19 years old and an apprentice weaver. After he had finished his training the next year, he felt a call to spread the Quaker gospel and for the next five years preached through Cornwall, Devon and Dorset, suffering imprisonment at least five times.' In 1664, as 'part of a sustained persecution led by Sir William Armorer' he was arrested at the Reading Quaker Meeting. Armorer's campaign of harassment 'saw most of Reading's Quaker men and women imprisoned.'

During this period Quaker worship was carried on by their children, who were themselves often subjected to physical abuse. 'As Quakers observe the Biblical injunction to "swear not at all" they were readily trapped by the authorities for refusing to swear the Oath of Allegiance.'

---

[90] Quoted from an account of Coale's life written for the *Reading Book of Days*. This was based on a biography by G. Whitehead and others, published in 1706: *Some account of the life, service, and suffering, of an early servant and minister of Christ, Joseph Coale, collected out of his own writings; who after near six years imprisonment in Reading - Goal, died prisoner for his Christian testimony*. London: printed and sold by T. Sowle. This also includes some of Coale's letters from prison. Mr Skidmore is preparing a collection of early Reading Quaker records for the Berkshire Record Society, due for publication in 2025.

In effect they became 'non-people' and their property and their very lives were forfeit. During the six years that Joseph Coale spent in Reading Gaol up to his death, he continued to write and publish Quaker literature.

21st century members of Reading's Society of Friends dressed in traditional Quaker costume

The reader will once again have noted the malevolent influence of Sir William Armorer. He is said to have taken it upon himself to march into Quaker meetings, whereupon a dialogue would ensue on the following lines:

'What a devil, are you met again? I will send you all to prison. What a devil, are you all dumb? Hath the devil cast his club over you and bewitched you?'

'We have learned of a better spirit, even the Spirit of Christ Jesus, which leadeth us to deny the devil and all his instruments.'

'Who a devil will believe you? Hang you, I could find in my heart to lay you over the pate with my cane. You are deluded by the spirit of the devil; I will send you all to prison.[91]

Manfred Brod characterises Armorer as 'drunken, foul-mouthed and not very intelligent' – a description borne out by this exchange.

The generally acknowledged founder of the Quakers was George Fox and he recorded a number of visits to Reading in his *Journal*[92] from which the following extracts are taken:

[1655] 'I travelled till I came to Reading, where I found a few that were convinced of the way of the Lord. I stayed till the First-day, and had a meeting in George Lamboll's orchard; and a great part of the town came to it. A glorious meeting it proved; great convincement there was, and the people were mightily satisfied.'

---

[91] Quoted by Alan Wykes in *Reading, A Biography*, but with no reference to source.

[92] The Journal was not published in Fox's lifetimes but was compiled after his death in 1691, including an element of 'reconstruction' on the part of the editor. There seems no reason, though, to suppose that the recorded visits to Reading are not actual events!

[1658] 'After a while I went to Reading, where I was under great sufferings and exercises, and in great travail of spirit for about ten weeks. For I saw there was great confusion and distraction among the people….And I saw how many were destroying the simplicity and betraying the truth.'

[1660] 'Now did I see the end of the travail which I had in my sore exercise at Reading; for the everlasting power of the Lord was over all, and His blessed Truth, life, and light shined over the nation. Great and glorious meetings we had, and very quiet; and many flocked unto the Truth. Richard Hubberthorn[93] had been with the King, who said that none should molest us so long as we lived peaceably and promised this upon the word of a king; telling Richard that we might make use of his promise.'

Alas! The King's word was not to be trusted and many Quakers, such as Joseph Coale, suffered for their beliefs under Charles II, along with other dissenters, so that in 1670 we find Fox writing thus:

'At Reading most of the Friends were in prison, and I went to visit them. When I had been a while with them, the Friends that were prisoners gathered together, and several other persons came in; so that I had a fine opportunity, and declared the Word of Life, encouraging them in the truth; and they were refreshed in feeling the presence and the power of the Lord amongst them.'

---

[93] Another of the early Quakers emanating from Lancashire, Hubberthorn[e] died in Newgate prison in 1662.

The earliest meeting house of the Quakers was in Sun Lane, the southern part of what is now King Street, close to the George Inn. Later they moved to Sims Court off London Street, where some fabric of the building they used survives and finally to Church Street, where a new meeting house was built in 1715.[94] William Penn, the founder of Pennsylvania, was for a number of years one of those who met for worship at Sims Court.

The meeting house site includes one of the finest Quaker graveyards in the country, which is perhaps also one of the most peaceful spots in our boisterous township. In line with Quaker principles all the tombstones are of similar size with a marked lack of ostentation in either design (no angels or other exuberant sculpture) or message (just the names and dates of the deceased.) The months are generally stated as first, second and third etc. in line with the Quaker practice of avoiding the pagan origins of the usual appellations.

---

[94] This remains the centre of Quaker worship in Reading, although the 1715 meeting-house was rebuilt in 1835.

9   Restoration to Revival

The eighty-year period following the restoration of the monarchy and prayer book was one of the least remarkable in the history of the Church of England and there is little to suggest that Reading differed in this respect. The abiding emphasis was on rational Christianity and thus preaching was characterised by 'prudential morality, based on reason rather than revelation, and appealing deliberately to sober common sense.'[95] In other words, the gospel was neglected and a rise in *in*sobriety and *im*morality resulted![96]

And yet this period was punctuated by an event that resulted in greater toleration in religious matters and arguably, therefore, greater freedom to preach the gospel. Reading played a significant part in the Glorious 'Bloodless' Revolution of 1688, for it was here on December 9th that the only battle took place between a force of 600 Irishmen loyal to James II and an advance guard of Dutchmen sent by William of Orange from Hungerford to head them off. The Irish lost 50 men to five of the Dutch and some of those who were slain were

---

[95] Quoted from Joseph Butler (1692-1752), Bishop of Bristol.

[96] Since these words were originally penned, I have become aware of a revisionist argument advanced by Dr Stephen Hampton in 2008 and taken further in 2022 by Dr Jake Griesel. Their writings suggest according to Edward Malcolm in the *Gospel Magazine* (2023) that reformed doctrines 'were very much alive in the Church of England' in the period 1660 to 1730 and that 'a large number of eminent Churchmen of the period…adhered to the old "Calvinianism" of the Protestant Reformers.'

buried in St Giles' Churchyard. Daniel Defoe included a graphic account of the battle (more of a skirmish) in his *Tour through the Whole Island of Britain*.

The clergy who served Reading's churches at this time seem to have been a fairly undistinguished group of men, although one, Phanuel Bacon[97] of St Laurence's, was at least noted for his extreme longevity in office. Presented in June 1688, just before the revolution, he saw out the reigns of William and Mary, Anne and George I and died in the fifth year of George II at the age of 80 years, of which over half had been spent as Vicar of St Laurence's. The young John Cennick sat under his ministry and seems to have experienced some stirrings towards conviction of sin although it was not until after he left Reading for London that he was truly converted.

Almost equally long-lasting was William Richards (1643-1712), Vicar of St Giles from 1678 till his death. During this period he was preferred to higher office as Archdeacon of Berkshire in 1689 and Salisbury in 1694. His name was frequently invoked posthumously during a long-running dispute between his successor, Samuel Torrent, and a parishioner over a funeral payment known as mortuary.[98]

Nonconformists began to enjoy the benefits of a measure of toleration following the Glorious Revolution through an act of 1689 'for Exempting their Majesties

---

[97] It is interesting to note that his son of the same name (1700-83) also took holy orders but was better-known as a minor dramatist and poet. His output includes a long comic poem on *The Snipe*, published in 1765.

[98] This saga is related at some length in Leslie Harman's history of St Giles'.

Protestant Subjects dissenting from the Church of England from the penalties of certain lawes.' These laws, which included the Conventicle Act and the Five Mile Act, had been enacted under Charles II and remained in force against Roman Catholics ('any Papist or Popish recusant') and any others[99] who could not be classed as 'Protestant dissenters.' The last clause of the act 'provided that no Congregation or assembly for religious worship shall be permitted or allowed by the said Act until the place of such meeting shall be Certified to the Bishop of the Diocese or to the Arch Deacon of that Arch Deaconry, or to the General or Quarter Sessions of the Peace.' The registrations that have survived have been collected by Lisa Spurrier for the Berkshire Record Society and make interesting reading.[100] One of the earliest from Reading in the collection is dated 1752:

> We whose names are underwritten, Protestant Dissenters well affected to his Majesty King George the Second, Do Certifie that a house in St Mary's Butts,

---

[99] These included Unitarians who are described in the act as 'any Person[s] that shall deny in his writing the Doctrine of the Blessed Trinity.' An act of 1813 extended the system of registration to Unitarian gatherings although the tendency during the 18th century for chapels registered as Independent (and including some General Baptist congregations) to depart from Trinitarian doctrine meant that many such had already entered through the proverbial 'back door.'

[100] With some modifications made in 1812, the system of registration continued until 1852 and those of which records survive are listed in Appendix Two. By the Protestant Dissenters Act of 1852 the responsibility for registering places of worship passed to the Registrar General.

Reading, in the county of Berks, late belonging to Silvester Richards,[101] deceas'd, & by his last will and testament bequeath'd to William Cudworth[102] and others, is Set apart for the Religious Worship of Protestant dissenters commonly called Independants [sic], And we do hereby request and desire that the Said house may be Licensed and registered in the Registry of the proper Ecclesiastical Court for that purpose according to Act of Parliament in that behalf made and provided. In Witness whereof we have set our hands the eight day of July in the year of our Lord one thousand Seven hundred and fifty two.

The document is signed by Cudworth and six of his adherents. It was not till late September that registration was completed although usually the process was shorter with most registrations finalised within two weeks and some within a few days of the application.

There is also a record of an earlier certificate, dating from 1728, for the Quakers meeting in Church Lane, the

---

[101] It seems possible that this is the same Mr. S. Richards who makes several appearances in John Wesley's *Journals*. See Chapter 12.

[102] Cudworth (c. 1716-63) was a follower of Wesley who broke with him in 1745 to form his own sect. He had another congregation in Arborfield, and also followers further afield in London, Norfolk and Suffolk. Professor Childs connects the Cudworthians, I think erroneously, with the theory of the 'corpuscular philosophy of light' advanced by the 17th century clergyman, Ralph Cudworth (1617-88). Even if William Cudworth was a descendant of Ralph, there is nothing to suggest that he took an interest in 'natural philosophy.'

original of which has not survived. A copy records that 'a certificate bearing Date ye Twenty Seventh Day of June in Ye Year of our Lord 1728, under the Hands of Abraham Bonifield and Josiah Collett, for appropriating a House in Church Lane in ye Parish of Saint Giles's in Reading in ye County of Berks, for a place of Publick Worship of Protestant Dissenters called Quakers, was Duely Register'd in the Archdeacon's Registry of Berks.' One can perhaps imagine Messrs Bonifield and Collett wincing at the use of the word 'June' rather than the preferred Quaker form of the Fourth Month![103]

As summarised in Appendix Two, the registrations are indicative of the rich variety of worship options open to the people of Reading, reinforcing the comment made by Judith Maltby[104] in relation to the effects of the 1689 religious settlement on English Christianity: 'By the end of the next century, the people of England could choose from an extraordinary range of Christian and other religious expressions which, despite establishment, made the society more akin to America than much of the rest of Europe.'

We referred in the previous chapter to the Quakers' move to Church Street in 1715. Behind this move, there lies an unfortunate history of schism in the movement which began in the late 1670s just as the pressures on dissenters from the Establishment were easing a little. This originated in London with two Quakers from Westmoreland named John Story and John Wilkinson who felt that George Fox was becoming too authoritarian in his

---

[103] Up until the switch to the Gregorian Calendar in 1752, June was regarded as the fourth month; thereafter as now the sixth month.

[104] In *Prayer Book and People* etc., p. 235.

leadership – some even compared him to the Pope! There were a number of other issues that bubbled to the surface, including the rule requiring abstention from payment of tithes, the holding of separate meetings for women and the question of whether or not members should flee persecution. Among the Reading Quakers, the Separatists siding with Wilkinson and Story included founder members, Benjamin and Leonard Coale and Thomas Curtis, who had funded the building of the Meeting House, while those who remained faithful to the leadership of Fox included William Lamboll and Abraham Bonifield. Curtis had at one time extravagantly referred to Fox as 'he who should come, not born of the Flesh, but of the Spirit' but now turned against him. For a number of years the dispute led to unseemly scenes with the 'Orthodox' locked out of the meeting-house and then to an endemic of pamphleteering on behalf of each side in the conflict. For a while both parties deserted the Meeting House but from 1693 the Separatists moved back into the building and the Orthodox crossed over to Sims Court. By this time the 'Pope' had died in 1691. Eventually, the Separatists came to the view that they had been in the wrong and the reunited Friends were able to meet together in the new building in Church Street.

During the first half of the 18th century the Baptists similarly went through a period of internal wrangling. Following the pastorate of Jonathan Davis from 1715-25, Peter Belbin also served for ten 'difficult and stormy' years. Much of the trouble seems to have involved a series of disputes with a deacon named Glover. Belbin complained that 'strife and contention, fickleness and cavilling, animosities and parties have for many years contributed to the weakening and ('tis more than probable) will by degrees effect the total destruction of this unhappy Society.' In 1733 arbitrators from Abingdon were called in but evidently failed to resolve the issues and in 1735 Belbin resigned (in desperation?) in order to conform to the Church of England! His successor, Thomas Flower, died after a few months in post, following which the church was without a pastor until 1741.

Things were little better among the Congregationalists meeting in Broad Street. Samuel Doolittle succeeded Thomas Juice in the ministry in or before 1707. His father, Thomas, had been an ejected minister of 1662[105] and had founded an academy at which his son had studied, along with the future Bible commentator, Matthew Henry, and the historian of the ejection, Edmund Calamy. Samuel served as co-pastor to Juice from 1700 before succeeding him. Described as being of delicate health, he seems to have had a poor opinion of his flock which he regarded as being made up of rough, country people 'who mind more that the form of words delivered to them be Wholesom and sound, than gay and eloquent.' He himself took on an assistant two years before his death in 1717. This was George Burnett, a native of Berwick, who succeeded him in the sole pastorate.

Strains had developed in the congregation towards the end of Doolittle's time and these soon issued in a split, with Presbyterians under Richard Rigby leaving to form a church in Sun Lane (now King Street). A dispute arose between the two assemblies over the right to possess the pulpit cushion. The secessionists who tended towards Unitarianism survived as a body until the late 18th century.

---

[105] His parish had been that of St Alphege, London Wall, in the City of London.

Burnett continued in office till his death in 1740, 'very much afflicted by gout, insomuch that he frequently went on crutches into the pulpit.' His son, John succeeded him but suffered the charge of plagiarism – preaching his own father's sermons! As a result the congregation 'grew very much dissatisfied with him.'

By this time at least things were stirring back in the Church of England as John Wesley made his first recorded visit to Reading in 1739:

> On Friday morning [9 March] I set out, according to [Mr Kinchin's] desire, and in the evening came to Reading, where I found a young man who had in some measure 'known the power of the world to come.' I spent the evening with him and a few of his serious friends; and it pleased God much to strengthen and comfort them.

The young man was John Cennick, then aged just over 20 and after William Laud and Charles Simeon perhaps the most important figure in English church history to have been born in Reading.

10 Reading's Great Awakening

The surprising thing about Reading's Great Awakening is that it almost did not happen! Readers may know John Wesley's most famous and not very flattering reference to Reading: 'How many years were we beating the air at this town? Stretching out our hands to a people stupid as oxen!' The story of John Cennick illustrates the obstacles that were met with during the early years of the Revival.

Cennick was born in Reading around the beginning of December 1718 and baptised in St Laurence's church on the fourth of that month, the son of George Cunnicke (one of several alternative spellings) and the grandson of Thomas Connick, a clothier who had espoused the Quaker faith after hearing George Fox and William Penn preaching. George, however, reverted to the established church following his marriage to Anne Groves in 1708. Their son, John, therefore, was brought up in the Church of England, strongly influenced by his mother. Anne Cennick was evidently a religious woman, albeit one who showed little empathy with the evangelical doctrines later espoused by her son.

Before he was 17, Cennick made the first of a number of forays into London in search of work and it was during one of these that he began to feel the first stirrings of a conviction of sin. A period of spiritual depression lasting two years followed, which has been compared to that described by John Bunyan in *Grace Abounding*, and then back in Reading, in his home church of St Laurence's on 7th September 1737 he heard the words of the psalm, 'Great are the Troubles of the Righteous, but the Lord delivereth him out of them, all! And he that puttes his Trust in God shall not be destitute.' Then he 'was overwhelmed with Joy, and [I] believed there was Mercy. My heart danced with Joy, and my dying Soul reviv'd! I heard the Voice of JESUS saying, I am thy Salvation.'

A chance remark led to Cennick's association with the Methodists. Taking supper with a neighbour he declined to join in a game of cards, whereupon a visitor from Oxford remarked, 'There is just such a stupid, religious fellow in Oxford, one Kinchin.' Almost immediately young John set off for the university city to find Charles Kinchin, who had been one of Wesley's colleagues in the Holy Club.[106] He succeeded in his quest and returned home determined to found a society in Reading. According to his sister and eventual supporter, Sally:

> We had heard of the awakening in Oxford, where my brother went, got acquainted with several, and brought Mr Kinching [sic] into our House...I was much perplex'd, in my own Mind at this rash (as I then thought) proceeding of my Brothers, fearing a Schism in the Church, but being convinced of the truth of their Doctrine, was soon as jealiously atatch'd [sic] thereto. But the Preaching being in our House, it made a great Stur [sic] in the Town & caused us much trouble and disgrace; So that My Mother hearing of it in London, came home & put a Stop to it.

Especially stirred to opposition were a Mr and Mrs Pigeon who accused Cennick of attempting the spiritual seduction of their son. Cennick, however, seems to have

---

[106] This was the originally pejorative nickname for a group of Oxford students that met from 1729 onwards for prayer, Bible Study and mutual encouragement. It is often seen as the origin of Methodism. For Charles Kinchin see also Chapter 12.

thrived on persecution and describes his experience in ecstatic language: 'The Lamb of God embraced me as a son of his Love! And the Holy Spirit moved Prolific on my Spirit, as it did once on the Confused waters in the Creation!'

In May 1739, Cennick left Reading, more or less for good, accompanied by his sister and by another female adherent, Kezia Wilmot, to join the Fetter Lane Society in London. From there he shortly after moved to Bristol to assist Wesley in his labours there and in the process discover the gift of preaching. He later separated from Wesley,[107] siding with George Whitefield in the doctrinal dispute that divided the movement and eventually in 1745 joined the Moravian Church, to which he devoted his labours for the ten remaining years of his life. Much of his work was done in Ireland but he died in London, having come over to visit his ailing mother.

The author has in his possession 'the substance of a sermon preach'd in Exeter in the year 1754 by John Cennick, late of Reading in Berkshire,' on the subject of 'Simon and Mary.'[108]

---

[107] For a more detailed account of the early progress of Methodism in Reading through John Wesley's visits to the town, the reader should turn to Chapter 12.

[108] The text of the sermon is given as Luke Chapter 7, v. 48: 'And [Jesus] said unto [the woman who had anointed his feet], Thy sins are forgiven.' It is notable that, whereas the gospel refers to an unnamed sinner, Cennick identifies her with Mary Magdalene or Mary of Bethany, sister of Martha and Lazarus. Although this was the common view in the Middle Ages, and evidently thereafter, the identification is refuted by most post-Reformation commentators, e.g. Bishop J C Ryle, who traces its

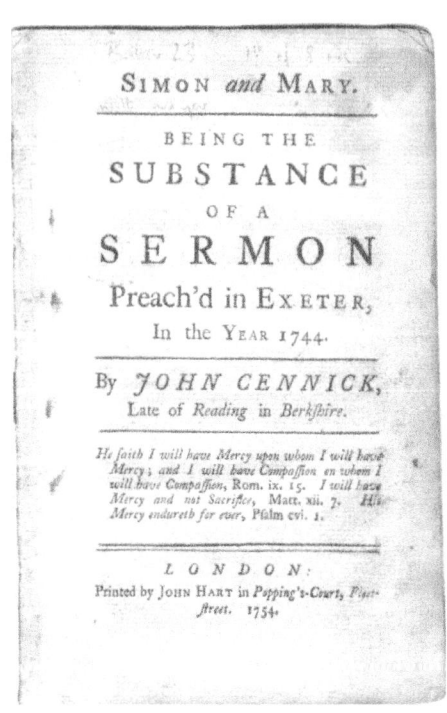

Title-page of John Cennick's sermon on Simon and Mary

It concludes with a moving prayer in which Cennick conveys something of his testimony and his faith in Jesus Christ, 'the Friend of Sinners':

> O Thou loving and merciful Saviour, who out of mere Pity to the Children of Men, once left thy everlasting Throne and Glory, and was made Man for

---

origin to Pope Gregory I (c.590). Perhaps surprisingly John Bunyan also identified her in a sermon with Mary, the sister of Martha.

the Sake of dying and redeeming them out of their lost Estate, be pleas'd still to be gracious in the same Way, and abide the Friend of Sinners. Take me to be thy Child, and behold me at thy Feet like Mary begging for Mercy and Forgiveness, nor send me empty away for thy Name's Sake. I am a poor Sinner who owes thee much; for I have failed and sinned in all I have done ever since I was born. I have no Righteousness to plead, but as a guilty Criminal before the Bar, so stand I before the Judge of all the Earth… I have nothing to pay, O freely forgive me all, and I will love thee much for ever and ever.

Perhaps Cennick's greatest legacy 270 years on lies in the handful of his hymns[109] which are found in hymnbooks today, including the Advent favourite, albeit much revised by Charles Wesley, 'Lo he comes with clouds descending.' Another still in common use is 'Children of the heavenly King.'

Progress in the dissenting congregations during the mid-century was slow and uneven. Among the Baptists, the turmoil that had characterised the first few decades came to an end with the brief but effective ministry of Daniel Turner from 1741 to 1748. Turner[110] seems to have exerted some discipline on the unruly factions within the church and the fact that 18 members were added suggests that some advance was made. However, in 1748 he received a call to Abingdon, where he laboured for 50 years

---

[109] For a longer account of Cennick's contribution to hymnody, see my booklet, *Some Hymn-writers connected with Reading*.

[110] Turner was also an accomplished writer of religious verse and the curious reader can find some notice of this in *Some Hymn-writers* etc.

to the end of his long life. The ministry of his successor in Reading, Thomas Whitewood (1749-66) was, however, marked by renewed decline in membership in spite of the building of a new meeting house in Hosier's Lane, first used for worship on Easter Sunday 1752. By the time the next minister, Thomas Davis, was ordained in 1768, the congregation had dwindled to only 41 members.

Whitewood's pastorate coincided with that of the Rev Evan Jones among the Broad Street congregation. Mr Jones arrived in Reading from Huntingdonshire in 1748 and was ordained on May 17th of the following year. It would appear that he alternated with Whitewood in conducting the Sunday evening service. Evidently, dissent was still treated with contempt by some, for the chapel accounts for this period refer to a sum paid to a person employed to watch the candle set up at the entrance to the chapel courtyard, to prevent it being snuffed out by mischievous passers-by! Evan Jones is said to have met with 'special difficulties' and in 1764 moved to Little Baddow in Essex, to be succeeded by Thomas Noon.

Noon was minister for some 30 years till his death in 1795 and appears to have steadied the ship during this period. He is said to have owed his conversion to a sermon by Whitefield and shortly afterwards to have excited the notice of the Countess of Huntingdon, who sought to secure him as a minister in her Connexion, which had not yet separated from the Establishment. However, young Noon 'strong in his adherence to his Nonconformist principles' declined the offer and instead studied for seven years at the Mile End Academy for dissenters. The Reading

MP, judge and playwright, Thomas Noon Talfourd (1795-1854), was his grandson.[111]

Again the experience of the Congregationalists was mirrored by those of the Baptists, who also enjoyed a long ministry under Thomas Davis, pastor from 1768 to 1796. Davis had been born in 1734 on the Isle of Wight, to a Welsh father and a mother of Huguenot lineage. His elder brother, John, three years older, became a Baptist preacher during the 1750s, whereas Thomas was by his own admission 'a thief, a most wretched liar, and a horrid sinner' during his early manhood. For a time he was the 'ringleader' of a gang in Woolwich that indulged 'in all kinds of wickedness,' including, it seems, smuggling. This continued till the early 1760s when Davis was wonderfully converted at a New Year's day service in Woolwich on Luke 13.7, becoming convinced that he was a cumberer of the ground like the fruitless fig tree in Our Lord's parable.[112]

---

[111] It is interesting to note that at the age of not quite 18 Talfourd, a prolific and precocious writer, authored *An Appeal to the Protestant Dissenters of Great Britain to unite with their Catholic Brethren for the Removal of the Disqualifications by which they are Oppressed*. This contributed to the general agitation towards greater toleration of worship outside the Establishment at this time and may have influenced some of the legislation relating to registration of dissenting chapels referenced in the previous chapter. Its author signed himself 'A Protestant Dissenter' but later after a Unitarian phase conformed to the Church of England.

[112] Davis's life and ministry is recounted in *Holy Spirit, now Descend* by Michael Haykin, 2022. This volume also reproduces Davis's personal confession of faith, delivered at his ordination to his charge in Reading on 14th September 1768.

Thereafter he became 'a fervent gospel preacher' and it was his custom on New Year's Day to give a lecture in which he detailed his own early 'wasted' life and his conversion on that day. His ministry in Reading was highly effective and the church grew considerably during these years; from his inheritance of 41 members bequeathed to him by Thomas Whitewood, he reckoned to have added 475 members by 1794, two years before his death. Davis was also instrumental in spreading the Baptist cause to some of the growing communities not far from Reading including Wallingford, Wokingham and Staines. In addition, he encouraged seven of his members to offer themselves for the ministry.

It was also in 1768 that things at last began stirring in the Church of England. To those who know St Giles today as one of Reading's leading churches within the Anglo-Catholic wing of the Church of England, it may be surprising to learn that it was the place where the Evangelical[113] Awakening began to move the established church within the town in 1768. In that year, William Talbot (1717-74) exchanged the living of All Hallows, Upper Thames Street in the City of London for that of St Giles-in-Reading which had been held from 1756 by James Yorke (1730-1808). The latter was very pleased to obtain a

---

[113] I suspect that this word 'evangelical' is one of the most misunderstood in the Christian dictionary today. Many, especially Christians of other traditions, associate it with 'happy-clappy' charismatic worship, including such novelties as speaking in tongues. Whatever may be said of such practices they are certainly not the essence of evangelicalism in which a belief in justification by faith, conviction of sin and personal need for salvation (being 'born again') through Christ's atoning death, are perhaps the most important elements.

prestigious city parish, which proved for him to be the stepping-stone to episcopal glory,[114] while Talbot, a convinced evangelical and associate of the Countess of Huntingdon, felt that a provincial urban parish was where the Lord was calling him to be. A product of Exeter College, Oxford, he took the living of Kineton, Warwickshire 'with a view to doing good before he could at all be said to be evangelical' but by the mid-50s is found 'itinerating' under the orders of the Countess. He moved to London early in the 1760s.

Talbot preached the gospel to great effect to the extent that his six years in Reading saw from 200 to 300 conversions to Christ. It was said of his preaching that it 'was accompanied by the sacred energy of the Holy Spirit, and hence it became the power of God to the salvation of many of his hearers.'

In a rather bizarre episode that took place in 1771 Talbot became involved with a scoundrel named Jonathan Britain, a confidence trickster and forger who had been apprehended in Reading for forging bank drafts to the sum of £45. Talbot visited Britain in the Compter gaol and at first seemed to feel that he was guiding him towards a confession of his guilt and a recognition of the dangerous state of his soul. However, it soon became clear that Britain was totally unrepentant and controversially Talbot turned detective, believing that only the prospect of facing the gallows would bring him to repentance. He was eventually instrumental in gathering the evidence that led to the felon's conviction and hanging the following year,

---

[114] As Bishop successively of St David's, Gloucester and Ely. However, even at the time of the exchange he was already Dean of Lincoln and thus clearly climbing up the greasy pole!

although all the evidence suggests that he died, a hardened criminal.[115]

In February 1774 Talbot was about to set off to London when he received a call to visit a sick parishioner. It would appear that he caught the same contagious fever that had laid this person low with the result that he was taken ill on his arrival in London and died at the home of a Mr. Wilberforce, uncle of the future anti-slavery campaigner. An affectionate tribute to Talbot appeared in *The Gospel Magazine* for April 1774 'by an intimate friend':

> How tender and compassionate, how full of bowels and sympathy to the poor! How ready to spend and be spent in his Master's cause! How often was his soul in travail for the conversion of others! In his family, a pattern of godliness. To his servants, a gentle and loving master. A FRIEND! One of a thousand; and as a husband none ever exceeded him in tenderness and love inexpressible!

St Giles was then a crown living in the gift of the Lord Chancellor who evidently on a whim decided to appoint the son of Lord Cadogan to the vacant living, although he had only recently graduated from Christ Church, Oxford. The various wheels were oiled after the 18th century fashion that enabled William Bromley Cadogan (1751-97) to become Vicar of both St Giles-in-Reading and St Luke's Chelsea in 1775. In the meantime, Talbot's recently appointed curate, John Hallward, kept up the ministry at St Giles.

---

[115] For a detailed account of this episode see the next chapter, 11.

The St Giles' congregation had grown to love Hallward and rather hoped that Cadogan would concentrate his activities on his fashionable London living and leave St Giles in the hands of the curate. However, Cadogan was a young man of hot temper and some considerable zeal, albeit misguided. As a student he had had an argument with an evangelically-minded contemporary and thrown a salt-cellar at him. He viewed evangelicals as men who courted popularity by throwing about their arms and making a great noise. He cast a petition urging him to retain Hallward's services into the vicarage fire and this was also the receptacle of a collection of sermons sent to him by John Wesley, Cadogan declaring that he 'would form his opinions from the Bible alone.'

At least that was a statement that persuaded some to hope that he would one day glimpse the truth and one woman in the congregation never ceased to pray for him, William Talbot's widow, Sarah. In the meantime, many of the former vicar's hearers drifted off to hear Thomas Davis at the Baptist Chapel or congregated in a chapel in the Butts acquired for the purpose through the offices of the Countess of Huntingdon. As the author of Her Ladyship's *Life and Times* puts it:

> Many naturally repaired to those places where the gospel was preached in their vicinity, where they could hear to edification; others, not satisfied with the doctrines preached by the new vicar, nor the form and discipline of the dissenting meetings, applied to the Countess of Huntingdon; and, having taken a place which would contain several hundred people, opened it as a chapel according to the forms of the Established Church, where they might worship God in their

customary way, and set again under the refreshing sound of Jesus Christ and his salvation.[116]

Informal meetings were also held in Mrs Talbot's house in Castle Street with visits from well-known preachers including John Newton,[117] William Romaine, Rowland Hill and Henry Venn, while Sarah herself continued to importune Cadogan, until he finally declared himself for the Gospel of grace. He later described Sarah Talbot as a woman 'wise in the things of God' and 'as a mother to me in love,' comparing her ministry to him with that of Priscilla to Apollos in Chapter 18 of the *Acts of the Apostles*.

From 1780, Cadogan began to preach the Gospel with great power from the pulpit of St Giles with the result that those that had flocked to other places of worship began to return. It was said that in spite of his learning and aristocratic pedigree Cadogan had the gift of communicating the great truths of religion with a simplicity that spoke to the hearts of even the most illiterate members of the congregation. Before preaching, he would always pray, 'Lord, send us not empty away.'

Nevertheless, he retained his earlier pugnacity, which was reflected in a forcible and rough manner of delivery in his sermons, together with a fondness for pointing out home truths, as in his address to his parishioners in 1785:

---

[116] From A C H Seymour, *Life and Times of Selina, Countess of Huntingdon*, London, 1840.

[117] It is evident from the diaries of John Newton, being progressively published by the John Newton Project, that Newton had known William Talbot and his wife, Sarah, from their time in Kineton before moving to Reading. There are also four letters from Newton to Sarah in Newton's *Cardiphonia*.

It is impossible to have been ten years your minister, and not to have observed the general neglect of those holy things, in which I am sent to minister among you; a neglect which is not only insulting to myself, but as it is dishonouring to God, and consequently bringing upon yourself swift destruction.

A specimen of Cadogan's preaching style is offered from his 'Thoughts on the Lord's Prayer,' based on a discourse given in St Giles.

Give us this day our daily bread.'

Man is composed of soul and body, of the breath of God and the dust of the earth, and this prayer is suited to his condition. Bread is the staff of life: the poor know too much, and the rich too little, that it is alone sufficient to support the animal frame; it may therefore be used here for food in general; 'feed me with food convenient for me.' The spirit of piety breathes in this prayer, teaching us to ask for whatever we have; it is true that they often have the most of this world's goods, who neither pray nor praise for any of them; but though their hearts are set upon the creature, they know not their use nor value, for 'they are sanctified by the word of God and by prayer.' Bread is sweet to a man, which is received as the gift of God, and comes to him as the answer to prayer. The little therefore the righteous hath, is better than great riches of the ungodly; the blessing of the Lord it maketh rich, and He addeth no sorrow with it; it turns bread into the most savoury meat, and water into the best of wine.

Cadogan exercised an effective ministry at St Giles over a period of around 16 years during which time galleries were installed in the church to accommodate the increased number of hearers. As well as providing spiritual meat he also made sure that the poor were fed with the 'staff of life' with 30 lbs of beef per week going into the vicarage stew-pot for this purpose.

Cadogan influenced a number of younger men, including: Reading-born Charles Simeon (1759-1836), for many years Vicar of Holy Trinity, Cambridge, who will be considered in a later chapter; William Marsh (1775-1864), likewise a Reading product, who became Curate of St Laurence's; and John Eyre (1754-1803), Cadogan's curate for four years and later one of the founders in 1794 of the pioneering London Missionary Society.[118]

However, early in 1797, Cadogan's all-too-short life came to a close, following an inflammation of the bowels and with it concluded St Giles' contribution to the Great Awakening. His death led to the foundation of what is now St Mary's, Castle Street, in 1798, but that again is another story, for which the reader will have to wait for Chapter 16.

---

[118] See also *Sent from Reading*, which covers in greater detail the part played by Simeon and Eyre in the formation of two of the major missionary societies, along with the later evangelistic endeavours of both Simeon and Marsh.

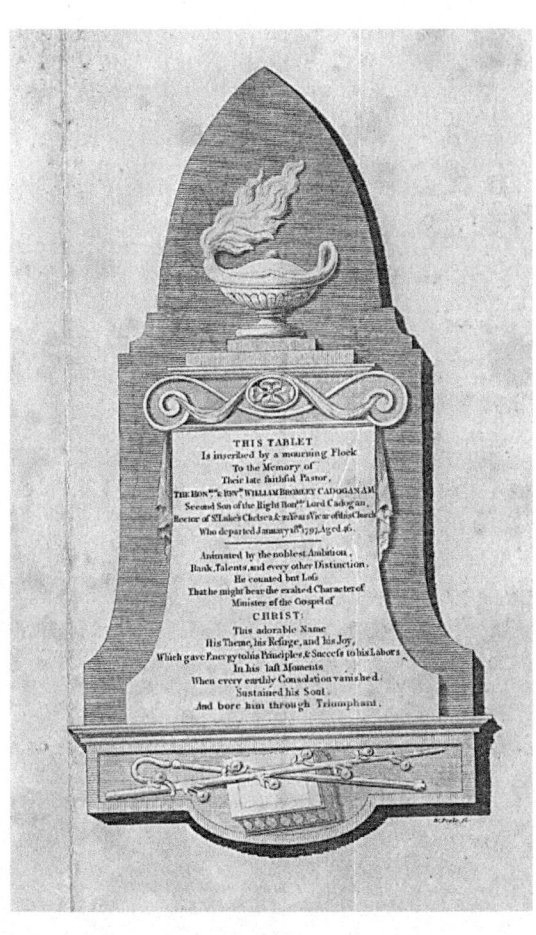

Memorial Tablet to William Bromley Cadogan
in St Giles' church

11   William Talbot and Jonathan Britain

It was during the writing of *The Church that Would Not Die* that I learnt of the relationship between the Rev William Talbot and the forger, Jonathan Britain, a man who faced the gallows in 1772. As indicated in the preceding chapter, Talbot was an important leader in the Evangelical Revival within the established church, though less well remembered today than such men as Newton, Romaine, Simeon and the Venns. Britain was described towards the end of his life as 'one of the greatest impostors that this kingdom has ever seen' but he too is largely forgotten, even in criminological circles.

William Talbot came from an aristocratic background and it is probable that initially he entered the church because it was the thing that younger sons of the nobility did rather than through any deep sense of vocation. As with many of his class, he owed his spiritual rebirth to the ministry of the Countess of Huntingdon and from that point on he was in the words of James Hervey of Weston Favell, a man 'baptized with the Holy Ghost and with fire - fervent in spirit and setting' his face 'as a flint.' Having held the livings successively of Kineton, Warwickshire and All Hallows, Upper Thames Street, London, Talbot came to Reading in 1768 as Vicar of St Giles, one of the three parishes that then served that town. Here Talbot's preaching of the Gospel was especially effective and, as we have seen, it was estimated that 200 to 300 souls were converted to Christ during the six years of his ministry.in Reading.[119] He was also much given to good works and,

---

[119] See A. C. H. Seymour, op. cit: 'two or three hundred seals,

as well as tending to the needs of the sick and the poor; this included prison visiting.

Jonathan Britain was a Yorkshireman, born in Thirsk, to respectable parents of limited means who, in the words of the *Newgate Calendar*, could not afford 'to give him a liberal education.' Instead, he was sent to work as an errand-boy at the office of an attorney in York. The latter recognised in young Jonathan 'marks of genius and ability' and promoted him to the position of articled clerk. Britain, however, was a restless youth afflicted by 'an impatience of restraint' who found it difficult to settle into any position for long. From the lawyer's office, he proceeded to a public academy where he was employed initially as a teacher of mathematics. Once again his talents achieved recognition and he was promoted to be the principal usher in the school.

It was not long, however, before the previous pattern of events repeated themselves and his next career move was destined to be his undoing, for he enlisted as a soldier in the 10th Dragoons.[120] Here it was his striking physical appearance rather than his intellect which brought him to the attention of his officers. Such attention 'very much flattered his vanity' and led him into an extravagant lifestyle through a vain attempt to emulate his superiors. As a result, he found himself in reduced circumstances and

---

such as shall be his crown in that day when the chief shepherd shall appear.'

[120] This regiment was later known as the 10th Royal Hussars and then amalgamated with the 11th to form the Royal Hussars (Prince of Wales's Own). Since 1992 it has been part of the King's Royal Hussars.

was tempted to dishonesty. As the *Newgate Calendar*[121] again puts it:

> He committed a variety of frauds, most of them of such artful contrivance as to elude all possibility of detection.
>
> He had a custom of introducing himself into the company of persons who had no suspicion of deceit, and then he would so far insinuate himself into their good opinion as to take undue advantage of their unsuspecting honesty.

We can thus sum him up as a 'con man' par excellence.

His career as a fully-fledged criminal commenced in Bristol where he passed a number of bank drafts which he had forged. From there, fearing detection, he proceeded to the capital where he wrote a series of letters to King George III, claiming that he had been implicated in a plot to set fire to the naval dockyard at Portsmouth. These were apparently disregarded, whereupon Britain addressed the Lord Mayor of London, offering to surrender himself and effectively turn King's Evidence. The promise of a pardon he requested was advertised in the *London Gazette* and on the strength of this Britain proceeded to Reading to meet his wife who had been sick. However, his continuing reduced circumstances induced him to offer further forged drafts totalling £45 and on this occasion he was apprehended and found himself in the Compter, one of Reading's several gaols. This was on Tuesday, 30th July 1771.

Shortly afterwards, while awaiting examination, Britain took a hefty dose of arsenic, evidently wishing to end his

---

[121] The *Complete Newgate Calendar*, 1926, page 87.

life rather than face a lengthy incarceration, awaiting trial at the next assizes. However, 'when his pains grew torturing, he submitted to the use of proper medicines, and listened to the advice of sending for some Clergyman to talk to him.'[122] Mr Blisset, a grocer, one of the victims of Britain's forgeries, was concerned for the state of his soul and asked William Talbot to visit him. Talbot was at first reluctant to undertake this duty, as the Compter was 'not within the limits of [St Giles'] parish' but St Laurence's. However, the urgency of the case persuaded him to ignore Anglican protocol in this instance. He found Britain 'not in the least degree sensible of the evil of what he had done' in attempting to take his life:

> I began to talk to him faithfully and roundly, and yet at the same time tenderly, of the extreme wickedness of the act he had been guilty of, and the perilous situation in every respect, in which I conspicuously discerned his soul to be; and to do the utmost in my power to bring him to a sight and a conviction of better things. By degrees, I obtained from him some seeming attention to me; and much conversation together, during the space of four or five hours, we had 'till every thing that I thought needful to be said had been, repeatedly and in the plainest manner, spoken to him.[123]

Talbot visited Britain again the following day and resumed his visits in mid-September after a period of convalescence on the South Coast. Britain continually

---

[122] Rev W Talbot, *Narrative of the Whole of his Proceedings relative to Jonathan Britain*, 1772, page 25.
[123] Talbot, op cit. page 26.

affirmed his innocence of the charges of forgery, both in Reading and (as these began to come to light) in Bristol. While in prison he also returned to his allegations concerning the alleged arson plot and wrote letters to several newspapers, claiming that Lord Mansfield, the Lord Chief Justice, the Earl of Halifax, Secretary of State, the Earl of Faulconbridge and other prominent persons had been bribed by the French to 'encourage the setting fire to the dockyard at Portsmouth.' He himself, together with a Captain Kelly of the Irish Brigades in France were the arsonists. Britain claimed to have a large quantity of incriminating evidence contained in a portmanteau sent on by him from Bristol to London.

Although at no time does Talbot appear to have doubted that Britain was guilty of deception in the matter of money, for a time he was at least prepared to give him the benefit of the doubt over the veracity of his claims concerning the dockyard fire:

> The steadiness of his assertions; the readiness with which he told his story; his being under no confinement when he originally made his offers of discovery; the certainty he had, tho' in gaol at present, of soon being at liberty again, added to the reasonable, and only request he had made, of being brought to a trial; together with his willingness to suffer death, if he should, upon that trial, be found an impostor: all these things together, did, for a little season, and 'till I had time to reflect, hold me in suspence; and there were moments, in the beginning of my enquiries, in which I was strongly inclined to believe, that there was truth, in some, at least of his pretensions; but the scale soon turned; daily discoveries of his falsehoods weakened

his credit with me more and more; 'till I was satisfactorily and perfectly convinced, that he was as errant a deceiver as DUDLEY himself.[124]

An extended stay at Bath from late October, while his wife, Sarah, received the benefits of the waters, enabled Talbot to take a trip over to Bristol to undertake enquiries. In regard to the alleged dockyard plot, he was able to satisfy himself that the portmanteaux was a non-existent figment of Britain's vivid imagination and 'that not a paper of consequence was he possessor of, any where; and that the whole of the correspondences he talked of was a scandalous fiction.'[125] He also succeeded in making the acquaintance of several people that Britain had defrauded in Bristol, most of them, like their counterparts in Reading, honest trades-people who had been taken in by Britain's plausible ways, which included the practice of 'diabolical deceptions, under the mask of religion'. One of these, a barber named Arthur Sandall was clearly a man of strong, religious convictions who had written to Britain, warning him of the terrors of hell that awaited him, of 'being confined in everlasting chains of darkness, there to be tormented with Devils and damned spirits, night and day forever.' This letter had evoked a response in Britain in which he described himself as 'the miserablest man upon earth' but the note of remorse was all part of his dissembling. The villain's activities in Bristol had not been confined to forgery but also encompassed drunkenness

---

[124] Talbot, op. cit. pages 54-5. It is uncertain to which Dudley Talbot is referring in this paragraph. A possible candidate is Captain Richard Dudley, a notorious highwayman, executed in 1681.

[125] Talbot, op. cit. page 70.

and riotings, together with sexual debauchery. He had also employed a number of aliases including that of William Johnson.

It was by now clear that the charges that had been made against him in Reading were unlikely to result in conviction, because material evidence had been inadvertently destroyed by his victims. Talbot, therefore, came to the view that it was his duty to encourage Britain's Bristol victims to combine together to bring him to justice.

I returned in the evening, to Bath; where I had leisure to ruminate upon all that I had discovered; and I was penetrated with the thought of the danger to society from such a man. So extensive a capacity and disposition to do mischief; such deep dissimulation and unsuspectable art; such unfeelingness of soul at the miseries he was creating; such treachery and baseness; and finally, so bold and daring, and malicious a spirit; all these pernicious endowments made him too dangerous to set at liberty again. I saw him also in the still more horrible light, of a diabolical incendiary, scattering, through the nation, firebrands and death; forging in his inventive brain, crimes of the deepest die; and charging them upon obnoxious names, without a shadow of their existence; poisoning thereby the people's minds, and inflaming their discontents; exciting them, so far as he could, to seditious, murderous insurrections; and throwing us all into the utmost confusion; and this, only to provide a chance of his own escape from the punishment due to the villainies of which he had been guilty. Having therefore regard enough for the public, and spirit enough for the undertaking, I resolved without delay, to stop him in his career.[126]

Talbot carried out his intentions and also terminated his visits to Britain who apparently remained in ignorance of his part in the proceedings against him until he was brought to trial. Following the collapse of the case against him in Reading, Britain remained in prison, a warrant of detainer having been served against him as a result of Talbot's efforts. Eventually, he was removed to Bristol by a writ of habeas corpus and there stood trial for his several acts of forgery. At this point, however, the case took another unusual twist.

....being put to the bar, he refused to plead, and held in his hand the *Gazette* which contained the offer of pardon, insisting that he had given information against his accomplices who had set fire to the dockyard at Portsmouth.

On this he was informed by the recorder that he could take no notice of the proclamation inserted in the *Gazette*. But Britain, instead of paying attention to this declaration, threw the *Gazette* upon the table where the clerk sat, and declared that a scheme was formed to deprive him of life, contrary to the due course of the law.[127]

Britain was warned that under a recent Act of Parliament he would be judged guilty if he continued to refuse to plead to the indictment. The trial was held up for two days while a special messenger was dispatched to

---

[126] Talbot, op cit. pages 73-4.
[127] *Complete Newgate Calendar*, page 88.

London to obtain a copy of the statute. When this had been procured, Britain was at last persuaded to plead not guilty and proceeded to conduct his own defence.

> He cross-examined the witnesses in a manner that gave sufficient testimony of his abilities; but the evidence against him was such as not to admit of a doubt of his guilt, and in consequence he was capitally convicted, and sentenced to die.[128]

Talbot's wisdom in breaking off his relations with Britain were vindicated by the prisoner's conduct, subsequent to his conviction. He put out a story that Talbot had deceived him into making a confession of his crimes and had then betrayed his confidence. In its most extreme version Britain alleged that 'hearing I was a Roman Catholic, [Talbot] came to me and told me he was a Romish priest, and then I confessed to him, and that is the way by which all these prosecutions have been set on foot.' In spite of the preposterous nature of these allegations, they were believed by a section of the public in both Bristol and Reading. As a result Talbot was obliged to rush into print with his *Narrative of the Whole of his Proceedings relative to Jonathan Britain*, designed to 'remove every blackening charge against me.' Even this does not seem to have satisfied all Talbot's accusers. One writer in the *Berkshire Chronicle*, using the pseudonym, Impartial (anything but!), was even moved to verse:

> A priest of late got Britain hanged.
>   Ye sufferers! Cease to mock:

---

[128] Op cit. pages 88-9.

> Who knows? When first he has harangued,
> Perhaps he'll hang his flock.

Talbot's primary aim in bringing Britain to justice was to rid the public of one whom he had concluded to be a dangerous criminal. However, initially, his concern had been for the security of Britain's soul, threatened as it then was by his attempted suicide. Although Britain exhibited, in the course of his relations with Talbot, a shameless lack of concern for his victims and no evidence of a repentant heart, the latter, nevertheless, retained a hope that when faced with the gallows he might still be saved from damnation. This is expressed in a letter to one of Britain's victims, Daniel Wait, written while he was awaiting trial in Bristol:

> I heartily wish something may be done for the good of his soul; but this, in his present state of mind and action, cannot be. If ever there will be an opening for this purpose, it will be when he is condemned, and has lost every hope of rescue.[129]

Alas! there is no evidence, in Britain's case, that the prescription was effective.[130] He was executed on the 15th

---

[129] Talbot, op cit. page 23. Quoted from a letter dated 11 April 1772.

[130] That the practice of preaching to the condemned could at times prove effective is suggested by the account in Charles Wesley's Journal of his ministry to the prisoners in Newgate. See *The Journal of the Rev Charles Wesley M.A. The Early Journal 1736-1739*, Robert Culley, 1909, page 185 et seq. and in particular page 189: July 12. – I preached at Newgate to the condemned

May, 1772 and, although he left 'a direct and full confession', withdrawing all his allegations relating to the Portsmouth fire, there was seemingly no indication of any softening of the hardness of heart that had afflicted him from the time of his arrest.

As for Talbot, he was determined to return to his parochial duties:

> I now gladly withdraw from the public stage, and go back to my parish; there to attend to the more pleasing, as well as more special and immediate duties of my calling; and, particularly, to the preaching of that *precious Name*, so deservedly *exalted above every Name*, JESUS; whose servant I am; to whom thankfully I ascribe whatever, upon this occasion, has been right in my spirit, principle, or conduct; from whom I derive all my supports and consolations here, and in whom I am looking for all my salvation hereafter.[131]

In conclusion, how are we to judge Talbot's actions in this matter? There are those today who would take a similar view to that of his 18th century detractors. One local Reading historian, the late Leslie North,[132] argued

---

felons, and visited one of them in his cell, sick of a fever – a poor black that had robbed his master. I told him of One who came down from heaven to save lost sinners, and him in particular… he cried, 'What! Was it for me? Did God suffer all this for so poor a creature as me?' I left him waiting for the salvation of God.

[131] Talbot, op cit. page 93. The italics are Talbot's own.

[132] Despite these reservations, the writer wishes to acknowledge the considerable assistance rendered to him by the late Mr North in tracking down the story of William Talbot and Jonathan Britain.

that he should have confined himself to seeking to bring Britain to sincere repentance and that in taking the measures he did to bring him to justice 'he went sadly astray - halter in one hand, crucifix in the other.' This, however, is to bring a modern, liberal Christian perspective to the issue. The 1770s seem a remote era to a society that can scarcely conceive that hanging criminals for forgery and theft was ever condoned and when the restoration of the death penalty even for murder seems an unlikely eventuality. The very cheapness of life in that age served, however, only to render the gift of salvation to eternal life even more precious to men. Talbot wanted both to save society from Britain and to save Britain from eternal punishment. At times, he may have accorded greater priority to the first than to the second motive but that appears to have been a question on which he exercised thoughtful, spiritual judgement rather than acting wilfully. Surely, in this instance, it could be said truly, echoing the 'intimate friend' quoted in the preceding chapter, that 'his soul [was] in travail for the conversion of' Jonathan Britain.

Note. This chapter has previously been published during the 1990s as a standalone piece, both in *Berkshire Old and New* (substantially as above), and in *The Churchman* with additional theological reflections on the subject of capital punishment.

12   John Wesley in Reading

John Wesley was a much travelled man who was estimated to have ridden 8,000 miles a year in the service of his Master during his long ministry from his conversion in 1738 till his death in 1791. Many of his journeys took him between Bristol and Bath in the west and London in the east, so that it is not surprising that he is found to make frequent visits to Reading, then as now, a major transport hub. There is, it would appear, surprisingly meagre documentary evidence about the early days of Methodism in Reading, so that the references to Wesley's visits in his Journals are key evidence in this regard. This chapter attempts to track these visits through their pages. Generally they only refer to the occasions on which he ministered, mainly through preaching. It is also clear from the diaries from which the more polished Journals were refined that Wesley made many other visits, often stopping an hour or two just to dine or to meet his associates briefly. A further primary source is the Sermon Register maintained by Wesley for a number of years, which indicates the text(s) on which he preached in the town.

Wesley's first reference to Reading in his journals takes place in the context of a journey from Oxford, where he was based during the first two weeks of March 1739, to Dummer in Northern Hampshire, where Mr Kinchin had 'earnestly desired me…to supply his church on Sunday.' This was the Revd. Charles Kinchin (1711-42), who had been a member of the Holy Club and was at this time[133]

---

[133] Like Cennick, he subsequently became attracted to the Moravian church, not long before his premature death in January 1742.

one of Wesley's most active supporters; he was a fellow (and later Dean) of Corpus Christi College, Oxford and Rector of Dummer. Thus Wesley writes:

> On Friday morning [9th March] I set out, according to his desire, and in the evening came to Reading, where I found a young man who had in some measure 'known the power of the world to come.' I spent the evening with him and a few of his serious friends; and it pleased God much to strengthen and comfort them.

The diaries identify the young man as John Senwick, clearly one of the many variants of Cennick. John Cennick (1718-55) was, as we have noted in Chapter 10, a native of Reading and at this time barely 20. His grandparents were Quakers who were imprisoned for their faith in the county gaol that formerly stood on the site of St Mary's, Castle Street, but his father converted to Anglicanism at the time of his marriage. Following his conversion Cennick heard of Kinchin's work in Oxford and sought him out, as also narrated in Chapter 10. Subsequently he became a staunch supporter of Wesley, joining the Fetter Lane Society in London for a brief period when things became too hot in Reading, before being appointed to teach at a school for the colliers' children established at Kingswood near Bristol. The diary shows that on a number of occasions, after Cennick removed from Reading to London and then Kingswood, Wesley called on Cennick's mother and on his sister, Sally, who as we can see from the letter to Whitefield quoted below was also by this time a convert.

In 1740, however, Cennick quarrelled bitterly with Wesley on the grounds that he 'did not preach the truth, in particular, with regard to election.' However correct his judgement may have been, Cennick's changed manner[134] towards Wesley was expressed in somewhat intemperate language, which recalls that of Toplady a generation later but is perhaps a little more excusable in the light of his youth. It is pleasing to be able to report that the two men were able to conduct an amicable correspondence some years later over the rival claims of the Methodists and Moravians, to whom Cennick now adhered, to a preaching-house in Dublin.

A letter of Wesley to George Whitefield[135] dated 16th March 1739 gives a slightly longer account of this first visit to Reading and also provides important evidence that there was considerable opposition to Methodism in the town, as elsewhere, not least from the clergy of the established church:

> On Friday accordingly I set out and came in the evening to Reading, where I found a young man, Cennick by name, strong in the faith of our Lord Jesus. He had begun a Society there the week before, but the minister of the parish[136] had now wellnigh overturned it. Several of the members of it spent the evening with us, and it pleased God to strengthen and comfort them. In the morning our brother

---

[134] Thus, under 16 December 1740, Wesley writes: 'I was greatly surprised, when I went to receive him, as usual, with open arms, to observe him quite cold, so that a stranger would have judged he had scarce ever seen me before.'

[135] Despite their differences Wesley and Whitefield also retained a great deal of respect for each other with the former preaching at the latter's funeral in 1770.

[136] This was the Revd. William Boudry, who was Vicar of St Laurence's, Reading, from 1733-42.

Cennick rode with me, whom I found willing to suffer, yea to die, for his Lord…

On Monday [i.e. on returning from Dummer]….we had appointed the little Society at Reading to meet us in the evening; but the enemy was too vigilant. Almost as soon as we went out of town the minister sent or went to each of the members, and, by arguing and threatening, utterly confounded them, so that they were all scattered abroad. Mr Cennick's own sister did not dare to see us, but was gone out on purpose to avoid it. I trust, however, our God will gather them together again, and that the gates of hell shall not prevail against them.

It was from Kingswood that Wesley's next substantial visit to Reading took place on 2nd November 1739. On this occasion his impressions were less favourable, although full of hope, even in adversity:

I set out, and the next evening came to Reading, where a little company of us met in the evening; at which the zealous mob was so enraged, that they were ready to tear the house down. Therefore I hope God has a work to do in this place. In thy time let it be fulfilled!

This record is augmented by that of the diary:

3.30 Reading, at the inn, in talk; 4 at Sally Cennick's. Mrs Cennick not [? at home], prayer, conversed, tea, read my Journal' 6.30 many came, Acts V. 8.30 supper, Journal, prayer; 11.

It was from Kingswood also that Wesley set out on 1st February of the following year, answering a call to London to see a young man who had been condemned to death for highway robbery.[137] On 4th February:

> I came to Reading, and met with a few hungering and thirsting after righteousness. A few more I found at Windsor in the evening.

He was back in Reading a month later, as the account for Monday 3rd March indicates:

> I rode by Windsor to Reading, where I had left two or three full of peace and love. But I now found some from London had been here, grievously troubling these souls also; labouring to persuade them (1) that they had no faith at all, because they sometimes felt doubt or fear; and (2) that they ought to be still; not to go to church, not to communicate, not to search the Scriptures 'because' say they, 'you cannot do any of these things without trusting in them.' After confirming their souls we left Reading.

On Friday 12th December Wesley set out from London bound for Kingswood at 4.30 am, accompanied by Cennick and two other assistants, Edward Nowers and a Mr Bond. The journey was rather protracted as the party was beset by 'some difficulty and danger, by reason of much ice on the road.' They reached Colnbrook at 8.15, Reading at 1, dining at Sally Cennick's, and Hungerford at 6.30.

The diary records further flying visits in January, March and May 1741. One of these (18th May) includes a tantalisingly brief reference to conversing with a stranger

---

[137] An interesting further example perhaps of the ministry to those under sentence of death explored in the previous chapter.

after arriving in Reading just after noon. The Journals then record an eastbound itinerary – Bristol – Reading – Windsor – in January 1743 but without incident in either of the two Berkshire towns.

The next visit recorded in the Journals is on 11th September 1747, following visits to Bath and Bearfield:

> We rode to Reading. Mr Richards, a tradesman in the town, came to our inn, and entreated me to preach at a room he had built for that purpose; I did so at six in the morning, and then rode on. It rained all the way we came to London.

Mr Richards' premises are believed to have been located at the top of London Street, near the Crown Inn, one of the coaching inns used by Wesley, according to the diaries.

In November Wesley is back in Reading, having travelled from London on this occasion:

> Mon. Nov. 2. I preached at Windsor at noon, and in the afternoon rode to Reading. Mr. J. R. had just sent his brother word, 'That he had hired a mob to pull down his preaching-house that night.' In the evening Mr. S. Richards overtook a large company of bargemen walking towards it, whom he immediately accosted, and asked, 'If they would go with him to hear a good Sermon!' telling them, 'I will make room for you, if you were as many more.' They said, they would go with all their hearts. 'But, neighbours, (said he,) would it not be as well to leave those clubs behind you? Perhaps some of the women may be frightened at them.' They threw them all away, and walked quietly with him to the house, where he set them in a pew.
>
> In the conclusion of my Sermon, one of them who

used to be their Captain, being the head taller than his fellows, rose up and looking round the congregation, said, 'The gentleman says nothing but what is good, I say so; and there is not a man here that shall dare to say otherwise.'

Wesley paid a third visit of that Autumn on 14th December but of this we learn only that he arrived in Reading, 'thoroughly weary and wet'. Further visits in the following year are equally briefly dismissed, as on 31st May when Wesley preached and on 20th June when he 'preached at noon, to a serious, well-behaved congregation, and in the afternoon rode to Hungerford.' Similarly on 12th September, he again 'preached at Reading and rode on to Hungerford' en route to Bristol.

On 14th November he visited both Windsor and Reading, where in each town he 'examined the Members of the Society', with visits to Wycombe and Brentford following on the succeeding days for the same purpose. The system of Societies and classes, which had its origins at the start of the Methodist movement, had been institutionalised in 1743[138] and clearly, despite the inauspicious history of Cennick's original Society, was in operation in Reading by the mid-point of the century. Wesley himself aimed to examine the society classes four times a year, although there is no evidence of this taking place on such a regular basis in Reading.

November 1749 sees Reading back on Wesley's itinerary during a busy round of preaching with sermons at Bath,

---

[138] *The Nature, Design and General rules of the United Societies in London, Bristol, Kingswood, Newcastle-upon-Tyne &* were published in that year.

Seend,[139] Reading and in London over three consecutive days.

The entry in Wesley's Journal for the end of February 1750 gives a further and vivid picture of the punishing schedule that the great evangelist set himself:

> Tues. 27. I at length forced myself from London. We dined a little beyond Colnbrook, spoke plain to all in the house, and left them full of thankfulness, and of good resolutions.
>
> I preached at Reading in the evening; and in the morning, Wednesday, 28, took horse, with the north wind full in our face. It was piercing cold, so that I could scarce feel whether I had any hands or feet, when I came to Blewbury. After speaking severally to the members of the Society, I preached to a large congregation. In the evening, I met my brother [Charles] at Oxford, and preached to a small serious company.

Further brief visits to Reading occur in September 1750[140] and June,[141] August[142] and October 1751, the last occasion being a Sunday when Wesley 'preached at one and five', before riding forward to London on the next day.

1752 saw one evidently brief visit in November,[143]

---

[139] A Wiltshire village close to Melksham and Devizes. A Methodist chapel was opened there by Wesley in 1775.
[140] Friday 7th September. Text: Daniel 9.7.
[141] Texts: Hebrews 10.19, John 17.3, Ecclesiasticus. 9.10, Ezekiel, 37.1.
[142] 19th August. Texts: Philippians 2.1, 1 Kings 18.21, 2 Kings 5.12, Philippians 3.20.
[143] The Sermon Register also records a sermon on Philippians 4.7 in February 1752.

following which the Journal is silent until October 1754, when Reading is visited en route from Salisbury, where Wesley meditates on the folly of the uninhabited city of Old Sarum still sending two members to the Parliament, an anomaly that continued until 1832. On this occasion he seems to have challenged a lapsed follower:

> Thursday. 3. I rode to Reading, and preached in the evening. Observing a warm man near the door, (which was once of the Society,) I purposely bowed to him; but he made no return. During the first prayer he stood, but sat while we sung. In the sermon his countenance changed, and in a little while he turned his face to the wall. He stood at the second hymn, and then kneeled down. As I came out he catched [sic] me by the hand, and dismissed me with a hearty blessing.

In 1755, the dog-days of August[144] find congregations in both Reading and Salisbury in a soporific mood:

> Sun. 17.....In the evening, I preached to a sleepy congregation at Reading, on, 'It is a fearful thing to fall into the hands of the living God;' and to much such another on Tuesday evening, at Salisbury, on, 'Harden not your hearts.'

Two months later he is again in Reading on Thursday 23rd October and we find him preaching on consecutive nights:

> Several soldiers were there, and many more the next night, when I set before them, 'The terrors of the Lord;' and I scarce ever saw so much impression made

---

[144] Again the Register records an earlier visit in March when Wesley preached on 1 Corinthians 1.24.

on this dull, senseless people.

The Journals are then silent about Reading for almost twenty years. This was certainly a period in which the world did very much become Wesley's parish, as he travelled extensively in Scotland, Wales, Ireland, the West Country and Northern England during this time. He was also wont to take more circuitous itineraries between Bristol and London, for instance, adopting a southern loop through Salisbury, Winchester and Portsmouth. However, this is not to say that Wesley did not visit Reading, at least in passing. He was certainly often in the Thames Valley, with a number of references to High Wycombe, Witney and Henley-on-Thames.

He seems to have found the inhabitants of Henley akin to those of Reading in terms of resistance to the gospel with references in 1764 to 'a wild, staring congregation, many of them void both of common sense and common decency.' This was in marked contrast to the folk of Witney: 'congregation…both large and deeply attentive…so remarkably diligent in business, and at the same time of so quiet a spirit, and so calm, and civil in their behaviour.' Henley had improved by 1768 when Wesley met with a 'considerable number of serious people. One or two of the baser sort made some noise, but I reproved them, and, for once, they were ashamed.'

Earlier in March 1762 Wesley had undertaken a journey from London to Bristol, which seems to have lasted 12 days, as he 'went slowly through the Societies.' It would be reasonable to assume that Reading was on this itinerary. However, the next specific reference to Wesley's presence in Reading comes in March 1775:

> March 1st, being Ash Wednesday, I took a solemn

leave of our friends at London, and on Thursday, 2nd, met our brethren at Reading. A few were awakened, and perhaps converted here, by the ministry of Mr Talbot,[145] but, as he did not take any account of them, or join them together, we found no trace of them remaining. A large room was presently filled, and all the spaces adjoining, and I have hardly ever seen a people who seemed more eager to hear.'

This is puzzling since, as outlined in Chapter 10, accounts of the ministry of William Talbot at St Giles-in-Reading suggest a rather different story, Talbot's converts being numbered at around 300 (perhaps only a few by Wesley's standards!) At this time the rift between Talbot's successor, Cadogan, and his congregation could only just have started, although negotiations with the Countess of Huntingdon regarding the use of her chapel in the Butts commenced in the following month. Wesley had perhaps only heard a partial account of the state of affairs. Certainly he became aware of the arrival of the zealous and high-minded but unconverted William Bromley Cadogan, for, as recorded in Cecil's life of the latter and also noted in Chapter 10 above, Wesley sent him a copy of a volume of his writings for his perusal, which along with a number of other items found their way into the vicarage fire.

He preached again in Reading on 19th November 1775 but makes no mention of events in the town. We then pass on to 1777 and Wesley's most famous reference to Reading:

---

[145] Wesley was previously aware of Talbot's character as a minister of the gospel for he is included among fellow-labourers listed in a letter of 1764 along with such names as Newton, Romaine, Fletcher and Berridge.

Mon 10 [March]. In the evening I preached at Reading. How many years were we beating the air at this town? Stretching out our hands to a people stupid as oxen! But it is not so at present. That generation is passed away, and their children are of a more excellent spirit.

**John Wesley, founder of Methodism and
a frequent visitor to Reading
– painted by J M Williams RA**

Of the next visit on 17th July 1780 we learn only that Wesley preached but it is also interesting to note that on this occasion he was accompanied by his hymn-writing brother. This is the only instance in which Charles's company on a visit to Reading is explicitly recorded.

Wesley's last recorded call of any substance occurred early in the following year. He was travelling from London by coach to Bristol and experienced one of the hazards of 18th century travel:

> Sun 4 [March]. At eight in the evening, I took coach for Bristol with Mr Rankin, and two other friends. We drove with two horses as far as Reading. Two more were then added, with a postillion, who knowing little of his business, instead of going forward, turned quite round on a sloping ground, so that we expected the coach to overturn every moment; so it must have done, but that the coachman instantly leaped off, and with some other men held it up, till we got out at the opposite door. The coach was then soon set right, and we went on without let or hindrance.

The fellow-traveller mentioned can be identified as Thomas Rankin (1738-1810), a Scotsman who had been converted at an early age while hearing George Whitefield preach in Leith but later attached himself to Wesley. He was a circuit preacher as early as 1761, served as Superintendent of the work in America from 1773 to 1778 and was ordained by Wesley for ministry in England in 1789.

The diary does record three later visits, which may be quoted here for sake of completeness:

1 March 1784:	preached at 12 on Matt 7.24, dinner, 2 chaise; 5 Newbury.
27 Feb 1786:	11.30 Reading, the Crown, dinner, within; 12.30 chaise,

	read Guthrie.[146]
7 Sept 1786:	12 Reading, chaise, 2.30 Newbury, dinner.

A further event of this last decade of Wesley's life that has an indirect connection with Reading is his meeting with Charles Simeon. Although the bulk of Simeon's life and work is bound up with his ministry in Cambridge, he was Reading-born[147] and was much influenced during his earlier years by his friendship with William Bromley Cadogan. He made a good impression on Wesley:

> 20 December 1784. I went to Hinxworth, where I had the satisfaction of meeting Mr. Simeon, Fellow of King's College, in Cambridge. He has spent some time with Mr. Fletcher, at Madeley; two kindred souls; much resembling each other, both in fervour and spirit, and in the earnestness of their address. I preached in the evening on Gal. VI. 14.

Simeon's own account in his *Horae Homileticae* of his interview with Wesley is of considerable interest since the Arminian Wesley and the moderate Calvinist, Simeon, find they have spiritually much in common.[148]

---

[146] This is believed to be refer to William Guthrie (1708-70), Scottish author of a *Geographical, Historical, and Commercial Grammar* (1770), as well as histories of England (1744-51). Scotland (1767) and the World (1764-7).

[147] For Simeon's career, especially as it involved his hometown, see next chapter.

[148] The following extracts from the interview are as quoted in Handley Moule's life of Simeon (p. 80 et seq.):

With rare exceptions such as that of Mr. S. Richards,[149] we know scarcely anything of the converts that Wesley made in Reading but happily the *Wesleyan Methodist Magazine* does record the life of one such in an obituary from 1835:

> Nov. 27 at Reading. Mrs Anne Smith aged 67. At an early period of her life she attended the ministry of Mr. Wesley and his assistants, received some spiritual good, and rejoiced in receiving the benediction of that eminent man. Methodist preaching being discontinued in Reading, she joined the church belonging to the people of the Hon. and Rev Mr Cadogan, and profited

---

'Sir, I understand that you are called an Arminian; and I have been sometimes called a Calvinist; and therefore I suppose we are to draw daggers. But before I consent to begin the combat, with your permission I will ask you a few questions. Pray, Sir, do you feel yourself a depraved creature, so depraved that you would never have thought of turning to God, if God had not first put it into your heart? *Yes, I do indeed.*

And do you utterly despair of recommending yourself to God by anything you can do; and look for salvation solely through the blood and righteousness of Christ? *Yes, solely through Christ…* And is all your hope in the grace and mercy of God to preserve you unto His heavenly kingdom? *Yes, I have no hope but in Him.*

Then, Sir, with your leave I will put up my dagger again; for this is all my Calvinism; this is my election, my justification by faith, my final perseverance…'

The comparison with John Fletcher of Madeley is also noteworthy, as he followed Wesley in his Arminianism.

[149] See, however, Chapter 9, from which it seems likely that subsequently Richards joined the followers of William Cudworth.

under the ministry of Mr Davies.[150] After the recommencement of Wesleyan preaching in this town, she joined the Society in 1818…

This is an interesting illustration of the extent to which many Christian believers in the 18th century were prepared to cross denominational boundaries in their desire to hear the Gospel. It also shows that, however hard Wesley worked at Reading, and in spite of the apparent breakthrough achieved in the 1770s, it was only in the early Nineteenth century, twenty years after his death that Methodism became firmly established here. A new Wesleyan society was formed in 1811 when the Revds. George Banwell and James Shoar[151] were sent to Reading by the Home Missionary department. Work had advanced sufficiently by January 1813 for the Wesleyans to register a schoolroom in London Street 'to be set apart and appropriated for Religious Worship for the use of His Majesty's Protestant Subjects being Dissenters of the Denomination commonly called Wesleyan Methodists.' This became popularly known as the 'Inkpot Chapel' on account of its previous use.

The work took off after John Waterhouse's arrival on the scene. Born in Yorkshire in 1789 and ordained to the

---

[150] This most likely refers to Thomas Davis, the Baptist pastor in Reading in the late 18th century. See also Chapter 10.

[151] George Banwell is listed in the *Methodist Magazine* for 1811 as serving in Southampton, part of the Portsmouth District, which also included Reading, where Joseph Scott is shown to be stationed as a missionary. A James Shoar entered the Methodist ministry in 1813 and later ministered in Cambridge but one cannot state with certainty that this is the individual referred to here.

Wesleyan ministry in 1809, Waterhouse came to Reading in 1815 and, assisted by his wife Jane, built up the congregation and established the first purpose-built Methodist chapel in Church Street in 1816-17,[152] using rented land formerly serving as a market garden. The foundation stone was laid by Joseph Butterworth, MP for Coventry and later Treasurer of the Wesleyan Methodist Missionary Society. One of the early guest preachers in January 1817 was the renowned Methodist leader, Jabez Bunting (1779-1858), perhaps an acquaintance of Waterhouse during his earlier ministry in the north of England.

Two years later in 1819 Waterhouse left Reading, subsequently ministering in London, Manchester, Halifax, and from 1839 in Australia where he served as General Superintendent of Wesleyan missions in Australia and Polynesia[153] until his death four years later.

Note. This chapter is based on a standalone pamphlet, entitled *John Wesley came to Reading,* which was originally published in 2003, to mark the tri-centenary of Wesley's birth. In that publication, the author acknowledged with gratitude the assistance rendered by Mr Geoffrey Spittal, then Librarian, during a visit to the library of the New Rooms, Bristol.

---

[152] This was registered in April 1817 on a similar basis to that of the Inkpot Chapel quoted above.

[153] See *Sent from Reading,* Chapter 13.

13   Charles Simeon and the Great Societies

Charles Simeon, born in Reading in 1759

Charles Simeon, who was born in the Forbury, Reading on 24th September 1759, became perhaps the most prominent leader of the Evangelical Revival in its second phase. It could also be argued that he was the most important churchman to be born in the town after Archbishop William Laud and one whose influence on the Church at large was as beneficial as Laud's was arguably pernicious. Yet Laud has been commemorated in the name of a new road while Simeon remains a 'prophet without honour in his own country!'

His father was the son and grandson of successive Vicars of nearby Bucklebury but himself became an attorney by profession. Charles was the fourth and youngest of his sons. Of the others, Richard, named after his father, died in early manhood, John became an MP for Reading and a baronet, while Edward was a wealthy merchant who served as a Director of the Bank of England. Edward Simeon is the best known locally as the benefactor who gave Reading the monument designed by Sir John Soane that still stands in the old butter-market; all three of Charles's brothers were brought to faith in Jesus Christ through his benign influence. Charles Simeon also had ecclesiastical connections through his mother, Elizabeth, whose family, the Huttons, had spawned two Archbishops of York.[154]

Like John Cennick, Charles was baptized at the nearby church of St Laurence and spent much of his early life in Reading; he was then educated at nearby Eton, before going up to Cambridge in 1779. It was there in that same year that he was converted to a living faith in Christ and it was there that his life work would be centred as a Fellow of King's College and Vicar of Holy Trinity Church. At Trinity he overcame considerable opposition, manifested in such petty actions on the part of his churchwardens as locking the pulpit door when he was due to preach. In time, he came to exert a mighty spiritual influence over the next generation of Cambridge students.

---

[154] Matthew Hutton was Archbishop from 1595-1606 and his namesake from 1747-57. The latter then succeeded to Canterbury but died a few months later.

We may quote from Simeon's *Memoirs* his own description of the circumstances that led to his conversion and consecration to the Lord's service:

> On my coming to College, Jan. 29, 1779, the gracious designs of God towards me were soon manifest. It was but the third day after my arrival that I understood I should be expected in the space of about three weeks to attend the Lord's Supper. What! said I, must I attend? On being informed that I *must*, the thought rushed into my mind that Satan himself was as fit to attend as I; and that if I must attend, I must prepare for my attendance there. Without a moment's loss of time, I bought the old *Whole Duty of Man,* (the only religious book that I had ever heard of) and began to read it with great diligence; at the same time calling my ways to remembrance, and crying to God for mercy; and so earnest was I in these exercises, that within the three weeks I made myself quite ill with reading, fasting, and prayer. From that day to this, blessed, for ever blessed, be my God, I have never ceased to regard the salvation of my soul as the one thing needful.
>
> I am far from considering it a good thing that young men in the university should be compelled to go to the table of the Lord; for it has an evident tendency to lower in their estimation that sacred ordinance, and to harden them in their iniquities; but God was pleased to make use of that compulsion for the good of my soul, and to bring me to repentance by means, which for the most part, I fear, drive men into a total disregard of all religion.

At the time of Simeon's conversion, as we saw in Chapter 10, the outstanding evangelical ministry in Reading was that of William Bromley Cadogan, Vicar of St Giles. Simeon, therefore, sought out Cadogan, who by then had begun to preach the gospel with great power, and also the widow of his predecessor, Mrs Sarah Talbot, who had played a key role in preserving the St Giles congregation during the period of Cadogan's antipathy to 'Enthusiasm.' These contacts were against the expressed wishes of old Mr Richard Simeon and Charles went so far as to promise his father that he would not undertake preaching duties for Cadogan.

In spite of his father's opposition, Charles Simeon and William Bromley Cadogan remained friends and, when the latter died in 1797, Charles was invited to preach his funeral sermon, taking as his text words from Hebrews 13 that Cadogan himself had chosen as the church's motto for the year: 'Go on....strong in the grace that is in Christ Jesus; and doubt not, but that you shall find the grace of Christ as sufficient for you, as it has been for him; and that what Christ has been for others in former ages, He will be to you, *the same yesterday, today and for ever.*' Simeon wrote afterwards concerning the funeral: 'The multitudes who attended his funeral with their sighs and tears, yielded a far more real honour to his memory, than all the empty pageantry of this world could possibly afford.'

As detailed more fully in Chapter 16, the death of Cadogan and the vicissitudes of the patronage system led to the withdrawal of most of Cadogan's hearers from St Giles and the foundation of the cause that began as an independent chapel outside the establishment but was eventually in 1836 accepted as a proprietary chapel within the Church of England, namely St Mary's, Castle Street.

Perhaps more than anyone Simeon strove to keep Evangelicals within the established church and to avoid further defections such as those of the Countess of Huntingdon's Connexion and the Wesleyans that had but recently taken place.[155] He owed his very conversion to the liturgical services of that church which had required him to examine himself rigorously before receiving Communion. Thus, although he clearly understood the exceptional circumstances at Reading that led to the events outlined above, they would certainly have grieved his heart. When in 1836 circumstances changed and the Castle Street Chapel was at last licensed for Church of England worship, one of the Trustees, Dr Thomas Ring, wrote to Simeon, inviting him to preach at the first service held in the chapel under the new dispensation. At that time, Simeon was only two to three months from the end of his earthly life and had perforce to decline: 'I happen to know the differences between 37[156] and 77; and I am content to discharge, as God shall enable me, the offices pertaining to the latter age…It is also a real joy to me also to see that Church, to which I am very deeply attached, prospering by the return of some of her best-loved friends to her Communion.'

---

[155] These occurred in 1783 and 1795 respectively. The Countess's secession was largely caused by increasing resentment towards her chapel-building programme from parochial clergy, supported by the episcopal hierarchy. The Methodist secession followed shortly after the founder's death, though the seeds can be found in Wesley's assumption of episcopal powers in ordaining ministers for work in North America.

[156] 37 was the age at which he had preached at Cadogan's funeral.

The first Sunday sermon at the episcopally recognised chapel was delivered by a former curate of Simeon, Professor James Scholefield,[157] and, although I am not aware of any direct evidence, it is reasonable to suppose that the first regular Anglican minister, Charles Joseph Goodhart, could have come under Simeon's influence while a scholar of Trinity College, Cambridge, during the 1820s.

It was the ups and downs of the gospel in Reading through the period from 1767 to 1836, exemplified in the pre-history and early history of St Mary's, Castle Street,[158] that inspired Simeon to take action by founding the Simeon Trustees. In 1814, his brother, Edward, died and under the terms of his will Charles – having declined a considerably larger sum – received a bequest of £15,000. This afforded him a comparative degree of wealth, which he characteristically put to the service of his Lord. One of the principal effects was the formation of the Simeon Trustees, with the aim of buying up the patronage of churches in provincial towns and so 'fixing the gospel there in perpetuity.' He also spoke of this work as 'purchasing spheres, wherein the prosperity of the Established Church, and the kingdom of our blessed Lord, may be advanced; and not for a season only but if it please God, in perpetuity also.' The Trust was founded in 1817 and by the time of Simeon's death it controlled 21

---

[157] 1789-1853. Professor of Greek at the university from 1825, he was also incumbent of St Michael's, Cambridge.

[158] See Chapter 16. It is also notable that the issue of patronage was likewise a concern for Evangelicals within the Church of Scotland, leading to the Disruption of 1843 that brought the Free Church of Scotland into being.

advowsons.[159] While at the time of the formation of the trust Simeon would have seen the principal opposition to evangelicalism coming from the anti-enthusiasm represented by men such as Joseph Eyre, the growth of the Tractarian (Oxford) Movement from 1833 with its increasing Romanising tendency clearly represented a further and potentially more serious threat.[160]

Simeon also played a key part in the establishment of one of the three great missionary societies that came into

---

[159] This subject is covered extensively in *Simeon and Church Order* by Canon Charles Smyth. A number of other trusts were subsequently formed with similar intentions, including the Peache Trustees and those now administered by Church Society and the Protestant Reformation Society. However, these good intentions have in many cases been frustrated in recent years by diocesan interference through the suspension of livings and the creation of large combined benefices whereby the various trusts take their turn to appoint the 'Team Rector.' As a result it is now quite possible for an Evangelical to be succeeded by an Anglo-Catholic with a Broad Church Liberal waiting in the wings! Currently the Simeon Trustees manage nearly 200 livings, including around 30 under the legally separate Hyndman Trustees. It is interesting to note that the patronage of St John's, Reading, hitherto coming under a private trust, was transferred to Simeon's Trustees in 1965.

[160] The Tractarians were so called after the series of *Tracts for the Times* authored by the leading members of the Movement. Professor Childs takes the view in his useful survey of Reading during the early 1800s that the town's churches were slow to come under its influence. A notice of the 'Oxford Tracts' in the *Reading Mercury* during 1838 is perhaps the first reference to the movement but it was not till 1856 that St Giles, now a very distinctive Anglo-Catholic stronghold, received its first Tractarian Vicar.

being during the 1790s. Although a number of Anglicans were prominent in the formation of the London Missionary Society (LMS), there were others in the established church who felt that it should have its own missionary society, dedicated to church principles, such as the Baptists already possessed through the labours of William Carey and others. This was also Simeon's view.

Simeon's missionary concerns were apparent even in the early years of his ministry. Early in 1788, he received an Address from Bengal regarding a mission to India, proposed by the Rev David Brown, who was then a Chaplain of the East India Company, based in Calcutta, and others including Charles Grant, Director and later Chairman of that company. As a corporate body, the East India Company, was very much for letting sleeping dogs lie and against disturbing the status quo in India but thanks to the presence of godly men like Brown and Grant the climate would change in favour of missionary enterprises. Simeon's support was solicited in the following words: 'We understand such matters lie very near your heart, and that you have a warm zeal to promote their interest. Upon this ground we take the liberty to invite you to become agent on behalf of the intended mission at home.' Although Simeon's reply has not been preserved it is evident from later correspondence that he responded with enthusiasm to the proposal.

Following the foundation of the LMS in 1795, Simeon was one among a number of prominent evangelicals who began to work towards the formation of a society within the Church of England and at a meeting of the Eclectics Society in February 1796 he posed the question, 'With what propriety, and in what mode, can a Mission be attempted to the Heathen from the Established Church?'

Three years later following much behind-the-scenes activity by Simeon and others what eventually became the Church Missionary Society was founded at a meeting held in the Castle and Falcon, Aldersgate Street. Perhaps surprisingly Simeon was not on the first committee but this was mainly a matter of geography, all those appointed being London-based men. Simeon was also much involved with missions to the Jews and the story of these and other societies, as they involved men and women from Reading, can be found in *Sent from Reading* (2021) by the present writer. The following paragraphs provide a brief summary of some of the material contained in that book.

It was not until the last decade of the 18th century that three of the great overseas societies that were to dominate missionary activity in the 19th were founded: the Baptist Missionary Society (BMS), the LMS and the CMS.

The BMS, founded in 1794, was the earliest of the three. Baptist activity in Reading in this regard seems to have begun with a deputation sermon by Dr John Ryland of Bristol who preached at the Hosier's Lane Baptist Church in 1811, when the collection amounted to £8 3s. 6d. This was during an interregnum in that church's ministry which was filled by a mission-minded man, John Dyer, then aged 30. After four years in Reading Dyer moved to London to become Assistant Secretary of the BMS and then a year later in 1818 it first full-time Secretary, thus beginning a tradition in Reading of supplying able men to undertake administrative roles in relation to foreign missions. As Secretary he clashed with the BMS' pioneer missionary, William Carey, who complained that his letters read like those of a 'Secretary of State,' and this led to a separation between the BMS and the Serampore Mission in India. Unhappily Dyer came under intense pressure towards the end of his life, caused by financial problems which the Society faced and these contributed to a severe depression that ended in his suicide in 1841.

One of the founder members of the LMS (1795) was John Eyre (1754-1803) who had been Curate of St Giles' under Cadogan from 1781-5 and was later Minister of Ram's Chapel in Homerton and founder of the *Evangelical Magazine*. Perhaps because of the connection with John Eyre there is evidence of an early interest in the LMS at the Castle Street Chapel. Its second regular minister, John Bickerdike, is recorded in the *Evangelical Magazine* for June 1804 as speaking at a meeting in Reading, when collections amounted to £70 (about £4,000 at present values) and also as one of those distributing the elements at a service of the Lord's Supper that concluded the Tenth Annual General Meeting of the Society on 11th May that year. The earliest Reading man so far traced as an overseas missionary was a co-worker of James Sherman[161] named John Ross, who was sent to British Guyana by LMS in 1834 but invalided home. Later Castle Street Congregational Chapel sent out the Revd W C Attwell who was a missionary in Madagascar from 1870 to 1887, followed later by the Revd W E Cousins.

In spite of Simeon's connection it was not until the mid-19th century that Reading came to play any part in the work of the CMS through Thomas Valpy French. French's father was born in Reading, the son of one of the founders of the Castle Street Chapel, and he himself, though born in Burton-on-Trent, received his initial schooling at Reading School. Called to the mission field while at

---

[161] Minister at the Castle Street Chapel, 1821-36 - See Chapter 16.

Oxford, he sailed for India as a CMS missionary in 1850 and devoted much of the rest of his life to overseas work, including serving from 1877-87 as the first Bishop of Lahore. He died in 1891 at Muscat, while exploring the possibilities of Christian mission in Arabia. His biography records that he read a paper at the Reading Congress of 1883, which was noted 'for the freshness and boldness of the views expressed in it.' Pleading for more 'apostles' he described missionary work as 'the work of the century' and called for 'the deepest contrition, humiliation, and genuine heartfelt confession on the part of the labourers for past neglects and defects.'

French's words were certainly taken to heart for in 1890, Hubert Brooke, minister of St Mary's, Castle Street, Reading, signed what became known as the Keswick Letter. A number of those participating in the annual Keswick Convention with an interest in missionary affairs wrote an open letter to CMS calling for a thousand missionaries 'within the next few years' to meet the needs of Gospel work in China, India and among the 'recently-discovered' African tribes. CMS largely responded to the call with the enthusiastic support of Archbishop Edward White Benson. In Reading, Brooke's vision inspired some 24 missionaries to go out over the next decade. The first of these, leaving Reading in 1891 were Thomas Simmonds for China and James Redman who was to work in what is now Tanzania. Redman went out as Castle Street's 'own missionary' but died of a fever shortly after arriving at his post the following year. Others called to the mission field included three daughters of Mr. Richard Bazett of Bath Road, Louisa, Mary and Sibella, who all went to East Africa. Mary married another of the 24, the Rev Harry Leakey, who had been a French master at Reading School;

their son was Louis Simpson Bazett Leakey, the renowned anthropologist.

Other evangelical churches, notably Greyfriars and St. John's, also responded to the challenge. From the former, the two daughters of Admiral John Venour Fletcher, Selena and Sophy, went to work in Hong Kong; from St John's, two curates, Walter Owen and Arnold Kay, worked in East Africa and India respectively.

Mission work was not confined to these three societies. Dr Livingstone's explorations in Central Africa under LMS led to the formation in 1858 of the Universities' Mission to Central Africa (UMCA) with support mainly from the more Tractarian-minded clergy. UMCA's first expedition in 1861 under the leadership of Bishop Charles Frederick Mackenzie was to the area around Lake Nyasa and the River Shire, territory now largely a part of modern Malawi. Mackenzie had previously been Archdeacon of Natal and evidently had some idea of the practical requirements of a mission in Africa, for he asked for three craftsmen to accompany him. The volunteers were Adams, who was an agriculturist, Blair, a printer, and Clarke, a shoemaker, who hence became known as the ABC of the mission. The 'C' – was Richard Martin Clarke, whose home church was St Giles-in-Reading. Of his work, Clarke wrote back: 'It being my province to superintend our African men in their work, the honour fell on me of building the first place devoted to the worship of God in this part of Africa. My prayer is that this may not be the last by many built in this land for the same great object, but I hope that they may be more worthy of being styled churches than the present. The structure was begun and finished in five days. I must tell you that we have no church bell and that the substitute for one is a native drum.' The mission, however, was something of a disaster as the party was overwhelmed by blackwater fever, which led to the deaths of several of the key participants, including the Bishop. Clarke himself came close to death but survived and later served as a catechist in Cape Town.

Other societies founded in the 19th century had connections with Reading and the Reading area. The South American Missionary Society had its origins in the life and courageous death of Captain Allen Gardiner, born in the village of Basildon, a few miles from Reading, in 1794. In 1808 he signed up as a naval cadet at Portsmouth and saw action as a midshipman in the latter years of the Napoleonic Wars. He subsequently arose to the rank of Captain but more importantly from our viewpoint underwent a conversion to the Christian faith which in turn inspired him to his heroic efforts to bring the Gospel to the Indian tribes of the southern tip of South America. It was in the course of this task that he perished, along with his helpers, from starvation on Tierra del Fuego in September 1851. In the following year, the Rev Charles Goodhart, who had been the first Incumbent of St Mary's Episcopal Chapel, moved to London to become Clerical Secretary of the society now known as the Church's Ministry among Jewish People (CMJ).

Many of these great missionary movements can be traced back to Simeon as one who had inspired the missionary spirit in Reading and in the country at large. Charles Simeon was indeed one of Reading's greatest sons and it remains a matter of considerable regret that there is little if any public recognition of that fact. Nor is this just a case of one formerly famous fading into the mists of time. That lively chronicler of Reading life in the 19th Century, W. S. Darter, recalls that at the time of the death of the 'brother of our late member[162] ...I heard one of our jocular members of the Corporation say that a greater than he has about this same time departed this life, viz. the Duke's horse, Copenhagen, which carried the Duke at Waterloo.' Alas, those who preach the true gospel must expect the scorn of cynical unbelievers.

---

[162] This refers to Sir John Simeon (1756-1824) who represented Reading for the Tories from 1797 to 1802 and 1806 to 1818. He was created a Baronet in 1815.

Statue in St Laurence's Church of Dr Richard Valpy,
Headmaster of Reading School

14   Education, Education, Education[163]

One consequence of the Great Awakening in England and Wales was its impact on Education. This was central to the movement in Wales where there was much illiteracy and thus education was perceived as a key element in facilitating the spread of the Gospel. In England it was perhaps seen most clearly in the commencement of the Sunday School movement, in which Robert Raikes of Gloucester is famed for his pioneering role. What of Reading? The 2019 volume in the Berkshire Record Society's series, entitled *Berkshire Schools in the Eighteenth Century*, provides us with an indication of the churches' part in the town's educational work in general, including that of leading evangelicals such as Cadogan, Simeon and Marsh. The following summary is mainly based on this account:

Reading School. This 'free' School or Grammar School had begun as an offshoot of the Abbey and was located in the Forbury up until its relocation to Erleigh Road in the later 19th century. We have already noted the part that two of its (head)masters, Leonard Coxe and Julins Palmer, played in Reading's Reformation. The school reached 'the pinnacle of its fame' under the long headmastership of the Rev Dr Richard Valpy (1781-1830), an ardent churchman. The staff at that time also included two other clergymen, Mr Boardman and W B Young MA (Oxon).

The latter also ran his own school in Church Street

---

[163] Thus spake Prime Minister Tony Blair on 23rd May 2001: 'Our top priority was, is and always will be education, education, education.'

where young gentlemen were trained up 'for trade, the accompting house, and the university on moderate terms' – namely 14 guineas per annum.

Bluecoat School. This school was founded by Richard Aldworth[164] in the late 17th century. It was then located in St Giles' parish. It is interesting to note that Charles Simeon's philanthropic brother, Edward, was one of those who later made a bequest that helped to fund the school's continuing activities. The school moved to the Bath Road in the mid-19th century, and finally in 1947 to its present site in Sonning.

Green Girls' School. This began as a joint initiative by Revs Charles Sturges, John Nicholls and William Cadogan, Vicars of the three parishes, in 1779. These gentlemen felt that the moral and religious education of girls should not be neglected and in 1782 the school, so called from the colour of the girls' dresses, opened in a house in the Butts, with an initial roll of just six girls, selected from the three parishes. Numbers reached a maximum of 24 in the 1790s. There was a strong religious element in the lessons and on leaving each girl received a Bible, Prayer Book, and copies of *The Whole Duty of Man*[165] and *Introduction to the Knowledge of the Christian Religion* by Henry Crossman.[166]

---

[164] A descendant of Thomas Aldworth, noted in Chapter 6 as a former Mayor of Reading and an early Puritan sympathiser.

[165] It is interesting to note that this was the 17th century work, published anonymously in 1658, which Charles Simeon consulted when he began to explore the faith, coincidentally in the same year that the Reading Vicars set their plans in motion.

[166] Crossman was Rector of Little Bromley, Essex. His work, published in 1819, comprises two parts: 1, An explanation of the most material words and things in the Church Catechism;

Neale's School. One Joseph Neale left money for charitable purposes in his will of 1705 and these were used to set up a school in Pottern, Hampshire, but quite legally under the terms of the trust were transferred to a school in Reading, some time after the Rev Francis Fox, Vicar of Pottern, moved to St Mary's, Reading in 1726. This establishment was in existence by 1744 and was still going nearly a hundred years later, with 25 children on the register in 1842.

The British School. This originated after a lecture given by the founder of the movement, the Quaker, Joseph Lancaster (1778-1838), in Reading Town Hall, in 1809. The name 'British School' is derived from the name later adopted by the society set up by Lancaster, the British and Foreign Schools Society (BFSS). Although non-denominational, there was initially a strong Anglican influence: funding was kicked off by Edward Simeon with a donation of £500 while the original committee included not only Simeon but also Dr Valpy and the Evangelical former curate of St Laurence's, William Marsh. The building which still survives was erected in Southampton Street in 1811. The scriptures and Isaac Watts' hymns for children were among the books used and a report in 1815 indicates that 160 boys had learnt to read the Bible. A Girls' School was set up in 1818.

The British School survived into the 20th century[167] and

---

and 2, An Explanation of the Two Covenants [i.e. that of Works, and that of Grace]; the Great Feast and Fasts of the Church; and some Religious Terms designed to prepare People for understanding Sermons, the Holy Scriptures, and other good Books, together with prayers etc.

[167] The British School was transferred to the control of the

was later used as a depot for the distribution of school meals. Threatened with demolition at the end of the last century, it achieved heritage listing through vigorous local campaigning and has since been converted to residential accommodation. Following the 1902 Education Act (see below) the school closed and was replaced by the new George Palmer School under the local education authority.

National Schools. Despite the Anglican influence indicated above, some churchmen objected to the non-denominational[168] emphasis of the Lancaster British Schools and championed the alternative 'National School' system devised by the Scottish episcopalian, Dr Andrew Bell (1753-1832), which included teaching of the Church Catechism and doctrines of the established church to the exclusion of other variants of the Christian creed. This movement also had to have its own society, the name of which was even more of a mouthful than the BFSS: the National Society for Promoting the Education of the Poor in the Principles of the Established Church. These worthy intentions were encouraged by the Bishop of Salisbury, John Fisher (1807-25), and following a series of meetings, including one at the house of Dr Valpy, a committee was formed, funds sought, and ultimately a school was opened within the walls of Reading Abbey in September 1813, with a capacity for 300 to 400 children but an initial intake of just under 100. By 1833, it had an attendance of 250 boys and 180 girls on weekdays with a few others on Sundays. A number of voluntary aided or controlled church primary

---

Reading School Board in 1901 and replaced by the George Palmer School in 1907.

[168] Enshrined in the phrase 'without any reference whatsoever to sect or party in religious opinions.'

schools remain in Reading that owe their origins to the NS movement, including St Mary and All Saints, New Christ Church and St John's, Newtown.

School of Industry. This school was founded in 1802 following an initiative by the widow of William Bromley Cadogan, Jane, who took out a 99-year lease on a cottage in Friar Street intended for use as a school. The intention was to instruct 'poor female children' in 'the Truths of Christianity according to the articles of the Church of England.' In 1806 the property was placed in the hands of four trustees who included Charles Simeon and William Marsh. The school could admit 34 girls with the object of making them 'good servants and useful members of Society.'

This was another cause to which Edward Simeon contributed and more generally this remarkably benevolent financier placed £2,500 in trust to Reading Corporation to provide clothing for pupils at the town's charity schools on the day before the Mayoral election. On the day itself they were required to attend divine service at St Laurence's with 400 in attendance in 1811.

Congregational School. Not to be outdone, the Congregationalists (or Independents) meeting at the Broad Street Chapel established their own day school for girls in 1802; the long-serving minister, Archibald Douglas,[169] was the principal mover in this. Evidently in order to discourage vanity, the girls were deprived of their curls on arrival at the school, the hairdresser being a formidable

---

[169] Douglas succeeded Thomas Noon in 1796 and served until 1839.

lady member of the congregation, Mrs Macalister.[170]

Jewish children. A school for the purpose of educating 48 children of Jewish parentage was opened in 1810.

Small day and Sunday schools were set up in connection with St Giles and St Mary's parishes. In the 1820s there were around 800 children educated at ten Sunday schools, of which three were run by the Anglican parishes, two each by the Countess of Huntingdon's Connexion, the Baptists and Independents. Other records refer to 142 children attending a Wesleyan Methodist Sunday school in 1833. St James Roman Catholic Church operated a day school for poor children at the time of the 1851 census.

The Sunday School movement was well-established in Berkshire by the time of the 1851 census (see Chapter 17). Analysis by Kate Tiller suggests that 65% of Anglican churches and one-third of nonconformist and Roman Catholic churches catered for Sunday scholars. The numbers reported in the census by Reading churches follow:

Bethel Wesleyan	32
Broad Street Independent	180
Castle Street Congregational	250
Kings Road Baptist	350
Salem Primitive Methodist	70
St Giles	300
St John's	50
St Mary's, Castle Street	220

---

[170] 'The first thing was to deprive them of their curls, enforcing excessive neatness, but tolerating nothing that she deemed fitted to encourage the vanity of the youthful mind.' (Quoted by W H Summers)

Trinity Chapel	200
Trinity Independent	111
Wesleyan Methodist	10
Wesleyan Methodist, Spring Gardens	47

TOTAL   **1,820**

Churches with no reported Sunday School provision included the Baptist congregation meeting near St Giles and St James RC.

Somewhat late in the day, **St Mary's, Castle Street** established a day school in the 1850s which met in buildings behind the chapel where there is currently an electricity sub-station. At its height this provided education for around 300 children but later faced competition from the new Board Schools set up in the wake of the 1870 Education Act,[171] introduced during Gladstone's first

---

[171] Often called Forster's Act, after William Forster, the Liberal MP, who sponsored it, the full title of the legislation was 'An Act to provide for public Elementary Education in England and Wales.' On account of the concerns of the nonconformists who feared that their children might be taught Anglican doctrines the Act ruled that 'No religious catechism or religious formulary which is distinctive of any particular denomination shall be taught in the school.' Parents with conscientious objections had the right to withdraw their children from 'attend[ing] any religious observance or any instruction in religious subjects in the school or elsewhere.' Some secularists were opposed to any religious element in public education but the spirit of the 1870 Act has largely survived through to the Butler Act of 1944 and RE remains a requirement under the National Curriculum: 'RE is an important curriculum subject. It is important in its own right and also makes a unique contribution to the spiritual, moral, social and cultural development of pupils and supports wider community cohesion.'

Liberal government. After declining to a roll of around 180 in the 1890s, it closed down in 1906. Other church schools were formed in association with the newer parishes to the east and south of the town centre; these, as noted above, remain active in the present day.

Following the advent of state education with the 1870 Education Act the place of religious affiliation in the education of children declined to some extent but as the following table indicates in 1887 the churches continued to play an important part in the process.

Elementary Education in Reading - 1887

Name of School	Affiliation	Nos of places	Average attendance
Religious Foundations			
All Saints Infant	CE	300	90
Christ Church	CE (National)	480	378
Greyfriars	CE (National)	850	440
St John's	CE	252	230
St John's Infant	CE	230	180
St Lawrence	CE (National)	600	400
St Mary's Episcopal	CE	300	180
St Mary's	CE (National)	572	412
St Stephen's	CE (National)	350	350
Trinity	CE	230	230
British School	Non-denominational	600	550
St James'	RC	217	100
Sub-total		4,981	3,490
Board Schools			
Silver Street	Secular	244	230
Coley Street	Secular	400	270
Katesgrove	Secular	631	531

Oxford Road	Secular	1,000	900
Newtown	Secular	1,580	1,390
Sub-total		3,855	3,321
TOTAL		8,836	6,811

Source: Kelly's Directory, 1887.

In 1887, the Board School system was still only 16 years old and did not yet cover all districts of Reading. Thus it is not surprising that the schools of religious foundation, principally the National Schools and the British School, still supplied some 56% of school places in the town, although in terms of attendance their share was a little lower at 51%. This may be due in some instances to the competition provided by the Board Schools, although there may be other hidden factors at work.

In 1902, further changes were made to the structure of education, this time under the Conservative government of Arthur Balfour, bringing both the board schools and the church schools under the wing of the local government authorities. While the church schools received funding from the local authorities they remained part of the 'voluntary' sector. As most were Church of England-associated, the measure was strongly opposed by nonconformists and by the Liberal opposition that tended to represent their interests, contributing to the fall of Balfour's government and the Liberal landslide victory that followed. Nevertheless, the Balfour legislation set the pattern for elementary education until the 1944 Act introduced the division between primary and secondary education which still exists in the present day.

Data from 1915 (by now including Caversham and Tilehurst) shows a striking change in the balance with numbers of places at secular schools increasing from 3,855 to 12,550, whereas, despite the addition of Caversham schools, children at denominational schools now numbered 4,991, up only ten on 1887. Thus, over 70% of places were now directly provided by the local authority, as against 28.5% by the various Anglican and Roman Catholic schools. These were divided between Voluntary Controlled Schools which are of Christian foundation but largely run by the local authority and Voluntary Aided Schools where the churches retain a greater influence in their governance.[172]

---

[172] The distinction between these two categories is aptly illustrated in Reading by the recent history of Christ Church Primary School, originally founded as a National School in association with the parish church of the same name in 1867. For many years it operated as a Voluntary Controlled School with a board of governors chaired by the Vicar of Christ Church or other church members but also with strong LA representation (including from 1993-99 the present writer representing the borough council – called 'the minor authority' - as a nominee of the Reading Labour Party). After being placed in special measures following an OFSTED inspection the school was taken more closely under the wing of the Diocese of Oxford in 2000 as a Voluntary Aided School with a fresh name, New Christ Church Primary School. According to the National Association of Teachers of Religious Education (NATRE) the National Curriculum makes the following distinction between aided and controlled schools in relation to RE:
- for foundation and voluntary controlled schools with a religious character, RE must be taught according to the Agreed Syllabus unless, parents request RE in accordance with the trust deed of the school; and
- in voluntary aided schools RE must be taught in accordance with the trust deed.

We may conclude this chapter with a reference to Reading's most celebrated school for girls, albeit not one of specific Christian origin.[173] This was the La Tournelle and St Quentin Boarding School, also known as the Abbey Gateway School, best known as the establishment where Jane Austen received her only formal education. This flourished from pre-1760 until 1794. Its principal interest in relation to our subject was that its pupils also included Martha Butt, later better known as Mrs Sherwood (1775-1851), a celebrated writer of children's literature with a strong evangelical influence. She attended the school from 1791-3, starting about five years after Jane Austen's departure.

The school had been founded by a Mrs Mapleton, assisted by Mrs Spencer, with the latter in sole charge from 1769-87. On her death in that year her assistant, Sarah Hackett, otherwise known by the more pedagogic name of La Tournelle, took over, joined in 1790 by Mrs St. Quentin, née Pitts, wife of the French teacher. These ladies sold up in 1794, moving to London where they continued to be involved in the education of girls. However, the purchaser, a Mrs Jesse, was also a schoolma'am and ran her own establishment on the premises till 1804 when she moved it to Castle Hill.

---

[173] Note, though, that both Jane Austen and Martha Sherwood were daughters of the clergy and thus it may be assumed that the school was deemed to be eminently suitable for the education of Christian girls. In addition, Sherwood's father, Rev George Butt, was a friend of Dr Valpy and in all likelihood sent his daughter to the Gateway School on his advice; Valpy's daughter, Carteret 'Carty' Valpy, was also a pupil at the school. Martha's cousin, Thomas Butt, was a pupil at Reading School.

In her memoirs, Mrs Sherwood has provided a very vivid and sometimes amusing picture of life at the La Tournelle and St Quentin Boarding School:

> It was late on a Sunday evening that we reached Reading and it was at a very late hour that I was taken across to the school. The person who received me was Mrs Latournelle; the school was not yet met, Mr and Mrs St Quentin were in London, and I was the first pupil who had appeared after the holidays. Mrs Latournelle was a person of the old school, a stout woman, hardly under seventy, but very active, although she had a cork leg; how she had lost its predecessor she never told. She was only fit for giving out clothes for the wash, making tea, ordering dinner, and in fact doing the work of a housekeeper…
>
> I found in addition to Mrs Latournelle, who was making tea almost by firelight, three teachers of whose existence I had not even dreamed… Miss Holt was a little, simpering English woman, very like a second-rate milliner of these days; she taught spelling and needlework. Miss Bournany was a dashing, slovenly, rather handsome French girl, and ran away with some low man a few months afterwards. Miss Trelishaw was, I think, a Swiss.

In later life, Mrs Sherwood authored many books on improving subjects, which included *The History of Little Henry and his Bearer* (1814), *Stories Explanatory of the Church Catechism* (1817), *The History of the Fairchild Family* (1818) and *Scripture Prints, with Explanations in the Form of Familiar Dialogues* (1831). It is reasonable to suppose that these found their way into the hands of many of Reading's 19th century schoolchildren.

15   The Roman Catholic Revival

Several episodes have passed since we recorded the end of papal supremacy in Reading, as elsewhere. At that point what became Roman Catholic worship went underground and so it remained for over two centuries. Nevertheless, there were many, particularly among the upper classes who continued to observe 'the old faith' and, as detailed in Tony Hadland's excellent history, *Thames Valley Papists,* such 'recusant' families were especially prevalent in our part of the world.[174]

We know most about those who belonged to the aristocracy and occupied some of the large country houses dotted around the Berkshire and Oxfordshire countryside near Reading. Two of these in particular, Mapledurham and Stonor, continue to belong to Roman Catholic families to the present day. Another was Englefield House, near Theale, the seat of Sir Francis Englefield (1520-96), who also held Whitley Park in what is now Reading as master of game and keeper of the park and lodge. His nephew, another Francis, later acquired Whiteknights Park, the present home of the University of Reading.

Conditions for those holding to Roman Catholicism worsened after the papal bull of 1570 which declared Elizabeth I a heretic and in effect invited her subjects to depose her[175] – or worse. The propagation of popery thus

---

[174] Hadland defines 'recusants' as those who refused to attend Church of England services.

[175] The wording was as follows: 'We do out of the fullness of our apostolic power declare the foresaid Elizabeth to be a heretic and favourer of heretics, and her adherents in the

became seen as a form of treason. This did not prevent courageous, if perhaps misguided, Jesuit missionaries from seeking to spread their faith and such famous figures as Saint Edmund Campion are known to have made extensive tours of the Thames Valley area, using Stonor as a base. In addition, and a little closer to Reading, Ufton Court, the home of Francis Perkins, became a safe-house for the missionary-priests. Thomas Vachell of Coley Park was yet another recusant, although his Reading home was regranted to Protestant relations and he moved to Ipsden in Oxfordshire. There he was convicted in March 1588 of not attending Church of England services and fined £50 (equivalent to around £5,000 today).

Feelings towards the old faith hardly improved with the accession of James I and the discovery of the Gunpowder Plot. William Alexander who then occupied Caversham Court was one of those said to have been implicated on the fringes of the affair, along with the Browne family who

---

matters aforesaid to have incurred the sentence of excommunication and to be cut off from the unity of the body of Christ.... And moreover (we declare) her to be deprived of her pretended title to the aforesaid crown and of all lordship, dignity and privilege whatsoever.' (Quoted from Dan Graves, Christianity.com.) Even the former King Consort, Philip of Spain, thought that the Pope, evidently moved by vastly exaggerated rumours of Elizabeth's unpopularity among her subjects, had taken leave of his senses. The ultimate outcome of the Pope's action was the Babington Conspiracy to place Mary Queen of Scots on Elizabeth's throne and the consequent execution of Mary in 1587. For an excellent if partisan fictional account of the Babington affair in the general context of the times see Monsignor Robert Hugh Benson's 1912 novel, *Come Rack! Come Rope!*

succeeded the Alexanders and were related by marriage to the arch-conspirator, Robert Catesby. The Alexanders had been patrons of Caversham Parish Church but following the Plot Romanists were deprived of such rights.

Conditions for Roman Catholics eased under Charles I as part of his marriage treaty with his French wife, Henrietta Maria. However, there was further deterioration under the Commonwealth[176] and, despite Charles II's marriage to another Catholic princess, conditions continued to worsen. In 1676 when lists were made of Recusants in the Thames Valley, only 0.1% of Reading's population was so identified, compared with 22% at nearby Ufton Nervet. The activities of James II provoked further reaction and Romanists were left at the end of the 17th century as the group benefiting least from the greater religious toleration that resulted from the 1688 Revolution.

Catholic involvement in the Jacobite rebellions was another factor that delayed progress towards the easing of the penal laws, although Vicars Apostolic and other Bishops appointed by the Pope to minister to his English adherents seem to have been able to move fairly freely in spite of them. In 1741 Bishop Richard Challoner (1691-1781), Coadjutor to the Vicar Apostolic, visited Whiteknights and recorded that there was at that time 'a large congregation of 300 Catholics in the neighbourhood of Reading'. This must have been based on a fairly broad definition of Greater Reading, as an official return of 1767

---

[176] Cromwell's government was generally tolerant of all shades of Trinitarian Christianity but Roman Catholicism was the exception that proved the rule.

recorded Reading as containing a mere 28 Catholics.[177]

Later in the 18th century, with the Jacobite threat passed, the way was open to a more tolerant attitude to Papists and in 1778 the first Catholic Relief Act was passed, removing some of the penal laws in return for Catholics denouncing Stuart claims to the throne[178] and denying any civil authority on the part of the Pope. A second Act of 1791 reopened the professions to Roman Catholics and gave legal existence to registered Catholic places of worship, on condition that clergy took an oath of allegiance to the Crown. Such chapels were not allowed to have steeples or a ring of bells, so that they might not be mistaken for churches of the Establishment.

Catholic advances in England received a further impetus from the anti-clerical sentiments of the leaders of the French Revolution. This led to a mass exodus of French priests from mid-1792 with a total of 5,000 fleeing across 'La Manche'. Some of the early arrivals found their way to Reading and were housed in Finch's Buildings in Hosier Street but the bulk were located initially in Winchester. Then, from 1796 Norman priests were dispersed to Reading with the town's grandest coaching inn, the King's Arms, Castle Hill, requisitioned by the government of William Pitt as a hostel for 340 of them. The inn's assembly

---

[177] According to Tony Hadfield, the total for Berkshire as a whole was 587 with a further 317 in southern Oxfordshire.

[178] Jacobites recognised an alternative line of succession following the death of James II in 1701: James III (the Old Pretender), 1701-66; Charles III (the Young Pretender aka Bonnie Prince Charlie), 1766-88; and his brother, Henry IX (Cardinal Henry Stuart), 1788-1809. Both brothers died without issue and the Stuart line then became extinct.

room was used as a chapel, accommodating 400 worshippers. Although conditions in France eased after the Concordat with the Papacy of 1801 and the evolution of the Revolution into Napoleon's papally approved empire, not all the exiled priests returned across the Channel.

Finch's Buildings then developed into an important mission centre served by some four or five priests, led by Father Jean Baptiste Longuet. He and his colleagues gave French lessons and with their earnings saved sufficient funds to acquire a plot of land near the Forbury, where in 1812 Reading's first purpose-built post-Reformation Roman Catholic place of worship was consecrated as the Chapel of the Resurrection. It served as such for less than 30 years and its site was long believed to have been occupied by the former Rising Sun public house in the Forbury; it is now thought more likely that it was located further north in the path of the Great Western Railway. The chapel is said to have served a congregation of around 170 comprising the few native Catholics in the town, along with converts, French émigrés and Italian traders. In February 1817 Longuet was the victim of a dreadful mugging incident, being attacked, robbed and murdered at what is now Norcot Junction on the way back from a visit to Pangbourne. He was buried in the Chapel of the Resurrection with his remains being removed to the new St James's church in 1841. After a gap of three years he was succeeded as priest at the chapel by Father Francis Bowland who served until 1837.

The next major step in the toleration of Roman Catholicism came in 1829 with the Catholic Emancipation Act, which was mainly designed to avert civil war in Ireland but clearly also had consequences for England. Catholics could now once more sit in Parliament and occupy most offices of state, provided they denied the Pope any non-spiritual jurisdiction.[179] The Prime Minister at the time was a man with strong local connections, the Duke of Wellington, whose country seat, Stratfield Saye, was seven miles south of Reading. An early consequence of the legislation was the election in 1831 of the Romanist Sir Robert Throckmorton of Buckland Park as MP for Berkshire.

Reading's premier Roman Catholic church of St James is one of the earliest and also most unusual works of the pioneering Gothic Revival architect, Augustus Welby Pugin (1812-52). By the time he was commissioned to design St James Pugin had already developed pronounced views on what was appropriate for church architecture and these did not encompass the Norman or Romanesque style that characterises this church. It is said that he was influenced in adopting this style for St James' by his patron, James Wheble, and that Pugin later repudiated the church as unworthy of him. Nevertheless, it is a pleasing building that has survived two extensions dating from 1925 and 1962.

On August 27th 1849 there happened in Reading an almost accidental occurrence that links the town with perhaps the most pivotal event in the history of British Christendom during the 19th century. On that day an Italian priest, named Father Dominic Barberi, was travelling by train from London to Worcester when he

---

[179] Article 37 of the 39 Articles of the Church of England states: 'The Bishop of Rome hath no jurisdiction in this Realm of England.'

suffered a severe heart attack between Reading and Pangbourne. His companions removed him from the train at the latter station but found that there was 'no room at the inn,' as the proprietors of the two hotels in the village, presumably the George and the Elephant, apparently suspected him of having contracted cholera which was then rife in the capital. So he was taken back on the train to Reading where he died at the more compassionate Railway Tavern in the Caversham Road. Father Dominic seems to have had a presentiment of his coming death and murmured 'Thy will be done' on reaching Reading.

Born in 1792 near Viterbi in the Papal States north of Rome, Barberi had been sent to England in 1841 as a member of the Passionist Order to propagate the Roman Catholic faith. In the course of these duties, he received a summons to visit a Church of England clergyman in Oxford called John Henry Newman. On 8th October 1845 Newman 'wrote to a number of friends': 'I am this night expecting Father Dominic, the Passionist... He does not know of my intention; but I mean to ask of him admission into the one Fold of Christ...' Afterwards Barberi wrote: 'All that I have suffered since I left Italy has been well compensated by this event, and I hope the effects of such a conversion may be great.'

Thus Newman set foot on a road that led to a Cardinal's hat in 1879 and ultimately in 2019 to papal canonization. 1845 was a watershed also for the Church of England. At the very least Newman's conversion called into question the idea of the national church as a via media between Rome and Protestantism, on which the early Tractarians had set so much store. Indeed Barberi himself had repudiated Newman's arguments in Tract XC for a Catholic interpretation of the 39 Articles. As Father

Dominic had hoped, numbers of converts followed Newman, especially after the Gorham controversy[180] at the end of the decade.

The increasing confidence of Roman Catholicism in Reading and elsewhere, boosted by the conversion of Newman and others of the Oxford Movement, led to the bold move in 1851 to create a diocesan structure for the church mirroring that of the Establishment; this was hotly contested by convinced Protestants[181] who labelled it not inaptly as the 'Papal Aggression.'

Reading was originally part of the RC diocese of Southwark under Bishop Thomas Grant and then from 1882 that of Portsmouth with John Virtue as the first bishop.

---

[180] This resulted from the refusal of the Bishop of Exeter to institute a clergyman named George Cornelius Gorham to a new living within his diocese. The outcome in Gorham's favour, following the intervention of the Judicial Committee of the Privy Council, convinced some Tractarians that the Church of England was irredeemably protestant in character and subject to the whims of the state. Earlier in his career, Gorham had been Curate of Maidenhead.

[181] Nearly 900,000 signed a petition against the move. This was at a time when the UK population was around 21 million, a third of what it is today.

16   A Tale of Two Chapels – and a Church

Proprietary chapels are almost but not quite a thing of the past. However, in the 18th and 19th centuries they provided a useful means, particularly for evangelically minded Christians, to get round the obstacles to the spread of the gospel posed by the rigidity of the parochial system and the unsympathetic attitude of many of the clergy. Provided the clergyman concerned was indifferent rather than downright hostile, a proprietor who might be a wealthy individual (such as the Countess of Huntingdon) or a board of trustees could obtain permission to build a proprietary chapel that was licensed for Church of England worship. These were chiefly operated independently of the parish system, although in some cases they might be technically classified as chapels of ease to a parish church and their ministry nominally subject to the authority of the parochial vicar or rector.[182]

There were two such chapels in Reading, both formed within the parish of St Mary's but today only one remains as a proprietary chapel, albeit outside the Church of England, while the other is now a parish church within that communion. St Mary's Castle Street or St Mary's Episcopal Chapel has its origins in a chapel founded in 1798 by a body of evangelicals who had been gathered at St Giles during the ministry of William Bromley Cadogan, already

---

[182] In a judgement of 1840 in the case of Hodgson v. Dillon, the Dean of the Court of Arches, Dr Stephen Lushington, expressed the view that a bishop could not lawfully grant a licence to the minister of a proprietary chapel without the consent of the rector or vicar of the parish. This ruling is now said to be enshrined in Canon C.8.

discussed. They found themselves unable to continue under that of his successor, Joseph Eyre, especially after he preached a sermon accusing them of 'zeal without knowledge.' They attempted to establish a proprietary chapel on the lines described above but the other town clergy sided with Eyre and permission was refused. As a result the New Chapel in Castle Street was founded as an independent chapel and remained as such for 38 years. Initially it had a strong link to the Countess of Huntingdon's Connexion[183] and, as in the Countess's own chapels, worship was according to the 1662 Book of Common Prayer.

Recently published[184] letters show that the veteran Evangelical clergyman, John Newton, encouraged the separatists, stating that Eyre 'could not have taken a more public and decided step, to justify your separating from the walls of St Giles.' ...As he has publicly arraigned your whole body, and charged your principles with being inimical to government, I judge that you are not only warranted but bound to vindicate yourselves from the assertion, and... show the absolute necessity you were under for building a Chapel and providing a Preacher, who would not contradict from the Pulpit, what you had been long accustomed and pleased to hear from the Desk.'

---

[183] The Connexion had come into being in 1783 when the Countess seceded from the established church. Three of the early ministers of the New Chapel, William Green, John Bickerdike and James Sherman, were sourced from the ordained ministry of the Connexion.

[184] Online by the John Newton Project from a collection of letters to Dr Thomas Ring, one of the Castle Street founders, and his wife, Sophia. Newton was at this time Vicar of St Mary Woolnoth in the City of London.

The chapel's early days were by no means smooth. The first minister appointed, William Green (c.1756-1802), fell sick and resigned and after brief pastorates by John Bickerdike and Henry Gauntlett the pulpit was largely supplied for 14 years by visiting preachers while prayer book worship was provided by the Clerk, Abraham Watkins, who was ordained for the purpose. In 1808 part of the congregation split away, apparently objecting to the Trustees' rigid adherence to the Church of England liturgy, and formed a new congregation, meeting in Minster St, at the Salem chapel, a building formerly occupied by Presbyterians.[185]

The Castle Street chapel entered a more stable period with the appointment in 1821 of James Sherman (1796-1862), who held the pastorate until 1836. Sherman was a gifted preacher, a notable scholar who brought out new editions of some of the near-forgotten works of the Puritans and a good organizer who succeeded in setting up a ring of satellite chapels in the villages around Reading.[186] Two of these at Binfield Heath and Caversham Hill are still active churches at the present day.

Further overtures were made to seek recognition by the establishment during Sherman's ministry and, when he left in 1836 to succeed the late Rowland Hill at the Surrey

---

[185] This story is told at some length in *The Church that would not Die* by the author, now out of print. See also Chapter 18 for the subsequent use of the chapel by the Primitive Methodists.

[186] More details of this aspect of Sherman's ministry can be found in the author's pamphlet entitled *Beautiful the Landscape*, available from St Mary's, Castle Street, and more generally Sherman's life and witness is recounted in *The Church that would not Die*.

Chapel in London, a licence was obtained from the Bishop of Salisbury and the Rev Charles Joseph Goodhart (1804-92) became the first regular Anglican minister. In the early 1840s the building of 1798 was enhanced by the addition of the distinctive portico and a chancel.

James Sherman, Minister of the Castle Street Chapel 1821-36

Although at this time St Giles enjoyed an evangelical ministry once again under John Cecil Grainger, as did those who worshipped at St Laurence's under John Ball and at the new church of St John's under Francis Trench, the period of 50 years under Goodhart (1836-52) and his successor, George Tubbs (1852-88), was undoubtedly Castle Street's hey-day. Goodhart reported 666 morning worshippers, 240 Sunday scholars and 825 evening worshippers to the religious census of 1851. Thereafter to some extent the chapel suffered from the restoration of Greyfriars as an evangelical powerhouse but of that development we shall have more to say later in this chapter.

The Caversham Hill Chapel, one of a number founded by Sherman in the villages round Reading

After a number of attempts to either associate Castle Street with a parish or conventional district or move to a new location in Southcote or Woodley came to nothing,[187]

---

[187] The Southcote proposal came about in the mid-1950s but did not get further than the proverbial drawing-board; an Anglican church, St Matthew's, eventually opened in 1967. This currently has an evangelical ministry, associated with that of Greyfriars, though that has only come about very recently. The proposal for a move to Woodley arose in the mid-60s and Castle Street people were involved in the foundation of a new church, St James, in the expanding district. Ultimately, however, St

the chapel became increasingly less comfortable with the establishment it had previously fought hard to join and in 1994, following the approval by the General Synod of the ordination of women, withdrew from the Church of England to become a constituent church of the Church of England (Continuing).

While Castle Street was governed by a Board of Trustees who were originally mainly members of the congregation that had decamped from St Giles, Trinity Chapel in the Oxford Road was built at the initiative of one man, the Rev George Hulme (1787-1845), in part to meet the needs of those living in the western area of the expanding town and also to provide burial vaults or 'catacombs' for those who preferred this method of entombment to churchyard burial. The church was built between 1825 and 1827 but was not consecrated until 1832. Hulme appears to have been on friendly terms with the trustees of the Castle Street chapel, for it was he who acted as a go-between for them in their negotiations with the Bishop in 1836. In 1840 he received a somewhat unusual additional appointment as Domestic Chaplain to the King of Hanover.[188] When he died he was described in the local press as 'a clergyman whose earthly career has been one of unabated zeal in that cause in which he early embarked.'

Mary's, Castle Street, 'refused to die.' This story is also related in *Beautiful the Landscape*.

[188] Up until 1837 the King of Hanover had for over 120 years also been King of Great Britain; because Hanover operated under the equivalent of the Salic Law, with the succession of Victoria to William IV as monarch of the UK, the title passed to the next eldest surviving son of George III, Ernest Augustus (1771-1851).

Hulme himself chose as his successor William Whitmarsh Phelps (1797-1867), who was then Curate of Sulhamstead and had formerly been a Curate at St Laurence's under John Ball, and Phelps was duly presented to the living by Hulme's sons. It cannot be often that a clergyman composes an epitaph for his predecessor, but William Phelps was moved to write the following eulogy for George Hulme.

> A Minister of Grace to sinful man,
> One steadfast aim thro' all his conduct ran.
> In doctrine, language, manner still the same,
> He strove the devious wanderer to reclaim,
> To build the just on faith's foundations up,
> And neutralize the gall in sorrow's cup.
> The brow of gravity that mark'd a mind
> Touch'd with the guilt and danger of mankind,
> The joyous eye that in his Master's cross
> Read the full remedy for nature's loss,
> The look affectionate, that won the heart
> Ere the kind accent could its charm impart,
> All spoke a soul enkindled from on high,
> To whom 'twas Christ to live, and gain to die.

Under Phelps, the original preaching box was enhanced by the addition of a new 'east front'[189] and bell-tower. He also built a Parsonage and some adjoining properties known as Hulme Villas.

An important change in legislation governing proprietary chapels had taken place just before the

---

[189] It is notable that both Reading's former proprietary chapels have a north-south orientation rather than the more usual and traditional west-east.

founding of Trinity which restricted their lifespan as autonomous institutions to 50 years[190] and as a result Phelps had the year 1875 fixed in his gaze, realizing that the church's evangelical ministry might thereafter come under threat. This threat not only affected Trinity; the three parish churches had all passed into the patronage of the Bishop of Oxford (from 1845 Samuel Wilberforce), who, despite or because of his parentage, was not on the whole sympathetic to evangelicals. Already Cecil Grainger of St Giles had been succeeded in 1857 by a man of 'higher' churchmanship.[191] Phelps, therefore, conceived the notion of replacing the chapel with a restored Greyfriars, a project that finally came to fruition just after he himself had departed to become Archdeacon of Carlisle in 1863. Holy Trinity duly became a chapel-of-ease to St Mary's and eventually in November 1875 a parish in its own right.[192] As Phelps had expected it also came

---

[190] My understanding is that this legislation was not retrospective and thus did not cover St Mary's, Castle Street, which was already established with a trust deed of 1807, revised in 1856, providing a firm legal framework for its continued existence. Whilst it was technically a chapel-of-ease to St Mary the Virgin, the latter rarely if ever sought to interfere in the ministry.

[191] This was Thomas V. Fosbery (1807-75), who served St Giles until 1870, having previously held the perpetual curacy of Sunningdale, Berks. Rather surprisingly, perhaps, he was a graduate of Trinity College, Dublin, which one tends to associate with the 'low church' end of the Anglican spectrum!

[192] This date is given by Ditchfield, though other authorities state it as 1870. It seems also to be the case that initially the parish area was defined as a district chapelry, as was the case

increasingly under the influence of the Oxford Movement, especially after 1894. John Cecil Grainger (1869-85), son and namesake of the former St Giles' Vicar, was the last incumbent appointed to Trinity as a proprietary chapel and under Henry Last (1894-1902) it became a thoroughly Anglo-Catholic stronghold.

To Reading citizens today it is perhaps most clearly associated with the incumbency (1967-89) of the late Brian Brindley, who converted to Roman Catholicism not long after his departure from the parish under a *News of the World*-engendered cloud. Brindley transformed Holy Trinity into an Anglo-Catholic shrine choc-a-bloc with rejects from other churches, including a pulpit from which Wesley once preached and a Pugin rood screen from St Chad's RC Cathedral, Birmingham. If Brindley through life often seemed to be courting notoriety his death in 2001 at the Athenaeum in London part-way[193] through a gargantuan lunch to mark his 70th birthday certainly hit the headlines.

In 2011, a later Vicar, Jonathan Baker (1996-2002) was consecrated to become one of the flying bishops introduced to cater for opponents of women priests; initially appointed to that of Ebbsfleet, he subsequently became Bishop of Fulham. In the same year, the serving Vicar, Rev David Elliott, and fifteen members of the congregation opted to join the Ordinariate established by Pope Benedict XVI for disgruntled 'traditional' Anglicans.

---

with Greyfriars, with full parish status following as early as 1876. See *London Gazette*, 29th October 1875 and 9th June 1876.

[193] Famously, or infamously, during the breathing-space between the stuffed crab and the boeuf en croute.

**Holy Trinity, the former Proprietary Chapel,
as it appears today**

The church that both replaced Holy Trinity in the evangelical 'camp' and displaced St Mary's Episcopal Chapel from its prime position within that camp was Greyfriars. As we have observed earlier in this chapter, the restoration of Greyfriars arose from the vision of William Phelps of Trinity, who is said to have thought out a scheme for a new district church in August 1860, seeing the fulfilment of his dream on 2nd December 1863 when the church was in Rev P H Ditchfield's words 'consecrated for the pure worship of the Reformed Church of England'. The architect for the reconstruction was W H Woodman, better known for his work for the dissenting community and also with his partner, W F Poulton, for that wondrous Gothic extravaganza, Wokingham Town Hall.

The restored Greyfriars church, as it appears today

The re-consecration ceremony was presided over by Bishop Wilberforce with a congregation of over 700 filling the church. Those present included the Mayor of Reading, Lewis Cooper, the Archdeacon of Berkshire, Ven. J Randall, the Vicars of the three ancient parish churches and other clergy. These included the Rev J R Woodford, who was one of the bishop's examining chaplains and later from 1873 Bishop of Ely.[194] Wilberforce's sermon took

---

[194] Woodford was also a noted hymn-writer, some of whose

Matthew 14. 16 as its text, from the evangelist's account of the feeding of the 5,000. The first evening service attracted an even larger congregation of 800/ 900, who heard Archdeacon Phelps preach and joined in the singing of John Cennick's great Advent hymn, 'Lo He comes with clouds descending.'

The first Vicar of Greyfriars, Rev Dr Shadwell M Barkworth (1819-91), served until 1874, when Seymour H Soole (1840-1912, V. 1874-1905) began the first of a number of exceptionally long incumbencies, which included in the 20th century those of the Revs. John C Rundle (1878-1967, V. 1924-47) and John K Page (1912-89, V. 1947-68). From the first Greyfriars was designed to be a citadel of Conservative Evangelicalism, use of the black Geneva Gown continuing long after it was abandoned by other churches of a similar stance including St Mary's Castle Street.[195] In the later 20th century, it moved towards a more charismatic style of worship.

---

compositions have survived into the 20th century, if not the 21st.

[195] A guidance note prepared in the 1950s for applicants to fill a vacancy in the incumbency of St Mary's, Castle Street, placed the chapel between Greyfriars at the conservative end of the evangelical spectrum and St John's, which was deemed to be more moderate. In the 1980s Greyfriars began to adopt more contemporary modes of worship, whereas Castle Street reinforced its emphasis on Prayer Book worship and revived use of the Geneva Gown. There was some traffic between the two churches – in both directions! – partly as a result of these changes.

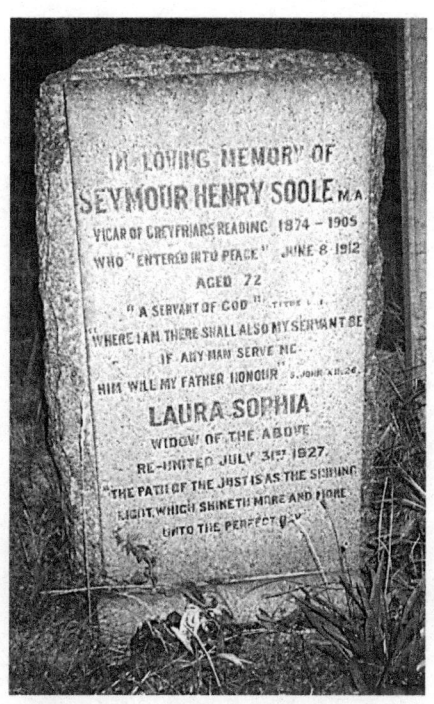

**Gravestone in Reading Cemetery of
Seymour Henry Soole, the first of many
long-serving vicars of Greyfriars, 1874-2005**

In August 1864, Greyfriars was assigned a conventional district, which was taken from 'certain extremities' of the parishes of St Laurence and St Mary. What was initially called 'the Consolidated Chapelry of the Grey Friars, Reading' took in an area bounded in the north by the railway bridge across Caversham Road, passing up Greyfriars Road and West Street, with Oxford Street going westward forming the southern boundary as far as Chatham Street and down into Great Knollys Street. Dr Barkworth was originally styled the Perpetual Curate but from 1868 he was accorded the title of Vicar of the new parish.

As had been expected there was a large influx of members from Holy Trinity as that chapel moved towards the orbit of St Mary's and, significantly too, the new church attracted the support of several leading citizens of the town including some such as Martin Hope Sutton[196] who had previously been strongly associated with St Mary's, Castle Street.

---

[196] Sutton was one of the trustees of St Mary's, Castle Street, named in the Trust Deed of 1855 and appears to have remained a trustee till his death in 1901. However, he also warmly supported Archdeacon Phelps' vision for the restoration of Greyfriars and seems to have been more closely associated with its ministry thereafter. Members of the Sutton clan, though, continued to serve on the St Mary's Trust well into the 20th century, the last being Mr Audley Sutton (1957-63) and Rev Richard Sutton (1964-80); other members of the family are found worshipping at St John's. Richard Sutton was one of the Castle Street contingent who helped to set up the new church in Woodley, serving later as a CMS missionary in Pakistan.

17   Religion in Reading 1851

1851 is probably most often remembered as the date of the Great Exhibition that took place in the Crystal Palace, a high Victorian celebration of the greatness of the British Empire, at a time when the amount of red on the world map was increasing year by year. Doubtless there were many who went up to London from Reading to Paddington to view the exhibits. 1851, however, was also the date of the first and only national census of religious activity[197] and as a result we have as complete a picture as numbers can give of the state of Christianity in Reading at the mid-century.

The following table sets out the results of that census as they affected Reading, both the town within the boundaries that then applied, together with those areas later assumed into modern Reading. I have also included in this some of those forming part of the Greater Reading conurbation such as Earley that remain outside the present boundary. In the table Old Dissent is a term widely used to denote the various denominations that arose during the 16th and 17th centuries, including the Baptists, Independents/ Congregationalists, Presbyterians and Quakers, while New Dissent denotes those that chiefly arose from the Evangelical Revival and later movements, notably the various strands of Methodism.

---

[197] Although census forms have included questions on religious identity since the 2001 survey, these have not attempted to establish how this related to actual numbers of worshippers.

No.	Category	Church	Adult A.M.	P.M	Eve
1	C of E	Chapel of Royal Berks Hospital	0	0	55
1	C of E	St Giles's Parish Church	700	0	750
1	C of E	St John's	500	450	0
1	C of E	St Lawrence's Parish Church	1,200	1,000	0
1	C of E	St Mary's Chapel	666	0	825
1	C of E	St Mary's Parish Church	700	0	900
1	C of E	Trinity Chapel	600	0	600
7	Sub-total		4,3,66	1,450	3,130
1	Old Dissent	Baptist (St Giles)	110	30	130
1	Old Dissent	Broad Street Chapel	403	308	341
1	Old Dissent	Castle Street Independent	520	0	460
1	Old Dissent	Society of Friends	80	0	58
1	Old Dissent	Kings Road Baptist	320	120	600
1	Old Dissent	Strict Baptist	50	0	0
1	Old Dissent	Trinity Independent	300	0	300
7	Sub-total		1,783	458	1,889

1	New Dissent	Bethel Wesleyan Methodist	30	0	45
1	New Dissent	Christian Brethren	30	0	40
1	New Dissent	Latter Day Saints	8	16	31
1	New Dissent	Salem Primitive Methodist	220	0	590
1	New Dissent	Wesleyan Methodist (St Giles)	210	60	247
1	New Dissent	Wesleyan Spring Gardens	0	18	15
6	Sub-total		498	94	968
1	Roman Catholic	St James	220	0	140
21	TOTAL		6,867	2,002	6,127

AREAS FORMING PRESENT-DAY 'GREATER READING'

No.	Category	Church	Adult		
			A.M.	P.M	Eve
1	C of E	Caversham Parish Church †	260	210	0
1	C of E	Mapledurham Parish Church	120	45	0
1	C of E	Shinfield Parish Church	160	111	0
1	C of E	St Andrew's Parish Church, Sonning	235	229	0
1	C of E	St Peter's Chapel, Earley	90	100	80

1	C of E	Theale Parish Church	200	350	0
1	C of E	Tilehurst Parish Church †	250	180	0
7	Sub-total		1,315	1,225	80
1	Old Dissent	Binfield Heath Congregational	0	40	50
1	Old Dissent	Caversham Independent †	0	0	60
1	Old Dissent	Chazey Heath Independent	0	0	27
1	Old Dissent	Sonning Congregationalist	0	0	30
1	Old Dissent	Tilehurst Independent †	24	0	46
5	Sub-total		24	40	213
1	New Dissent	Bethesda Countess of Huntingdon, Tilehurst †	59	127	0
1	New Dissent	Shinfield Primitive Methodist	0	0	40
1	New Dissent	Woodley Primitive Methodist	36	0	45
6	Sub-total		95	127	85
21	TOTAL		1,434	1,392	378

† Within present day borough.

Source: Kate Tiller/ Berkshire Record Society (see Bibliography).

The results from the areas forming the Oxford Diocese (i.e. Berkshire, Buckinghamshire and Oxfordshire) are of particular interest because the Bishop of Oxford, Samuel Wilberforce, took a rather extreme line, opposing the whole idea of a religious census. He was convinced that the Nonconformists, of whose scruples he clearly had a very low opinion, would use it in an effort to 'bump up' their numbers in order to make them look good, when compared with those of the Established Church. He instructed his clergy to do all they could to prevent co-operation with the census. As a result, we find a number of returns where minimum information is given, returns filled in by the parish registrar instead of the incumbent and conversely returns that are quite substantial in their content, indicating implicitly and sometimes explicitly that the clergyman concerned thought his Bishop was in the wrong! Thus in Reading the return for St Mary's Parish Church is a brief one of three lines, signed by Frederick West, Registrar and Master of the Coley Workhouse, but is followed by a 17-line epic on St Mary's Chapel, Castle Street, signed by the Minister, Charles Joseph Goodhart. Here are two examples falling within these extremes from both sides of the denominational divide, but both containing detailed information:

TRINITY CHAPEL. Chapel of Ease in Parish of St. Mary. No district. *When consecrated* 1828. Additional church. *How erected* by Rev George Hulme. *Cost* private benefaction £5,000. *Endowed* £100 in 3 per cent stock, pew rents £250. *Free sittings* 450; *other sittings* 650. *On 30 March*: morning general congregation 600; Sunday scholars 200; evening general congregation 600. *Average attendance*: morning general congregation 600;

Sunday scholars 200; evening general congregation 600. *Signed* W. Phelps, Perpetual Curate, Reading. 31 March 1851.

BAPTIST CHAPEL. Kings Road Baptist Chapel. Parish of St Lawrence. *Erected* 1834 in lieu of another Chapel but not on the same site. A separate building used exclusively for worship. *Free sittings* 140; *other sittings* 560. *On 30 March*: morning general congregation 320; Sunday scholars 140; afternoon general congregation 120; Sunday scholars 170; evening general congregation 600; Sunday scholars 40. Signed John Jenkyn Brown, Minister, 5 The Abbot's Walk, Reading. 30 March 1851.

The following entry indicates that the disciples of John Nelson Darby, known as the Christian or Plymouth Brethren, were now established in Reading:

CHRISTIANS who meet simply as such, Queens Road, Parish of St Giles. A separate building not used exclusively for worship. *Free sittings* about 100; *standing room* about 20. *Remarks* from 30 to 40 persons usually meet together on Sundays in the morning for breaking bread and in the evening for worship upon the principles stated briefly in the accompanying paper [not apparently submitted]. There is full liberty for the exercise of any gift for service or Ministry, but Ministerial Office and station is unknown amongst us. *Signed* S. W. Spurr, 134 London Street, Reading. 29 March 1851.

In fact there is truly little evidence that the Nonconformists were any less honest than the Anglicans in their submissions – for instance, the admission by the

Brethren above that they had room for 100 but expected around 40 attendees seems very frank. Both groups complain about the bad weather on census day preventing more people from being present. So how do the results pan out? If we take Reading, as then constituted, total attendance, including no doubt some who attended more than one service, came to 14,996, just over two-thirds of the town's population of 22,175. Of these, 60% attended Church of England places of worship, 27.5% chapels of old dissent, 10.4% those of new dissent and 2.4% the RC Church of St James. In the rural areas around Reading, the Established Church appears much stronger with nearly 82% attending, compared with less than 8% for old dissent and 9.6% for new dissent. Among the latter it is particularly notable that the Primitive Methodists are strong, a phenomenon that is repeated in other parts of Berkshire; we will consider this further in the next chapter.

At least one aspect of religious practice in 1851 is in sharp contrast to that of the early 21st century: in the churches of both Old and New Dissent evening worshippers outnumber those attending in the morning. This is also in contrast to Anglican worship where numbers were greater in the morning, although attendance at evening worship could not be called negligible. Today, many churches, whether Anglican or Nonconformist, have abandoned evening services altogether and where they survive (with, of course, honourable exceptions) it is often a case of 'two or three being gathered together.'

Before looking at the consequences of 'the numbers game,' there was another aspect of mid-Victorian religion which can be analysed from the results of the census and that is the extent of the funding of church activity by pew rents. Except in those cases where incumbents followed the Bishop's lead or in the case of dissenters where meetings took place in rented accommodation, the census forms provide an indication of the balance between free sittings and sittings attracting pew rents. As the following table shows, rented sittings outnumbered free sittings by a proportion of 59% to 41%, although the balance in individual churches varied considerably. As a general rule, the independents are shown as more reliant on pew rents since the churches of the establishment benefited from other income sources such as tithes and endowments.

Category	Church or Chapel	Free Sittings	Rented Sittings	Pew Rents if known (£)
C of E	St Giles Parish Church	582	736	25
C of E	St John's	400	400	250
C of E	St Lawrence's Parish Church	527	450	
C of E	St Mary's Chapel	412	740	450 to 500
C of E	Trinity Chapel	450	650	250
Old Dissent	Baptist (St Giles)	80	40	
Old Dissent	Broad Street Chapel	120	470	
Old Dissent	Castle Street Independent	125	500	
Old Dissent	Caversham Independent	200	0	
Old Dissent	Kings Road Baptist	140	350	

Old Dissent	Tilehurst Independent	200	100
Old Dissent	Trinity Independent	150	350
New Dissent	Bethel Wesleyan Methodist	24	100
New Dissent	Countess of Huntingdon, Tilehurst	216	14
New Dissent	Christian Brethren	100	0
New Dissent	Latter Day Saints	100	0
New Dissent	Salem Primitive Methodist	89	331
New Dissent	Wesleyan Methodist (St Giles)	114	421
New Dissent	Wesleyan Spring Gardens	30	0
Roman Catholic	St James RC	96	166
TOTAL		4,155	5,928

Source: Kate Tiller/ Berkshire Record Society

Whatever Wilberforce may have said of the census there can be little doubt that he took notice of the results across the diocese and locally in Reading. It is, however, a cause of regret that such a great bishop with so many outstanding achievements should have maintained his deep prejudice against nonconformity for in 1863 he pronounced 'bad cottages, beer houses and dissenters' as the greatest obstacles to his work! Considering that Nonconformists were more likely than Anglicans to rally to the cause of temperance this does seem an extraordinary statement and it need scarcely be added that it caused outrage among leading free churchmen such as William Legg, minister at Broad Street.

The remainder of Wilberforce's episcopate is characterised by a great period of church building and restoration to cater for the needs of the expanding population, to ensure that if folk attended the dissenting chapels it was out of choice rather than necessity. During this period in Reading we see:

1854	St Michael's, Tilehurst, reconstruction.
1857	St Peter's, Caversham, new vestry.
1861-2	Christ Church, Whitley, commenced.
1862-3	Greyfriars restored as a place of worship.
1863	St Peter's, Earley, enlarged.
1863-4	Restoration and extensions, St Mary the Virgin.
1865	All Saints, Downshire Square, commenced.
1867-8	St Laurence restored.

These words from Wilberforce's sermon at the re-consecration of Greyfriars[198] illustrate his thinking on the subject: 'You know that in this great and growing population there has been hitherto very little accommodation for the poor for Christian worship in our churches. This is an attempt... to provide for this

---

[198] As quoted in Malcolm Summers' *History of Greyfriars Church, Reading*.

necessity. It is providing for these people the bread of heaven ...'

The feverish pace of church development certainly did not cease with Wilberforce's translation to Winchester in 1869. The 1870s and 1880s were further great periods of church building and the Nonconformists, not to be outdone, also built a number of new chapels during this later period in particular. We shall return to this theme in Chapter 21.

18 Dissent post-1800

As discussed in the previous chapter, the 1851 census revealed just over 40% of Reading church-goers[199] worshipping outside the Church of England with 27.5% representing Old Dissent, 10.4% New Dissent and the remaining 2.4% the Roman Catholics. In this chapter we consider the progress of protestant dissent up to and beyond that momentous year.

If we take the results of the census recorded above, it is evident that in 1851 the six principal nonconformist churches in Reading then were:

Denomination/ Location	**Total attendance**
Baptist – Kings Road	1,080
Congregational – Broad Street	1,052
Congregational – Castle Street	980
Salem Primitive Methodist	810
Congregational – Trinity	600
Wesleyan Methodist	517

Together these six represented 89% of all nonconformist attendances on the census day and 34% of all attendances including Anglican and Roman Catholic. While the Kings Road Baptists marginally outdid the Broad Street Congregationalists by 28 attendances, the three Congregational churches together with 2,632 attendances outnumbered them by nearly three to one.

We left the Baptists in Chapter 10 under the long and fruitful pastorate of Thomas Davis (1768-96). Davis was

---

[199] In Reading as defined by the boundaries then in force.

followed by John Holloway who ministered for 14 years till 1811, a period described by historians as one of 'great restlessness' in the church, mitigated by the establishment of a Sunday School. Next, following an interregnum of three years, John Dyer (1784-1841) came briefly to Reading, leaving in 1819 to become the Secretary of the Baptist Missionary Society (BMS).[200]

Dyer was succeeded by John Howard Hinton (1791-1873), whose father, James Hinton had preceded Dyer at the BMS. Hinton junior is best remembered in Reading for overseeing the move, which took place in 1834, from the 1752 chapel in Hosier's Lane to the new site in King's Road. Hinton was an imposing figure, 'six feet in height, of spare and severe form, his countenance calm and thoughtful, touched with sadness.' He was a noted preacher, known, like his contemporary, James Sherman, for his open air preaching during the Reading Cheese Fair In 1837 Hinton moved on to become pastor of Devonshire Square Chapel in London, also serving as Secretary of the Baptist Union from 1841.[201] Later

---

[200] The story of Dyer's controversial and ultimately tragic career as a mission administrator is told in *Sent from Reading* by the present writer.

[201] Ian Sellers, writing in the *Baptist Quarterly*, 'John Howard Hinton, Theologian,' characterises Hinton as follows:' Rarely has such a polymath occupied high office among the Baptists, for Hinton could write with expertise on theology, economics, politics, ecclesiology, philosophy, psychology and law, and had a close, first-hand acquaintance with the affairs of northern Europe and North America. A vigorous and voluminous controversialist, he left no opponent unscathed. Like so many early Victorians, he was assured of the rightness of his own case

ministers during the 19th century included John Aldis (1855-69), William Anderson (1872-86) and C A Davis (1887-94) who wrote the first history of the Baptist movement in Reading in 1891. Davis unfortunately left under something of a cloud when he was accused of travelling on the railway without a valid ticket.

Aldis was President of the Baptist Union in 1866 and also from 1859 secretary of the newly formed Berkshire Baptist Association. After his departure for Plymouth in 1869 the church underwent an uneasy period during the brief ensuing pastorate of Thomas Collins Page, marked by disputes over whether membership should be extended to those who had not received believers' baptism, which also affected the Berkshire Association. However, the church's effectiveness was restored under William Anderson (1848-86); during this period, the number of Reading's Baptist churches began to multiply with the foundation of Wycliffe (1881) and Grovelands (1886), following that of Carey in 1867. A Baptist cause also commenced in the transpontine town of Caversham in 1865. By the time of the early death of Anderson the King's Road church was in a healthier position with a membership of 568 (1890), making it the largest in numerical terms in Berkshire. In 1904 another church was

---

and the wrongness of everyone else's. More than a little arrogant, he claimed never to have changed a single opinion from youth to old age, and to be the author of a body of systematic divinity which no-one had ever previously expounded. 1 His figure was angular, his delivery nervous and staccato. Few people knew him well and most felt uneasy in his presence. 2 No-one, however, could dispute the thrustfulness of his intellectual penetration, even though the contradictions and inconsistencies in his thinking are never far from the surface.'

opened in the East Reading suburb of Earley, named the Anderson Memorial Church after William Anderson.

1796 also saw the appointment of a new minister to Broad Street after the long pastorate of Thomas Noon concluded with his death the previous year. In contrast to the Baptists, the Congregationalists continued to be blessed with long-serving ministers beginning with Archibald Douglas (c.1767-1839). Douglas had been born in London but was, as his name suggests, of Scottish parentage. After studying at the Mile End Academy he ministered in Newmarket before his call to Reading. He is described as a man of action, who reversed a decline in attendance during the latter years of Noon's ministry and set about the rebuilding of the meeting house in 1798. He also established a Sunday School and a day-school for girls[202] and was instrumental in the founding of the Berkshire Association for nonconformist ministers in or around the year of his arrival in Reading. He was a founder member too of the London Missionary Society (LMS)[203] and on the home front joined with others in starting the Reading Evangelical Society which began the process of evangelizing the villages around Reading, work later taken up by James Sherman in the 1820s, as we saw in Chapter 16. Over time Douglas acquired the nickname of 'Archibald Ironsides' – an allusion no doubt to that other arch-independent, Oliver Cromwell or 'Old Ironsides.' The later years of Douglas's long ministry were marred by the mental illness that afflicted his wife.

---

[202] See Chapter 14.

[203] See *Sent from Reading* for an account of the part played by Douglas and other Reading ministers in the early history of the LMS.

Douglas was also troubled by a partial failure of his voice which led him from 1823 to seek assistance in the ministry. Two such assistants, Thomas Stamper and Thomas Everett, came each for a few years and then in 1831 William Legg was invited to become co-pastor after a three months' probation and was ordained on the 14th of December of that year. Legg was not only Scottish-bred but also born – at Monquhitter, Aberdeenshire, in 1800. Having been apprenticed to a saddler at Peterhead, he was called to the ministry and studied at Aberdeen University and the Congregational Academy at Glasgow. On Douglas's death in March 1839 he became the sole pastor of Broad Street chapel.

A few weeks earlier, Legg had been involved in a notable event which attracted the attention of the Reading public at large, a debate in the Town Hall in which he crossed swords with the redoubtable Socialist pioneer, Robert Owen (1771-1858). At this time Owen's beliefs can be characterized as vaguely deistic or agnostic, although towards the end of his life he espoused spiritualism. Owen visited Reading to propagate his views in 1838 and issued a challenge to the ministers of the town to engage with him in public debate. Legg, perhaps as a 'doughty Scot,' seems to have been the only one to have accepted the challenge and the tournament took place over two days from 4th March. The debates were chaired with firmness and impartiality, we are told, by Dr Cowan, who practiced medicine in London Street and was a member and trustee of St Mary's, Castle Street. It seems that far more wanted to attend the debate than could obtain admittance and allegedly students from Oxford offered to pay elderly ladies a guinea for their shilling tickets but without success!

Legg seems to have believed that he won the day and the *Reading Mercury* agreed with him. But of course prejudgement may well have influenced its reportage and even the 'impartial' Dr Cowan subsequently expressed himself vehemently opposed to the 'depravity' of socialism. Geoff Sawers speculates that Owen, at 68, may have been 'a little past his prime,' although still a formidable speaker, in contrast to the comparatively youthful Legg.

**Broad Street Chapel
as it appeared for most of the 19th Century**

In the 1860s history repeated itself. Legg, by now in his 60s, began to feel his powers fading, and like Douglas before him took on a series of co-pastors. The first of these, Daniel Mossop, was a great help and evidently much missed when he departed for Queensland. However, his 24-year old successor, Samuel Clarke Gordon, like Legg a graduate of Aberdeen University, proved to be the source of much contention following his ordination as co-pastor in September 1866. Before long this led to litigation between Gordon, who claimed that he had been appointed for life, and the chapel trustees, who demurred. The latter were successful but as a result the congregation suffered a damaging split. Seventy-three members, termed by one wag 'the left Leggs,'[204] followed Gordon when he was dismissed in 1868 and subsequently in 1869 founded a new chapel, the Augustine Church in Friar Street.

Shortly after this disruption, Legg himself resigned his ministry, being presented with a silver inkstand and a purse of £100 by his grateful hearers. He died in 1871. Later ministers at Broad Street during what remained of the 19th century were: George Colborne (1870-2), Charles Goward (1873-80), Thomas Ross (1881-7) and Herbert Sewell (1888-1903). During the first three of these pastorates the chapel experienced a continuing decline in numbers but under Sewell, an Irishman, something of a revival took place. Among other innovations he instituted a society for Pleasant Sunday Afternoons and presided over the reordering of the chapel, including the construction in

---

[204] Geoff Sawers ascribes this term to the Augustinians whereas Summers applies it to those who seceded to form Trinity Chapel (see below). Quite probably it originated then but was revived for the later secession.

1892 of the present façade, now Messrs Waterstones' shop window. As for the Augustine Chapel that was of brief duration[205] and following its closure in 1886 the building was converted into a theatre in 1893. Gordon had departed the scene in 1875 after which two brief pastorates intervened before the congregation combined with that of Castle Street (see below).

Broad Street also had two 'satellite' chapels during the 19th century, at Tilehurst (from 1842) and at Toker's Green, outside Caversham (from 1846). At the very end of the era, in 1899, Arborfield was added to this number.

The Castle Street Chapel was a by-product of the licensing of what became St Mary's Episcopal Chapel for Church of England worship in 1836. Particularly under James Sherman's ministry the chapel had attracted a large number of dissenters who had no wish to become Anglicans. These numbered at least 200 for this was the number that attended a meeting in the vestry of the Broad Street Chapel in September 1836 to discuss the formation of a new Congregational Chapel. This was duly opened, on the opposite side of the road from the Episcopal Chapel, in October 1837 with the Rev Spedding Curwen from Newbury as its first pastor. Evidently the church flourished for by 1851 it was attracting a morning congregation of over 500. Curwen died in 1856 and later ministries included those of Thomas Horton (1857-62), Richard Bulmer (1863-70), John Wood (1870-82) and George Stewart (1887-95).

---

[205] Malcolm Summers has written an excellent short history of the Augustine Church, which can be found in the *History of Reading Society Newsletter,* No 60, Spring 2023.

The new Castle Street Chapel also inherited the care of the village chapels around Reading, chiefly founded by the Rev James Sherman, namely Caversham Hill, Binfield Heath, Pound Green, Sonning, Woodley and Wargrave, together with a mission hall at Coley, which was later taken over by the Salvation Army.

The third Congregational chapel in our 'Top Six' originated in a dispute that developed at Broad Street in the late 1840s. In 1845 'serious differences' arose between William Legg and leading members of the congregation including three of the deacons. The total number who seceded is put at 27 although they must have attracted other dissidents from elsewhere for by the end of March 48 were recorded as 'desiring to form a new church.' Initially this met at the 'New Hall' (now the Hotel 1843 in London Street) but eventually moved to a new building in Queen's Road. This was opened in March 1849, notable attendees including the Rev William Legg. The numbers recorded in 1851 indicate that the new church rapidly gathered support under its first pastor, W Guest (1847-50). Later ministries included those of Christian Bateman (1855-61), John Frederick Stevenson (1862-74) and Ambrose Shepherd (1891-98). During Shepherd's pastorate the church celebrated its golden jubilee. Taking the chair on this occasion was Sir Peter Spokes (1830-1910), a noted banker, benefactor and onetime Mayor of Reading. According to W. H. Summers he was one of the original seceders from Broad Street, although he must have been rather young at the time! As Mayor in 1869, he attended Trinity Church in his robes of office, the first time, reportedly, that a Mayor of Reading had thus honoured a dissenting place of worship.

We move finally to the two strands of Methodism represented in our Top Six. We left mainstream (i.e. Wesleyan) Methodism in 1817 with the construction of its first purpose-built chapel. Following John Waterhouse, early ministers in Reading included John Anderson, George Galland and Thomas Squance. Research by Lisa Spurrier[206] shows that during the 1820s and 30s the congregation included craftsmen and tradesmen and their families, along with representatives of the gentry and professional classes.

The Church Street chapel sufficed until 1873 when the new Wesley Methodist Church in Queen's Road came into being, built to seat 900. Wesley remains the principal Methodist church in Reading at the present day when it also hosts a Chinese language congregation. Unusually perhaps the church was designed by a Wesleyan minister, named Johnson, and constructed under the supervision of the Reading architect, Joseph Morris.[207]

Up until the death of John Wesley in 1791 Methodism comprised two main strands, the Wesleyan or Arminian Methodists, deriving their doctrines from those of the Wesley brothers, and the Calvinistic Methodists who looked back to George Whitefield and various Welsh leaders of the Revival such as Howell Harris and Daniel Rowland. After 1791 the Arminian strands began to multiply, through a perceived ossification in the leadership of the Wesleyans as well as the divisive influence of powerful personalities. In particular, three new sects came into being: the New Connexion (founded in Sheffield in

---

[206] See *Berkshire Old and New, No. 40*, published by the Berkshire Local History Association in 2023.
[207] See Chapter 19 following.

1791 by Alexander Kilham), the Bible Christians (founded by William Bryan in Cornwall in 1815) and the Primitive Methodists (founded in Staffordshire in 1807 by Hugh Bourne). The New Connexion and the Bible Christians were mainly confined to the northern and western counties respectively.

The Primitive Methodists, however, spread to the south of England during the 1820s and 30s largely through the evangelistic efforts of two men, John Ride (1790-1862) and Thomas Russell (1806-89). Following the foundation of the first Berkshire society at Upper Lambourn in 1829, the two men are said to have met together in a wood in the following February where they joined in prayer that 'God would give them Berkshire.' Ride then declared a *fait accompli*: 'Yonder county is ours and we will have it!'

The first recorded Primitive Methodist meeting in Reading was in the grounds of the Forbury in April 1835, whence they moved to a room in London Street in October and four years later took over the Salem Chapel[208] in Minster Street. Numbers increased rapidly from three ministers and 300 members in 1836 to 14 ministers and 1,039 members in 1841 and by 1844 membership had topped 1,500 with an additional three ministers.

In 1841 the Salem Chapel was the location of the first southern conference of the Primitive Methodist movement with the founding fathers, Hugh Bourne and William Clowes, addressing meetings commencing at 5 a.m. John Ride was the first resident minister in Reading but later moved to London as a visitor of the Home Missions and in 1849 was sent to Australia to head up the

---

[208] See also Chapter 16.

mission there.[209] Later ministers in Reading included Edward Bishop, G. E. Butt and Peter Coates.

As the table shows, by 1851 attendances exceeded those at the Wesleyan church; by 1866 they had outgrown Salem and moved to the former Mechanics Institution in London Street, now the Hotel 1843. This remained the focus of Primitive Methodist activity in Reading until the union of the various strands of Methodism in 1932 rendered it redundant.[210] In the meantime, however, local churches were established in Cumberland Road serving Newtown (1871), Friar Street (also 1871) and Oxford Road (1878).

That concludes our 'Top Six' but we should perhaps add a brief word about the later history of the other principal representative of 'Old Dissent' – namely the Quakers or Society of Friends. Having settled in Church Street near St Giles in the early 18th century they rebuilt their Meeting House on or near the same site in 1835. During the 1800s Quakers became famous for the number of firms set up by members of the Society for the manufacture of chocolate and other supposedly nourishing foods. Rowntrees of York, Cadburys of Birmingham and Frys of Bristol remain household names to this day. Reading was not to be left out and the firm of Huntley and Palmers grew from humble beginnings in London Street to become perhaps the most renowned biscuit-making enterprise in the world.

---

[209] This Reading missionary connection was regrettably missed by the author when compiling *Sent from Reading*.

[210] It is a mark of the strength of the Primitive Methodist movement that it remained independent until the general reunion of Methodism, whereas the smaller Bible Christian and New Connexion branches had united in 1907 with a later breakaway group to form the United Methodist Church.

The interest in chocolate-based drinks to some extent reflected the strong temperance tradition that developed among Quakers, and it has also been suggested that the denial of entrance to the universities encouraged them to concentrate on the practical skills and inventiveness that enabled them to thrive in the business world; these skills were further enhanced by such pastimes as solving mathematical puzzles that took the place of more hedonistic forms of pleasure.[211]

In common with the other firms mentioned above, H&P acquired a reputation for what has been called 'benevolent paternalism'[212] – for instance, by setting up a Sick Fund' as early as the 1840s with pensions (for men only), and recreational and holiday provisions following.

Tombs of members of the Huntley and Palmer families can be found in the Quaker graveyard next to the Meeting

---

[211] This last point was made by Matthew Callow of the Reading meeting in a presentation to the History of Reading Society in January 2024. The theme is explored more generally by Amanda Thomas in *The Nonconformist Revolution*, Pen and Sword, 2020, p. 118: 'The Quaker network linked an extraordinary number of the greatest innovators of the industrial age.'

[212] Clearly there were some workers at H&P who found this regime too authoritarian for their tastes. For instance, the consumption of alcoholic beverages and trade unionism were two activities strongly discouraged, while membership of temperance bodies such as the Band of Hope was to be welcomed. There is also some, largely oral, evidence to suggest that when a rival biscuit manufacturer, Serpells, opened in Reading in 1899, it was able to recruit from disaffected H&P workers. That said, a great many more spent their entire working lives happily working for the firm.

House.[213] It is, however, probably true to say that in the course of the 20th century the Quaker influence faded, as later generations of the Palmer family espoused Anglicanism, a tendency also found in other Quaker enterprises, such as Cadburys.[214]

Another famous name is the architect, Alfred Waterhouse, who lived in Reading from 1867-77 and designed the new Reading School and parts of the Town Hall; some of his relatives are also buried in the Quaker graveyard, although Alfred himself was baptised into the Church of England in 1877.

In the 20th century Reading's most famous Quaker was perhaps Phoebe Cusden 1887-1981) who as Mayor of Reading in 1946-7 was instrumental in setting up the town's close links with the city of Dusseldorf in Germany. These remain strong in the present day through the Reading-Dusseldorf Association.[215] In 2023 Dusseldorf named a road Phoebe-Cusden Platz after her in a

---

[213] There is a larger collection of Palmer tombstones at the Friends' Meeting House in Long Sutton, Somerset, where George Palmer was born in 1818. The author visited this in 2013 with the Chapels Society.

[214] This was not just a 20th century phenomenon. As illustrated in the following chapter through the Morris family, dissenting families sometimes converted to Anglicanism, often as a means of joining the local elite and sending their sons to university. These factors no longer applied in the 1900s when perhaps the change in the character of Quakerism to a more radical form of politics might have been a deterrent to captains of industry.

[215] In 2022 the author had the privilege of showing members of the Reading Dusseldorf Churches Group, an allied body, round St Mary's, Castle Street.

ceremony at which the British Consul-General called her the 'mother of town-twinnings.'

Quakers have also been much involved in the field of education and one fruit of this is Leighton Park School at Whiteknights, founded in 1890, with its original boarding house designed by Alfred Waterhouse. Perhaps its most famous alumnus is the former Labour leader and cabinet minister, Michael Foot (1913-2010), who won his first election at the school as the Liberal candidate at a mock election in 1929. His father, Isaac, was elected for Bodmin in the real election of that year, also as a Liberal.

19 Reading's Second Coming

Joseph Morris (1836-1914) was one of the leading architects practising in Reading during the late 19th century, although his work in the town was mainly secular in nature; as County Surveyor, he designed many of the police stations, schools and other buildings required by public bodies, as well as shops, offices and private dwellings. Through him, however, Reading, has a connection with one of the more extraordinary of the apocalyptic sects that flourished during that era.

Morris's family came from Bedfordshire where they had lived at least since the second half of the 17th century. They were Quakers and on at least one occasion moved towns to evade persecution. One branch of the family seems to have progressed to Reading around the turn of the 18th century. Certainly Joseph Morris's father, Thomas, was in business in Reading in 1827 as a woollen draper with premises at 11 Market Place. There, we may assume, Joseph Morris was born in 1836, the youngest of a family of ten.[216] The father, Thomas Morris, was Mayor of Reading in 1846/7.

He was thus quite an establishment figure and, while the attractions of the greasy pole may not have influenced his change of heart, it is certainly interesting that his Mayoralty followed shortly after the family's decision to withdraw from the Society of Friends and join the Church of

---

[216] It is interesting to note that another son, Charles, married into the Cocks family, makers of the celebrated Reading Sauce, and became owner of the company.

England.[217] Thomas Morris and his wife, Anne, with their two eldest children were baptised at St Lawrence's in 1844 but certainly by 1846 they were associated with St Mary's Episcopal Chapel since in that year the remainder of their children were baptised by the Minister, Charles Goodhart. Quite a number of the leading lights of St Mary's, Castle Street, had premises in the Market Place and one wonders whether that influenced the choice of church in any way. In 1876 Morris designed extensions to the episcopal school[218] which was then run by the chapel, buildings that were demolished in the late 1950s.

The 1851 census indicates that Joseph Morris had become articled to the local architect, J B Clacy, whom he was later to succeed as County Surveyor. After leaving Clacy he may have practised in London for a short while but certainly by 1860 he was back in Reading. His first recorded work is St Paul's Church and Vicarage at Highmoor, near Henley, dating from 1858/9. It seems likely that a cousin of Morris, who was a minister in the Church of England may have been instrumental in assisting him to achieve this breakthrough. This same gentleman, Rev William Marten Shewell, officiated at his marriage in 1868 to Emily Partridge of Wandsworth.

Joseph and Emily had four children, two of whom, Francis Edward and Violet Shewell Morris, followed in their father's footsteps as architects. From 1871 until 1905,

---

[217] The repeal of the Test and Corporation Acts in 1828 removed the legal hindrances to dissenters taking public office but it is arguable that local prejudices might still have prevented such an appointment. Repeal of the Acts was bitterly opposed by many 'hard-line' Tories.

[218] See Chapter 14.

Joseph Morris was County Surveyor of Bridges and Buildings for Berkshire.

From 1875 to 1886, Morris was in partnership with a slightly younger architect, Spencer Slingsby Stallwood (1844-1922), who had been born in Marlow but had hitherto been practising in Folkestone. It seems that the Rev W M Shewell may also have been instrumental in bringing the two together. This was an interesting partnership, inasmuch as Joseph Morris is assumed to have been an evangelical churchman at this time whereas Stallwood's sympathies were very much with the Anglo-Catholics. He was Churchwarden of St Giles for over 25 years. Among the works and buildings which he produced independently of the partnership with Morris are St Agnes, Silver Street (demolished c. 2000), which was a daughter church to St Giles – see illustration, page 262.

Although Morris and Stallwood were able to work together as evangelical and catholic, it does appear that it was Morris's change of allegiance in 1884 that led to their break-up two years later. Quite what possessed him to join the Agapemonites is not very clear but what is certain is that his new-found faith profoundly influenced the rest of his life and work. At this point we must, therefore, examine the history of this curious sect. The reader may notice some analogies between the Agapemonites and the better-known Catholic Apostolic Church (Irvingites), founded in the 1830s. It should be noted, though, that the former strayed much further in the direction of heterodoxy than did the latter. Both sects emerged in the context of a general revival of interest in the branch of theology known as eschatology – the science of the last things. There was a widespread expectation that the return of the Lord Jesus Christ (the Second Coming) was imminent and this was held by orthodox ministers such as Charles Joseph Goodhart and Hubert Brooke at St Mary's Episcopal Chapel. It is conceivable that as a youth Joseph Morris may have heard sermons on this theme by Goodhart, which influenced his later beliefs.

The Agapemonites were founded by Henry James Prince who lived from 1811 to 1899. Prince was an apothecary who later took orders in the Church of England. During the period of his training at Lampeter in Wales he was noted for his austerity and perfectionism. From 1840 to 1841 he was curate to the Revd. Dr Samuel Starky at Charlynch near Bridgwater in Somerset. Apparently he was responsible for a revival in the area but in May 1841 his licence was revoked by the Bishop of Bath and Wells. He moved to another curacy in Suffolk where his conduct also came under episcopal scrutiny and he was suspended by the Bishop of Ely. He returned to Somerset and along with his former vicar began preaching in barns, 'drawing huge crowds.' In 1843 he declared himself to be the personification of the Holy Ghost but on another occasion he claimed to be the prophet Elijah. He and Starky also called themselves the Two Anointed Ones, in reference to the two witnesses of Revelation Chapter XI.[219] Letters to Prince were addressed to 'The Holy Lord God of Spaxton.' At various times he seems to have regarded himself as more of a John the Baptist figure sent to prepare for the Second Coming of Christ, at others as the incarnation of the Holy Ghost taking flesh.

---

[219] 'And I will give power unto my two witnesses, and they shall prophesy a thousand two hundred and threescore days, clothed in sackcloth.' (Revelation, XI. 3)

They also instructed their devotees to sell their property and give them the proceeds on the basis that community of goods was binding upon believers. This enabled them to purchase land in the village of Spaxton near Charlynch where they set up the Agapemone, Greek for the Abode of Love. 'Wealthy believers were encouraged to deposit their money in the Bank of England under the name of "Brother" Prince and to join the community.' Prince's former austerity seems to have rather deserted him at this point, for the Agapemone was noted during its early existence for the 'dissolute and ostentatious life of great luxury' enjoyed by Prince and his followers. There was apparently some doctrinal basis for this behaviour, since he taught that neither he nor his followers would die nor even suffer sickness and grief. 'Luxury and enjoyment had become theirs by right.' Prince was apparently much given to riding around in a carriage that had once belonged to the late Queen Adelaide driven by four cream horses and accompanied by bloodhounds.

This all came out when a former female member of the sect, called Nottidge, sued Prince for the return of her property. The case was heard in the Court of Chancery in 1860 and amid the resulting publicity 'the movement was generally discredited.' 'In the handsome chapel which had witnessed the Great Mystery,' we are told, 'the most prominent object now was a billiard table.'

Prince seems to have been somewhat chastened by the scandal and subsequently lived a quiet life at Spaxton. In the 1880s he set out his beliefs in two books, proclaiming the withdrawal of the Holy Ghost from the church and the world into himself and the Agapemone. This process was referred to as 'the doom of Christendom.'

Absurd as they may appear, these writings were effective in reviving interest in the sect – hence perhaps the conversion of Joseph Morris. Several members of the Salvation Army are also reported to have joined it in the 1890s. In 1892 the movement decided it needed a church in London and the following year Morris was commissioned to design the Church of the Ark of the Covenant – built at a cost of £16,000, largely sourced from the contributions of the faithful. By this time Frank Morris, having been articled to his father's firm since 1887, was a partner and is understood to have assisted Joseph in the design. Godwin Arnold and Sidney Gold described it thus in their monograph on Morris and family:

> The church is sited near the edge of high ground, its spire conspicuous from the Lea Valley below. Its gothic style is far more vigorous than was the accepted taste in the 1890s. By then High Victorian muscular gothic was well out of fashion and a more delicate neo-Perpendicular style was customary. The church is designed as a simple wide hall with a single-span high-pitched roof, a shallow semi-octagonal chancel and a western tower and spire.... The artwork both inside and outside the church is of fine quality. Around the base of the tower...are the four winged creatures of the Book of Revelation, carved in white stone. Crowning the tops of the buttresses in the place of pinnacles are the same four creatures - the lion, the ox, the eagle and the man - commonly interpreted as the symbols of the four Evangelists....Two wind vanes on pinnacles at the outer ends of the aisles are in the form of the fiery chariot of Elijah and the flying scroll of Enoch - the

two witnesses, since they were translated to Heaven without death, for the expected return of Christ.

It perhaps goes without saying that the decoration is very much dictated by the particular apocalyptic convictions of the Agapemonites.

The preacher at the opening ceremony in 1896 was another former evangelical, the Rev John Hugh Smyth-Pigott (1852-1927) who had been Curate of St Jude's, Mildmay Park[220] before joining the Salvation Army. It may seem puzzling that so many of the leaders of the Agapemonites from Prince and Starky onwards had started out as ardent evangelicals. As we have already noted, there was a keen interest among those of the evangelical party[221] in the study of eschatology in the mid-19th century; evidently at times this took some of them in a heterodox direction. Smyth-Pigott had earlier in the 1880s been an adherent of the unhealthy perfectionist tendency which had characterised the Keswick movement during its early years.[222]

---

[220] It is interesting to note that the Vicar of St Jude's around this time, the Revd Daniel Bell Hankin, later retired to Reading and served as a trustee of St Mary's, Castle Street from 1905 till his death in 1914. He lived at Mildmay Cottage, Christchurch Road. Smyth-Pigott was curate at St Jude's in 1883-4.

[221] By way of analogy, Edward Irving had been an evangelical minister in the Church of Scotland.

[222] See Sir Marcus Loane's short life of Handley Moule, pp 74, 78. Archbishop Loane's references are largely derived from J. C. Pollock, *The Keswick Story*, 1964. Moule was one of those who helped to set Keswick on a more even keel, along with Hubert Brooke of St Mary's, Castle Street.

Smyth-Pigott emerged as the natural successor to Prince as leader of the Agapemonites on the latter's death in 1899 and three years later he proclaimed himself to be Jesus Christ and the new Messiah. On Sunday 9th September 1902 he ascended the altar steps at the Church of the Ark and proclaimed the news:

> And I who speak to you tonight – I am that Lord Jesus Christ who died and rose again and ascended into heaven. I am that Lord Jesus, come again in my own body to save those who come to me from death and hell. Yes, I am He that liveth, and behold I am alive for evermore.

The official announcement stated: 'Jesus Christ has come again and is upon the earth!'

This news was also proclaimed in Reading at Morris's home at Ampthill, 3 Craven Road, where he and the forty Reading members of the Agapemonites held their meetings. The press became excited and Morris was asked his opinion on the matter by a *Reading Chronicle* reporter. The steadfastness of Morris' faith in Agapemonism is clear from his reply: 'That is not an opinion. I testify that is a fact!' At this time apparently the activities of the sect in Reading caused some controversy as it was alleged that they tried to separate husbands from their wives who were forbidden to wear their wedding rings. 'The blighting influence has been felt in more than one Reading home,' stated the *Chronicle*. 'Apparently the young men may not marry.'

Smyth-Pigott proved to be just as non-immortal as Henry Prince and after his death in 1927 the movement gradually died out. The Church of the Ark of the Covenant was acquired by the adherents of another peculiar sect called the Ancient Catholic Church who renamed it the Church of the Good Shepherd; in more recent years it has passed to the Georgian Orthodox Church and is now known as the Cathedral of the Holy Nativity.

By the time of the famous pronouncement from Craven Road, Joseph's daughter, Violet, born in 1878, was also practising as an architect, though she does not seem to have been formally connected with the family firm. This came to an end in December 1905, the month after Joseph resigned his position as County Surveyor on the grounds of ill-health. Frank Morris remained in Berkshire and also practised in London until his untimely death in 1908, while the remainder of the family moved to Spaxton to be close to Joseph's beloved Agapemone. It was here that Joseph Morris died in 1913 and we may conclude this chapter by quoting his obituary from the local rag, the *Bridgwater Mercury*:

> The death took place last week after a brief illness at his beautiful residence at Four Forks, Spaxton, of Mr Joseph Morris, a well-known and highly respected resident of this parish. The deceased gentleman, who was aged 76, had resided in a house adjacent to the Agapemone of which he was a prominent member for some years.
>
> Mr Morris was a man of great culture and kindly personality, and his demise is keenly regretted by a wide circle of friends...
>
> The funeral took place on Sunday morning in the deceased gentleman's garden, and according to the rites of the sect of which he was a faithful adherent.

Emily Morris predeceased Joseph by four years and Violet Morris continued to live in Spaxton until her death in 1958.

Note. This chapter is partly derived from a talk on Morris as Architect originally delivered by the author to the History of Reading Society in 1996 and later repeated with variations to other local societies including the Caversham Heights Society and the Berkshire Family History Society.

20 Bishops for Reading

For most of its history Reading has had a Bishop – even if he wasn't usually called the Bishop of Reading. But just what is a Bishop? To my reformed mind, he (or indeed she) is best seen as a priest or presbyter (elder) who is consecrated (i.e. set apart) to be a guardian of the faith and the faithful. Bishops are essentially shepherds, hence the crook, and to be a shepherd of the flock and a pastor to pastors is surely a good thing. A lot of the trouble with bishops came with the onset of prelacy from a Latin word[223] meaning to be set above somebody, thus introducing the concept of the Bishop as lord and master rather than servant. This view prevailed before the Reformation and has certainly not been eradicated from the church in the intervening years, as can be seen by the almost universal practice of wearing a mitre, even among supposedly evangelical bishops. Writing this, I realise that my Anglo-Catholic friends have a different view and do indeed tend to revere their bishop as one set over them in that mediaeval sense of the word.[224]

---

[223] Strictly speaking the immediate source is the Old French word *prelat*, but this is itself derived from the Latin *praelatus*, from the past participle of the verb *praeferre* (to prefer).

[224] Nevertheless, it was reassuring to read the following remarks by a prominent Anglo-Catholic clergyman, Barry Orford, made in *New Directions* during 2021: 'Whatever means we employ for making episcopal appointments, they must have at their heart the conviction that a bishop is to be above all someone whose priorities are prayer, sacramental worship, the pastoral care of their clergy, learning, and absolute dedication to helping parishes flourish under hard-working priests. It is not enough

It was in 1889 that Reading first acquired a bishop of its own but that did not, of course, mean that there was thitherto no Bishop *for* Reading. As we saw in Chapter 1, Christianity came to this part of the world the second time around through St Birinus who established his see at Dorchester-on-Thames in the mid-seventh century AD. This arrangement did not last long, partly because there were tensions between the bishops and the Kings of Wessex and also because Dorchester itself became part of Mercian territory in 672. After an uncertain period the diocese was finally established at Winchester (then the royal capital) in 705, although Bishop Hedde had largely ruled his see from the city before that date. On his death, Bishop Daniel (705-44) took over with responsibility for an area comprising Hampshire, Berkshire and Surrey with the eastern parts of Wiltshire.

Berkshire remained part of the Winchester diocese until 931 and thus bishops responsible for Reading (such as it then was) during that period included the meteorologically renowned St Swithun (852-62), his successor, Ealfrith, who was promoted to Canterbury in 872, and Denewulf (879-909), described as a protégé and councillor of that great Berkshireman,[225] King Alfred the Great. Some rather dubious mediaeval traditions suggest that Denewulf was originally by profession a swineherd and that it was his wife's cakes that the somnolent Alfred famously burnt!

---

for such ideals to be recited at episcopal consecrations, only for new bishops immediately to become functionaries of the present Church Managerial.' Hear, hear!

[225] Alfred was born in Wantage, then and until 1974 part of Berkshire.

In 931 Alfred's grandson, King Athelstan, and his archbishop, Plegmund, decided that the Winchester diocese was unwieldy and divided it into two, Berkshire forming part of the new see of Ramsbury in Wiltshire. None of the bishops of Ramsbury are particularly well-known but they included three who went on to Canterbury: Oda in 942, Sigeric in 990 and Aelfric in 995.

In 1058, further change brought about the union of Sherborne and Ramsbury, with the result that Dorset now formed part of Bishop Herman's territory. In 1075 the two dioceses were formally united and at the same time the Bishop's seat was moved to Old Sarum and from thence in 1219 to New Sarum, better known as Salisbury. In 1974 Ramsbury was revived as the seat of one of the suffragan bishops in the Salisbury diocese.

Although there were various boundary changes during the next six centuries, Reading remained part of the Salisbury diocese until 1836. There were many notable bishops during this period including:

St Osmund (1078-99);
Hubert Walter (1189-93), later Primate;
Robert Hallum (1407-17), a Cardinal but one who was sympathetic to modest reform;
John Jewel (1560-71),[226] best remembered as an apologist for the reformed Church of England;
John Davenant (1621-42), a theologian who had been one of the English church's representatives at the Synod of Dort in 1619;

---

[226] Shortly after taking office, Jewel undertook an episcopal visitation of Reading and preached a sermon at St Laurence's church.

Gilbert Burnet (1689-1715), the noted church historian; and

John Hume (1766-82) who was strongly opposed to the evangelical movement.

Gilbert Burnet is of particular interest since, like the town of Reading, he played a key part in the revolution of 1688. He was unusually perhaps a Scotsman, born in Edinburgh in 1643, the son of Robert Burnet, a moderate Episcopalian and a mother described as 'a violent Presbyterian' – perhaps after the example of Jenny Geddes, who famously threw a stool at the minister who had the temerity to use Laud's Prayer Book in St Giles' Kirk in 1637! Her brother was a leader of the Covenanters, who opposed the reimposition of episcopacy on the Scottish church under the Stuarts.

Gilbert seems to have taken more after his father, for following studies at Aberdeen, where he took his MA at the age of 13, and a period of travel during which he learnt Hebrew from a Jewish Rabbi, he was ordained in 1665 by the Bishop of Edinburgh. He spent five years in parochial ministry near Edinburgh and then three as Professor of Divinity at Glasgow before moving across the border in 1673, becoming first Chaplain to King Charles II and later lecturer at St Clement Danes in London. During this period he began his *History of The Reformation*, which engaged him from 1679 onwards and was not finally completed till the year of his death. He had a somewhat tempestuous relationship with Charles II, on one occasion writing him a letter advising him that a change in his heart and course of life was needed.

On the accession of James II he travelled on the Continent and during this period became intimate with the

Prince of Orange. He landed with the Prince at Torbay in 1688 at the start of the 'Glorious Revolution' that led to James's abdication. It was not perhaps surprising, therefore, that when the Prince became King William III Burnet was swiftly preferred to the vacant see of Salisbury in March 1689. He took part in the abortive Commission to produce a revised prayer book which became known as the 'Liturgy of Comprehension' designed to lure nonconformists back into the established church. Like many products of Royal Commissions over the centuries it was kicked into the long grass.

As a bishop Burnet was extremely diligent, spending eight months of the year in Salisbury and the remaining months in the archdeaconry of Berkshire, based in Windsor. He held confirmations at 275 churches in the diocese over a twenty-year period. He also found time to work on his *History of his Own Times,* the work for which he is most remembered, published posthumously in 1723 and 1733. In private life he made up for his predecessor, Seth Ward's celibacy by marrying three wives, outliving them all, the second marriage producing seven children. He offended Queen Anne by rushing from William III's deathbed to inform her of her succession. Although she implemented his scheme for the remuneration of clergy which became known as 'Queen Anne's Bounty' she regarded him as a buffoon and in 1713 derided his warnings of the possibility of a Jacobite invasion. Gilbert Burnet died in March 1715, a few months before the fulfilment of his prophecy under Anne's successor, George I.

His successor at Salisbury was William Talbot who was translated from Oxford in 1715 and went on to Durham in 1721. He was born in 1658, the son of William Talbot of Lichfield, who was a distant relative of the Talbots, earls of Shrewsbury. He was a graduate of Oriel college, Oxford and was preferred in 1682 to the rectory of Burghfield, near Reading, where the Shrewsbury Talbots happened to be patrons. The deanery of Worcester followed in 1691 and then in 1699 he became Bishop of Oxford. His son, Edward Talbot, became Archdeacon of Berkshire in 1717.

William Talbot was also a relative, as well as namesake, of William Talbot, Rector of St Giles-in-Reading from 1767-74 and, as we have seen, the first parish clergyman in Reading to espouse the doctrines of grace taught in the Evangelical Revival - and a noted private detective. Bishop Talbot, however, was a man of a different theological character, being characterised as a Latitudinarian (i.e. Broad Church). His sermons are said to have been influenced by the theology of Samuel Clarke, whose hold on Trinitarian doctrines was somewhat tenuous at times.

Born in 1703, or according to other sources 1706, John Hume was the son of a clergyman in Devon. He studied at Merton and Corpus Christi Colleges, Oxford. He was successively a Canon of Westminster Abbey and St Paul's Cathedral in the 1740s, holding the latter position with the Rectory of Barnes. In 1756 he was raised to the episcopal bench as Bishop of Bristol but after two years moved to Oxford, where his duties enabled him also to serve as Dean of St Paul's. Finally from 1766 until his death in 1782 he was Bishop of Salisbury and Chancellor of the Order of the Garter (ex officio). He is described as an ardent anti-Methodist and this position was revealed especially in 1768 by his part in the notorious expulsion of six students from St Edmund ('Teddy') Hall, Oxford, on account of their evangelical principles. Although any jurisdiction he might have had as Bishop of Oxford had by then ceased, in those days the borders of Berkshire came almost up to the city and one of the students had taken part in what he regarded as unacceptable evangelistic activity across the border, giving Hume his pretext to interfere in the controversy. It has been said that the Bishop held it 'a crime to attract a great auditory and be blessed in the conversion of many.'

The last Bishop of Salisbury responsible for Reading was Thomas Burgess (1825-37), a man much more sympathetic to the gospel than Hume, and the one who granted St Mary's, Castle Street a licence for Anglican worship in September 1836.

This must have been almost his last act in connection with Reading for by an Order in Council of 10th October 1836 the county of Berkshire was transferred to the Diocese of Oxford. That diocese had been formed by Henry VIII, carved out of the vast Lincoln diocese in 1542. For the first three centuries of its existence it was one of the smallest, comprising the city and county of Oxford. But then in 1836-7 it became geographically one of the largest with the further addition by an Order of July 1837 of the county of Buckingham, also formerly part of Lincoln. In the last 175 years it has also become one of the more populous, following the demographic changes that have occurred in the south-east of the country,. with a current population count of around 2.4 million, compared with 351,000 in 1801. It is currently exceeded only by London (4.4 m), Chelmsford (3.25 m), Southwark (2.9 m), and Leeds (2.8 m).

The first Oxford bishop with responsibility for Reading was Richard Bagot (1829-45) who was, it seems, very reluctant to accept the aggrandisement of his diocese, perhaps feeling that he had quite enough on his plate dealing with the controversies resulting from the Oxford

Movement. It was on his translation to what the editors of his successor's diocese books characterise as the 'quieter waters' of Bath and Wells in 1845 that Samuel Wilberforce, son of William, came on the scene, stamping his personality on the diocese over the next 24 years. We have seen something of his character and influence in previous chapters. We are fortunate in possessing his notebooks, published jointly by the Berkshire and Oxfordshire Record Societies. A few choice extracts follow, illustrating both his care and compassion towards his clergy but also his sometimes authoritarian attitude towards those who stepped out of line:

> **St Mary**. [c. 1846] S W Yates,[227] able man of business... a very excellent man, most courteous – very well off much in earnest: very good preacher.
> Confirm in this Church March 12 57. Yates I fear poor as a parish priest etc.
> 1860. Poor Yates Paralytic seizure... He intends next year to resign... He is to have a third curate besides Calverley & William Romanis.[228]
> A P Cust.[229] Appointed by me, 1862.
> I preach for Diocesan poor boys, Nov 2 62. Great congregation & good coll[ection].
> Nov 1 63. Lay first stone of **All Saints** Church.

---

[227] Vicar of St Mary's, 1835-61.

[228] William Romanis – also a minor hymn-writer – see my booklet, *Some Hymnwriters etc.*

[229] Arthur Perceval Purey Cust was Vicar of St Mary's from 1862 to 1875 and later served as Archdeacon of Buckingham and Dean of York. His grand-daughter, Margaret (or Peggy) was the object of the very young John Betjeman's affections.

St Lawrence. [c. 1846] John Ball.[230] Moderate… Great ability & Frankness. Love of [Joke? People] like him very much.

Rev J Ball. Who very fussy kind & pleased at my confirming here as well as at St Mary's March 12 57.

March 23/63 confirmed here, a really nice confirmation & J Ball very cordial.

St Giles. [c. 1846] Cecil Grainger,[231] also very bad health for 2 or three years, rather less sense than preceding but pleasing & well-behaved.

Cecil Grainger. March 57, very ill with stone & nervous depression. Dies soon after - & after thought & prayer I offer it to T. V Fosbery,[232] who accepts & which may God bless. Nov 17/57 I visit him there. Meet clergy. Great SPG[233] meeting in the Town Hall. Next morning early go round the parish.

St Mary's Castle Street. Goodhart. Curate C D Bell[234] to be licensed Jan 1846.

1856. <u>Rev G. I. Tubbs, Incumbent, St. Mary's Chapel.</u> [Noted along with Grainger and Francis Trench (see below) – also underlined – as a pall-bearer at the funeral of Spedding Curwen of the Congregational

---

[230] Vicar of St Laurence's, 1834-65.

[231] Vicar of St Giles, 1835-57. 'Than preceding' presumably refers to John Ball in the previous entry.

[232] Vicar of St Giles, 1857-70.

[233] Society for the Propagation of the Gospel, the oldest Anglican mission society, by this time mainly supported by the high church party, later combined with a smaller African mission to form the United Society for the Propagation of the Gospel (USPG), subsequently renamed United Society Partners in the Gospel – thus retaining the time-honoured acronym.

[234] Charles Dent Bell, also a minor hymn-writer.

Chapel, Castle Street. Wilberforce evidently regarded this as tantamount to fraternising with the enemy.]

George Ibberson Tubbs, longest-serving minister of St Mary's, Castle Street 1852-88 and one who crossed swords with Bishop Wilberforce

G. I. Tubbs. A good deal done that was nice in the look of his candidates March 5 1860. He celebrates evening communion after I write to him my objections. Declines Mission 60.
Drops evening celebration with a snarl.

Caversham. Rev Josh. Bennett.[235] A very conscientious man & wishing to do his duty, but cold & dry & very little spiritual work in the place.

In 1860 the Bishop conducted a mission in the three historic Reading parishes. He sought the support of all the clergy of the town but it is recorded that not only Tubbs but also William Phelps of Trinity Chapel and the clergy of St John's[236] declined to take part. In the case of the latter the bishop surmised that this was to their 'regret but they fear their party.' Here Wilberforce almost seems to be extending his dim view of dissenters to the evangelical party within the Establishment!

Notable bishops since Wilberforce have included:

- William Stubbs (1889-1901), a leading constitutional historian, author of the *Constitutional History of England*;
- Charles Gore (1911-19), founder of the Community of the Resurrection[237] and also of the Liberal school of Anglo-Catholicism, which has often seemed to dominate the hierarchy of the

---

[235] Perpetual Curate (later Vicar) of Caversham 1843-82.

[236] William Payne, Vicar of St John's (1857-92), and Frederick Blenkin, Curate (1857-62), plus the former Incumbent, Francis Trench. Like Tubbs, Blenkin fell foul of Wilberforce over the matter of holding communion services other than in the morning but was 'well behaved' about it.

[237] Established at Oxford before moving with Gore to Radley, Berkshire, this monastic institution later settled at Mirfield in Yorkshire where it remains to this day. It also acts as a theological training college for Anglican clergy.

Church of England in recent decades (Ramsey, Runcie, Rowan et al); and

- Kenneth Kirk (1937-54), representing the more advanced strain of Anglo-Catholicism.

The most recent bishops, John Pritchard (2007-14) and Steven Croft (from 2016), might be characterised as 'Open Evangelicals', following on from the Liberal, Richard Harries (1987-2006), subsequently a Labour 'working peer' as Lord Harries of Pentregarth. However, in his recent controversial statements on same-sex marriage, Bishop Croft's views do not seem to differ all that much from those of the Lord Harries.

Suffragan bishops, assisting the diocesan bishop, were first permitted to be appointed in 1534 but only for towns that were specified in an Act of that year. In 1888 the passing of the Suffragans Nomination Act permitted the extension of the practice to other towns, as required, and the Rt. Rev Dr James Leslie Randall (1829-1922), first Bishop of Reading from 1889 to 1908, was thus one of the first to be appointed under this new legislation. In recent years suffragan bishops have generally been restyled 'area bishops' – perhaps in consequence of the church's espousal of 'management-speak' under recent Primates: diocesan bishops may be compared to regional managers and suffragans to area managers.

Randall was the son of the equally long-lived James Randall, Archdeacon of Berkshire from 1855-69, while his brother, Richard, was also preferred as Dean of Chichester. He was educated at Winchester and New College, Oxford. Ordained in 1853, he served as Rector of Newbury from 1857 to 1878. From 1880 to 1902 he was successively Archdeacon of Buckingham and Oxford, holding these posts concurrently with his bishopric.

After Randall's retirement, he was not replaced but suffragans were appointed to Buckingham from 1914 and to Dorchester from 1939. It was Kenneth Escott Kirk who decided that the diocese would be best served by a system of three suffragans, each representing the three archdeaconries covering the historic counties. That for Oxford was easily filled by reviving the old see of Dorchester and appointing to it the Archdeacon of Oxford, who was already in Episcopal orders as formerly Suffragan Bishop of Sherborne. In November 1941, at Kirk's behest the Diocesan Conference passed a resolution welcoming the immediate revival of the see of Reading and providing the necessary funds. Finally in February 1942 (at 'Candlemas') the Vicar of St Mary's, Reading, Canon Arthur Groom Parham (1883-1961), was consecrated Suffragan Bishop of Reading by Archbishop Lang[238] in St Paul's Cathedral. The following month he was also appointed Archdeacon of Berkshire on the retirement of Richard Wickham Legg.

Bishop Parham was born in 1883 and educated in Oxford at Magdalen College School and Exeter College. He then trained for the ministry at Leeds Clergy School, an institution closely allied with Leeds Parish Church, leading to ordination in Rochester Cathedral as deacon (1909) and priest (1910). He served his title in Bromley, Kent and then in 1912 moved back to Oxford where he was for nine years Chaplain and Precentor at Christ

---

[238] This was almost but not quite Cosmo Gordon Lang's last significant act as Archbishop. He retired on the 31st of March 1942, three days after confirming the future Queen Elizabeth.

Church, and also Chaplain of his old school. This service was, however, interrupted by a period as a temporary chaplain to the Forces, being mentioned in despatches and awarded the Military Cross.

In 1922 he returned to parochial ministry as Rector of Easthampstead, moving in 1926 to become Vicar of St Mary's, Reading. Initially he held all three appointments as Bishop, Archdeacon and Vicar in tandem but in 1946 he resigned as Vicar. He continued with his episcopal and archdecanal duties until 1954 when he retired through ill-health, moving to Long Wittenham, where he died in 1961.

His successor, Eric Knell (1903-87) was also expected to 'multi-task', holding the bishopric concurrently with the archdeaconry and the benefice of Christ Church, Reading. He was another Oxford graduate (Trinity) and his postings prior to his consecration included the charge of his old college's mission in Stratford, East London. In the 1960s he played a key part in the formation of the Reading Civic Society. After 18 years as Bishop of Reading, Knell retired, making way for the formidable Eric Wild (1914-90).

Born three months after the outbreak of hostilities, Wild was educated at Manchester Grammar School and Keble College, Oxford. Apparently about the time of his retirement he astounded the Oxford Diocesan Synod by referring to his having been a card-carrying member of the Communist Party as a young man! He was ordained in 1938, serving his first curacy in Liverpool and then after war service in the RNVR he was appointed to successive incumbencies in Wigan and nearby Hindley. He came south as Director of Religious Education for the Diocese of Peterborough, then to London as Secretary to the Board of Education. In 1968 when the decision was taken to split the posts of archdeacon and suffragan he was appointed

Archdeacon of Berkshire, succeeding Eric Knell, whom he also followed as Bishop four years later. Unlike the two previous bishops who were more 'middle of the road,' Eric Wild was a decided Anglo-Catholic.

Wild served as Bishop for ten years and is remembered for his sometimes controversial empathy with the Anglo-Catholic wing of the church, as exemplified by an ordination service at Holy Trinity, Reading, in 1975 when all the newly ordained priests were obliged to 'concelebrate' the Sacrament with him, irrespective of their churchmanship.[239] He also made the front page of the *Sun* newspaper after administering the Sacrament at a pop festival with the words 'Phew, now I could do with a beer!' reported as issuing from his lips.

Following his retirement Eric Wild continued as an Assistant Bishop in the Oxford Diocese where his ministry was especially appreciated by those churches that shared his Anglo-Catholicism. It must have been after one such visit to St Giles that I was introduced to him as Church Warden of St Mary's, Castle Street, which brought forth the comment in Eric's characteristically deep voice: 'To be the Church Warden of St Mary's, Castle Street, is not *necessarily* the unforgivable sin.'[240]

---

[239] The author attended this service as a supporter of the Rev Trevor Williams, then curate of St Mary's Maidenhead, and himself later a bishop – of Limerick and Killaloe in the Church of Ireland. The service took place during the incumbency at Holy Trinity of Brian Brindley, who was also much in evidence.
[240] The reader should not, however, take this to mean that Eric Wild had no time for Evangelicals. He played his part in the preservation of St Mary's, Castle Street in the 1970s and in a Good Friday sermon at St Giles, according to my diary, he

With his successor, Graham Foley, we were firmly back in the centre of the highway. The only things he seemed to have in common with his predecessor were his origins in the North-west of England and the fact that he had also served as a Diocesan Director of Education. Ronald Graham Gregory Foley was born in Cheadle Hume, Cheshire in 1923 and educated at Wakefield Grammar school, King Edward VI's School, Aston and King's College, London. After ordination in 1951 he served a curacy in Blackpool and was then Vicar of St Luke's, Blackburn, until 1960 when he moved to Durham as Director of Education. He then returned to parochial ministry as Vicar of Leeds Parish Church (Leeds Minster) from 1971 until 1982 when he was elevated to the episcopate to succeed Eric Wild.

As Bishop he tried to steer a middle course but upset the Anglo-Catholics who had prospered under Wild's episcopate without earning too many 'brownie points' from the Evangelicals. Early on in his episcopate he introduced an open-air deanery eucharist in Reading. Leeds Minster was known for its strong musical tradition and the new Bishop rather hoped that St Mary's, Reading (i.e. the church in the Butts) would follow suit. To what extent this occurred I am unable to judge; it has certainly adopted the name, Reading Minster. Two years into his episcopate, Bishop Foley mutated from a Suffragan to an Area Bishop. After retirement in 1989, he served as an assistant bishop in the York diocese until 2007. He died in 2017, aged 94.

---

referred to 'those splendid early Evangelicals' who 'used to say, No Cross, No Crown.'

His successor, John Bone, held office from 1989 to 1996. John Frank Ewan Bone was born in 1930 and educated at Monkton Combe School, St Peter's College, Oxford, and Ely Theological College. After ordination in 1956, he served curacies at St Gabriel's, Pimlico, and Henley, followed by incumbencies in Datchet and Slough. He was also Rural Dean of Burnham, Bucks. In 1978 he obtained preferment as Archdeacon of Buckingham and then after 11 years in this post he was consecrated to become the next Bishop of Reading. Like his predecessor he served seven years as Area Bishop and then like Eric Wild continued in retirement as an Assistant Bishop in the diocese.

One episcopal trait that John Bone shared with many of his peers was a love of railways and as part of his retirement present he was treated to a trip to Paddington in the driver's cab of a train, driven by a near-neighbour of mine – needless to say emerging at the terminus, highly delighted. He was also a great admirer of Bishop Samuel Wilberforce and in 2005 led a service in St Mary's Minster Church to celebrate the bicentenary of the bishop's birth, which I attended. He died in 2014.

Hitherto the area episcopate of Reading had been a 'dead end' for clergy before retirement but the next two bishops both went on to higher things. First off was Dominic Walker, whose original Christian names were reportedly Edward William Murray, born in 1948. Previously Rural Dean of Brighton, he was appointed bishop in 1997 and served six years before succeeding Rowan Williams as Bishop of Monmouth, when the latter became Primate of All England. He retired in 2013, later assisting with episcopal duties in the Llandaff diocese. He is a notable supporter of animal welfare and also performs as an exorcist with a strong interest in the paranormal.

Bishop Dominic's preferment to Monmouth led to a bitter controversy over the appointment of the next Bishop of Reading. The diocesan bishop, Richard Harries, whose liberal position on same-sex relationships has already been noted, appointed the openly gay Welsh cleric, Jeffrey John. Although it was claimed by his supporters – and indeed his partner – that the relationship was celibate, in accordance with the principles set out by the Lambeth bishops in 1998,[241] John was clearly an advocate of homosexual rights, and ultimately of same-sex marriage. The proposed appointment, therefore, sparked an outcry within the episcopal area of Reading, leading to the formation of an organisation called Anglican Mainstream, in which Dr Philip Giddings, a lay reader at Greyfriars, played a prominent part. As a result and at the request of Archbishop Williams, John withdrew his acceptance of the area see. He was later preferred to the deanship of St Alban's but the episcopal mitre continued to elude him, despite a number of further attempts by his supporters.

Dominic Walker's eventual successor, Stephen Cottrell (born 1958), was destined for even greater preferment. Coming to Reading from a residential canonry at Peterborough Cathedral, he served from 2004 to 2010, when he became Bishop of Chelmsford for ten years and then from 2020 Archbishop of York. At Reading, he is said

---

[241] In particular Resolution 1.10 (b) which states that 'in view of the teaching of Scripture, [this conference] upholds faithfulness in marriage between a man and a woman in lifelong union, and believes that abstinence is right for those who are not called to marriage.'

to have displayed considerable ability in 'trouble-shooting' difficult pastoral situations and also distinguished himself as a temporary chaplain to one of the race-meetings at Ascot!

The next bishop, Andrew Proud (born 1954), was the first to be already in episcopal orders at the time of his appointment in 2011, having been consecrated in Addis Ababa, Ethiopia, in 2007 as Area Bishop for the Horn of Africa in the Jerusalem diocese. On Bishop Andrew's retirement in 2019, the see of Reading was for the first time graced by a lady bishop, Olivia Graham (born 1956), formerly Archdeacon of Berkshire (2013-19). Following her retirement in 2024, it was announced that another woman priest, Canon Mary Gregory (born 1970), a former prison governor, would take her place. Bishop Mary was consecrated by the Archbishop of York and former Bishop of Reading, Stephen Cottrell, early the following year.

Appendix I provides a full list of the Bishops during the ages having responsibility for Reading, including those from the Roman Catholic hierarchy. I have taken the timeline back to 634, although it must be acknowledged that in the early centuries Reading was never much more and perhaps rather less than 'a geographical expression.'[242]

We should also in conclusion briefly acknowledge the role of archdeacons. In earlier times, as we have seen, these often doubled with the suffragans but now the two offices are firmly distinct. Olivia Graham's long-serving predecessor, Norman Russell (1998-2013), was much liked, while a number of others attained episcopal status,

---

[242] As Count Metternich said of Italy in a somewhat different context.

notably John Brown (1978-86), later Bishop of Cyprus and the Gulf, and Mike Hill (1992-97), successively bishop of Buckingham (1998-2003) and Bristol (2003-17). In between came David Griffiths (1987-92), who devoted his retirement to a comprehensive study of the bibliography of the *Book of Common Prayer*, published in 2002.[243] The present Archdeacon is Stephen Pullin, previously Vicar of St Mary's, Reading.

If we go back in time, perhaps the most distinguished Archdeacon of Berkshire was John Morton, famous for Morton's fork, a theory of taxation rather than a species of cutlery. The future Cardinal Archbishop of Canterbury (1486-1500) was Archdeacon for the county in 1476; he seems, though, to have been something of a 'serial archdeacon' since he also at various times served as such for Chester, Huntingdon, Norfolk, Leicester and Winchester!

---

[243] As his tenure of office coincided with much of my own as a churchwarden I saw quite a lot of him at the annual swearing-in ceremonies, as well as attending the launch of his magnum opus at Lambeth Palace.

21 Building for an Expanding Town – the Case of St Luke's

We made a brief reference in Chapter 17 to the rash of church-building that began in the 1850s and 1860s partly in response to the Religious Census and the energetic activity of Bishop Wilberforce, while Chapter 16 covered the restoration of Greyfriars. We will revert to the subject of church-building in greater detail in the current chapter. At the time of the first census in 1801 the population of Reading was 10,791 and by 1901 it had risen to 72,946 – an increase of 576%. In the next hundred years it did not quite double to 143,124. Although the two proprietary chapels came into being during the early part of this period, the only other new Anglican church founded before 1851 was the original St John's Church, which was built in 1837. Francis Chenevix Trench (1805-86) had been curate of St Giles from 1834 under John Cecil Grainger and arranged with him the formation of a Conventional District serving the area of new development centred on Watlington Street. Trench was wealthy enough to fund the building, costing £3,500,[244] and served as Perpetual Curate until 1857 when he became Rector of Islip in Oxfordshire. During his time at St John's he published *Sermons preached at Reading* in 1843. He remained the patron of the church and thereby ensured

---

[244] Photographs show that this was built in the typical 'Gothick' style that characterised the 'Commissioners' Churches' erected following the 1818 Church Building Act in the two decades before the influence of Pugin's more authentic Gothic style became all-pervasive. Despite the Gothic trimmings, its interior resembled an 18th century preaching-box with a central three-decker pulpit, as in St Mary's, Castle Street.

that the evangelical tradition that he had established continued when plans for a new and larger church were formed in 1869. Trench was described by W S Darter as 'an excellent gentleman and deservedly beloved in Reading.'[245] Darter also considered that Trench had a poor manner of reading the scriptures with no apparent control over his voice. His younger brother, Richard, was Archbishop of Dublin at the time of the disestablishment of the Anglican church in Ireland.

The architect, William Allen Dixon[246] (1821-93), designed a church in the French Gothic style of the 13th century, which was consecrated by the new Bishop of Oxford, John Fielder Mackarness, on 6th November 1873, although the tower and spire were not completed until the following year. I confess to having regarded it until recently as a rather hideous edifice but its restoration by the present occupants, the Polish Roman Catholic community, has transformed it into a stunningly attractive building. The first Vicar of the new parish, also formed in 1874, was the Rev Canon William Payne, who also assumed responsibility for the church of St Stephen, which

---

[245] Unattributed quotation in John McKechnie's history of the church. Thanks to Malcolm Summers for spotting the source.

[246] Dixon was largely known as a designer of nonconformist chapels e.g. Potters Bar Baptist and St John's seems to be his only commission from the Church of England. The former Congregational Church at Southend bears some resemblance to St John's. With most of the prominent contemporary architects active in the Gothic Revival largely adhering to Tractarian principles (including Woodyer and St Aubyn – see below) he perhaps commended himself by his protestant dissenting connections. The choice of Woodman (see Chapter 16) for Greyfriars' restoration may be compared.

had been built 1864-6 as a chapel-of-ease to St Giles to serve the growing community of Newtown. St Stephen's was an example of the work of the important Gothic Revival architect, William White, and its wanton destruction as part of the rebuilding of Newtown in the 1970s is a matter of some regret.

Also carved out of St Giles was the new parish of Christ Church, Whitley. The church was consecrated on 7th August 1862 with the Rev W F Addison as the first Vicar. The building was designed by the distinguished Gothic Revival architect, Henry Woodyer, and it is arguably Reading's finest Victorian church, especially noted for its lofty chancel arch filled with reticulated tracery (rather like a window). The original building was enlarged in 1874. In 1868 a National School was built nearby and remains to the present day, associated with the church. Currently Christ Church represents what is sometimes called the Liberal Catholic tradition within the Church of England and appears to appeal to those members of the University staff who choose to worship.[247]

The early 1860s also saw the revival of Greyfriars which could be said to serve the 'west end' of Reading; the same was also true of All Saints, Downshire Square, built in 1865-74, initially as yet another chapel of ease to St Mary the Virgin, to serve a 'newly built district of large stuccoed

---

[247] During the 1990s the author found himself somewhat unexpectedly a governor of the school, now known as New Christ Church Primary School, associated with Christ Church. His fellow-governors included a former Professor of Botany at the University, Jeffrey Harborne, who worshipped at the church, as well as the then Vicar, Eric Essery – both delightful people though I suspect we might have disagreed on several points of Christian doctrine!

villas lining the Bath Road.' The architect was a Cornishman, James Piers St Aubyn, who was also responsible for the 'restoration' of St Giles in 1873 and later for the church of St Luke, Erleigh Rd, built in 1882-3 to serve the Redlands area. I have chosen the last-named as what might be called a case study.[248]

Originally the parish of St Luke's was part of one of the three mediaeval parishes of Reading, that of St Giles. In 1758 St Giles' is recorded as covering an area of 2,760 acres, or 1,117 hectares under the yet to be begotten metric system. In the course of the 19th century, as Reading and its population expanded, parts of the ecclesiastical parish of St Giles were hived off, originally as daughter churches or chapels of ease but eventually becoming separate parishes in their own right. The churchmanship of these new parishes was influenced by the prevailing ethos of the mother church. As we have seen, St John's (1837) came into being during the time that Cecil Grainger, an evangelical, was Vicar of St Giles and has continued to reflect that end of the Anglican spectrum. However, by the time Christchurch (1862) and St Luke's (1878) were founded, the mother church had come under the influence of the Oxford or Tractarian Movement and these churches reflected this 'higher' churchmanship. In the case of St Luke's it was noted in 1878 that 'there are at this moment nearly two hundred new inhabited houses upon the [Redlands] estate, in other words a population of nearly a thousand, situated a mile distant from the church.' This led to the decision by St Giles to 'secure a site in the centre of the new district, and to erect a temporary building.'

---

[248] This is largely based on notes prepared for a visit to the church by the History of Reading Society in 2021.

This was an iron church, erected in 1878 at a cost of £354 19s. The permanent brick church followed in 1882-3, built at a cost of £7,000 by John Bottrill of Reading. It was consecrated for worship on 6th June 1883 by Bishop Mackarness. Fund-raising for the new church included a concert at the Victoria Hall, Fatherson Road, in 1880, where such popular songs as *Dolly Varden* and *The lark now leaves his watery nest* were performed, the latter sung by the curates of St Giles, who seem to have been four in number at this time. That is the sort of story that makes one wish that video cameras had been invented earlier!

The architect, James Piers St. Aubyn (1815-95), was of Cornish descent and many of his earlier buildings were in the west country. However, he came to enjoy a national reputation as an architect. He had already worked in Reading and the surrounding area, having designed All Saints, Downshire Square (built 1865-74), as well as restoring Aldworth Parish Church (1871) and St Giles, Reading (1873). The latter was a very thorough-going 'restoration' of the kind that William Morris abhorred and John Betjeman mocked in his parody of a well-known hymn:

> The church's restoration
> In Eighteen-Eighty Three
> Has left for contemplation
> Not what there used to be.

Despite or because of his love of Cornwall, Betjeman is rather scathing about St Aubyn's restorations, describing them as practical but unattractive; he is more non-committal regarding his original designs.

The work at St Giles doubtless recommended St Aubyn as architect for the new church. As remarked by Godwin

Arnold, St Luke's was quite unlike his previous work in Reading, not least in being built in red brick. It is described as follows in the latest edition of the Berkshire volume in *The Buildings of England* series:

> A tall church of strongly urban character... Red brick with yellow bands, and a little stone. Lean-to aisles, continued across the west front. Also a pointed-roofed south-east. Bellcote on the chancel arch, just west of the small transepts. Polygonal apse. Former school attached to the North.

Although he was by now nearly 70, St Luke's was by no means St. Aubyn's last work for he continued designing churches to the end, two being completed after his death.

He lived to see the installation of the first of the series of stained glass windows, dated 1892-1930, which are sometimes regarded as St Luke's greatest attraction. These are mostly the work of Charles Eamer Kempe (1837-1907) and the firm founded by him. Kempe was greatly influenced by William Morris, Pre-Raphaelitism and the Tractarian movement, and like Morris was originally expected to become a priest but abandoned that vocation. In Kempe's case, it was a persistent stammer that led him to the conclusion that 'if I was not permitted to minister in the Sanctuary I would use my talents to adorn it.' Altogether around 4,000 windows were designed by his firm, to be seen in great cathedrals as well as the humbler parish churches. In Reading his work is also found at St Mark's, Kensington Road – one of his last works, dated 1905-6.[249]

---

[249] Kempe's work is the subject of a recent book entitled *Espying*

St Luke's Church, Erleigh Road, one of the churches built to serve the expanding town

According to the Victorian Reading church historian, Rev P H Ditchfield, in the early days of St Luke's, Sunday services were Holy Communion at 7.45, Mattins at 11, Children's service at 3 and Evensong at 6.30 pm. There was an additional communion service at 12 noon on the last Sunday of the month and Evensong at 7.30 pm. each Friday. The church could accommodate 600, three times the capacity of the iron church. In 1912, St Luke's was constituted a separate parish with the Revd Francis Howard, formerly priest-in-charge instituted as the first Vicar.

The original 'plant' also included school rooms adjoining the church and fronting Donnington Road,

---

Heaven: The Stained Glass of Charles Eamer Kempe by Adrian Barlow, published by Lutterworth Press.

intended for use as a church school. Following the opening of Redlands School in 1891 they were used for uniformed organisations and even keep fit classes until sold off for housing development in the 1980s.

The eastward expansion of Reading that created Newtown was matched in the west by the appearance of the slum area of Coley but it was not until 1887 that a permanent place of worship was built to serve this community. Designed by local architects, Brown and Albury, St Saviour's replaced a 'tin tabernacle' that had formerly served as a mission church and was consecrated in August 1888. It is one of the few Anglican churches in Reading never to have acquired a parish of its own, operating initially under the aegis of St Mary's and, in later years, St Giles. In 1986, despite the large Coley Park estate that had been built to its south, following the demolition of most of Old Coley, St Saviour's was deemed to be redundant. Happily this charming little brick church with a round apse was then acquired by the Elim Pentecostal Church and continues to serve them to this day, in spite of talk of demolition to build a larger church more in keeping with modern styles of worship.

A little earlier in 1877 a new parish was carved out of the vast parish of Sonning at the extreme east of Reading; this area was then a part of Earley but became a district of Reading in 1888. According to Ditchfield, the parish initially consisted 'mainly of operatives at Messrs. Huntley and Palmers' Biscuit Factory and a few villa residents.' The church of St Bartholomew was built to a design by Alfred Waterhouse, architect of Reading Town Hall, and consecrated by Bishop Mackarness in April 1879. The first Vicar was the Rev C. Robertson Honey. In 1992, the parish was combined with that of St Luke and in addition to

Church of England services the church caters for some of the more exotic Christian communities to be found in Reading. The present writer attended a Serbian Orthodox funeral there some years ago.

Moving west again, 1882 saw the parish of St George's taken out of that of Tilehurst with a population, including the troops in the nearby Brock Barracks, of 1,400. Ditchfield characterises the parish at this time as 'migratory' and of 'extreme poverty.' As at St Luke's, initially from around 1880 it was served by an iron church; a permanent brick structure was erected in 1885-6 and extended in 1893. Across the river too the expansion of the village of Caversham into what became known as Lower Caversham was served by a new church, St John the Baptist, on the Gosbrook Road, a flint and stone building of 1887-8.

In many cases the activities of the established church were mirrored by those of the free churches and there follows a list, which is not exhaustive, of those built mainly during the latter decades of the 19th century according to denomination:

Baptist: Providence, Oxford Rd (1859);[250] Zoar Strict Baptist, South St (1860); Carey (West Central Reading, 1870-1); Caversham (1865-6, replaced on adjacent site, 1875-6); Wycliffe (East Reading, 1880-1); Grovelands (West Reading, 1899).
Brethren: Bridge Hall (West Reading, 1890).
Congregational: Trinity (East Reading, 1848); Tilehurst (1888).

---

[250] This was opened as a Strict Baptist chapel, was later used by a Pentecostal church and is understood to have been acquired by the Brethren c. 1983.

Methodist: Primitive Methodist (London St, 1866, converted from the former Mechanics' Institute); Wesley Methodist (East Reading, 1872-3); Gosbrook Road (Caversham, 1898); Oxford Road (1893).
Presbyterian: St Andrew's, London Rd (1880); St Paul's, York Road (1898-1901).

Of the churches listed above all are active with the following exceptions: Zoar (demolished); Grovelands (later used by the Gate Christian fellowship but currently of uncertain future); Bridge Hall (replaced by Argyle Chapel and put to secular use); Trinity (demolished); Primitive Methodist (converted to a hotel and pub); Oxford Road (demolished); St Andrew's (rebuilt 1971-3 for United Reformed Church); St Paul's, York Road (demolished).

Although church building did continue in the 20th century to serve Reading's expanding population, it was generally at a slower pace and at the same time, as suggested above, town centre and/ or denominational decline led to the closure of some redundant churches.

It can probably be said that, following this powerful extension of capacity, Christian provision in Reading reached its zenith in the latter years of the 19th century. The supply of church services can be determined from the pages of Ditchfield's *Ecclesiastical History of Reading* (1883), supplemented by Kelly's Directory.[251] This I have endeavoured to do in Appendix Three. It will be seen from

---

[251] This is necessary because for Reading's answer to the Venerable Bede the term 'ecclesiastical' would seem to refer to the Church of England only, perhaps as that part of the 'Holy Catholic and Apostolic Church' established in England.

this that most Anglican churches offered on Sundays[252] a eucharistic service at 8, a late morning service at 10.30 or 11, either Mattins (Morning Prayer) or Communion, an afternoon service designed for children and evening service, normally Evensong (Evening Prayer), at 6.30; most also held midweek services. For the nonconformists services at 10.30/ 11 and 6.30 are also typical; afternoon and midweek services are less frequently found. The Nonconformists have also seen more of their churches closed down, although some have been replaced by churches in the new suburbs; nonconformist tendencies have also been satisfied by house churches and conversions of cinemas and the like, as detailed in our next and concluding chapter.

---

[252] Not necessarily on all Sundays.

Interior of St Agnes Church, Silver St – photo from the collection of Michael Penfold

22   The Twentieth Century and After

As I draw near to the close of this story of Christianity in Reading, I will not try to cover everything that happened in the century past and will concentrate on the earlier part of it. Some aspects of its history have already been touched on, notably in the chapter covering the Bishops of Reading.

It could be said that the century began with the church in a confident mood, continuing on from the High Victorian era. Reading saw its biggest expansion just before the 1914-18 War with the incorporation of Caversham and most of those parts of Tilehurst not consumed in an earlier expansion in 1887. One or two areas of modern Reading such as Emmer Green followed after the Second World War.

The confident mood was reflected in further bursts of church-building during the earlier part of the century to serve the expanding population and new suburbs. For the Anglicans St Mark's, Kensington Road was built in 1904-5, designed by Edward Hoare and Montague Wheeler, and around the same time the church of St Bartholomew, London Road, was extended in 1902-5 to designs by G. F. Bodley. As noted in Chapter 19, S. S. Stallwood designed St Agnes, Silver Street (1904), as a chapel of ease to St Giles. A tin tabernacle, St Paul's, in Lower Whitley followed in 1911. The Roman Catholics also received a new church at this time, St William of York, Upper Redlands Road, built in 1905-6, identical in date to the new Wesleyan Mission Hall in Whitley Street. Methodism was also served by the slightly earlier and now demolished Elm Park Hall in the Oxford Road, dating from 1904-5. The Presbyterians likewise received a new church, dedicated to

St Paul, in 1901, in York Road, serving the newly built up area between the railway and Caversham Bridge; this was another church that did not survive long into the 21st century.[253] The expanding suburb of North Caversham was served by the Caversham Heights Methodist Church, opened in 1907 and St Andrew's Church of England, which followed in 1910-11. Both churches were designed by the firm of Ravenscroft and Morris[254]. Down in Lower Caversham Scoles and Raymond designed the RC church of Our Lady and St Anne, commenced in 1902 but not completed until 1921.

First in after the 1914-18 war were the Congregationalists with the Park Church, adjacent to Palmer Park, built in 1923 to the design of W. R. Morris. The very impressive English Martyrs RC church by Prospect Park dates from the same era, designed in an Italian Romanesque style by W C and J H Mangan (1925-6), the former of whom also designed extensions to St James' around the same time. An Italian style was chosen too for the new Anglican church built to serve the Northumberland Avenue (Whitley) estate in 1938-9, dedicated to St Agnes,[255] and designed by Frederick

---

[253] St Paul's was demolished in 2001 but has been replaced with New Hope Church, a daughter church/ church plant from Greyfriars. I am indebted to Malcolm Summers for this information.

[254] The Morris here has no relation to Joseph Morris (Chapter 19) but refers to William Rickards Morris (1863-1950). For the story of the Methodist church see David Cliffe's *Praise in the Heights*.

[255] This took over the dedication of the former chapel-of-ease

Ravenscroft. The same period saw the closure of the Primitive Methodist chapel in London Street, rendered obsolete by the merger of the various strands of Methodism completed in 1932.

As we have seen, the war years were marked by the resumption of Reading's suffragan bishopric. This in part recognised the town's position as the leading centre of a county that had been transformed from a predominantly agricultural area into one of light industry and dormitory towns serving the London commuter-belt. In Christian terms, however, the post-war period was largely one of decline. A number of churches closed, notably Castle Street Congregational Chapel in 1956 and perhaps most significantly the mother church of Reading dissent, Broad Street Congregational (by now United Reformed) in 1983. The former was replaced by a new church in Southcote for the Congregational community, now known as the Grange United Reformed Church.

Among the Anglicans, St Mary's Castle Street came close to being closed in the 1960s but happily survived plans to move its ministry to the new town of Woodley on the borders of Reading.[256] The redevelopment of Newtown in the following decade led to the demolition of St Stephen's and the closure of St John's in Watlington

---

to St Giles in Silver Street, which was deconsecrated. At the time the Vicar of St Giles, Hugh Bonsey, noted that 'the majority of the people whom [the old St Agnes] used to serve have removed to Whitley' and expressed the hope that furnishings from the Silver Street site could be incorporated in the new church. (Report in *Reading Standard, February 25, 1938*, brought to my attention by Whitley historian, Dr Margaret Simons.)

[256] This story is told in the author's pamphlet, *Beautiful the Landscape*, which can be purchased from St Mary's, Castle Street.

Street, replaced by a combined church in the midst of the new housing estate, St John and St Stephen, opened in 1977 and incorporating some of the stained glass from St Stephen's. As noted in the previous chapter, the old St John's was later reopened as an RC Church serving Reading's burgeoning Polish community and dedicated to The Sacred Heart. Roman Catholics on the Whitley estate were served by the church of Christ the King, built 1958-9, and those resident in and around Earley and Whiteknights, received their own church, dedicated to Our Lady of Peace and Blessed Dominic Barberi, in 1976.

Other new Anglican church building projects included St Mary Magdalen, Kentwood (1962), St Matthew's in Southcote (1967), designed by the architect of Coventry Cathedral, Basil Spence, and St Barnabas, Elm Rd (1966-8). Greyfriars consolidated its position in the town centre with the addition of the West End in 1973 and Greyfriars Centre ten years later, both replaced in the 2020s. The seventies also saw the rebuilding of St Andrew's Presbyterian Church (now URC) in 1971 and the replacement of the King's Road Baptist Church by the Abbey Baptist Church on an adjacent site in 1979.

In the latter years of the 20th century and the early years of the 21st the Methodists underwent further consolidation, firstly with the closure of the Whitley Street Mission Hall, which was converted into a Hindu temple, then with the closure and/or demolition of two churches on the Oxford Road, replaced in 2005 by Emmanuel Methodist Church. The Oxford Road church (i.e. the one nearer the town centre) served for a time as the home for a Pentecostal congregation but was regrettably demolished a few years back. The Elim Pentecostals ensured continuing use for St Saviour's, Berkeley Avenue, after it had been declared redundant by the Oxford diocese in the 1980s, while the Central Evangelical Church, off Howard St, became an offshoot of Carey Baptist Church as the Carey Centre. Carey also acquired a neighbouring pub, the Oasis (formerly the Eagle), with a view to engaging with the local community – though not, I hasten to add, with the aid of alcoholic beverages! Another Pentecostal group, Life Spring Church, took over a building in Oxford Road that opened in 1929 as a cinema and later served as a snooker hall until transformed early in the 21st Century into the Pavilion Church. This followed a pattern set by the New Testament Church of God when it acquired the former Glendale Cinema in Caversham c. 1983.

This closing chapter has been mostly about bricks and mortar, perhaps because we cannot yet fully assess the part played by Christian people in moulding 20th – let alone 21st - century Reading. Some significant names have been mentioned in earlier chapters, among them Canon Brian Brindley of Holy Trinity (1966-89) and the Revs J C Rundle and J K Page of Greyfriars. There were substantial ministries also by Gordon Fairbairn (1902-30) at Kings Road Baptist, F J C Gillmor (1911-34) and Anthony Boult (1966-88) at St Giles, Richard Bell (1928-48) and John McKechnie (1968-85) at St John's and St Stephen's,[257] the latter overseeing the moved to the new church in the New Town redevelopment area. Others included Selwyn Morgan (1968-86) and Jonathan Stephen (1987-2006) at Carey Baptist Church, Richard Kingsbury (1983-2007) in the Caversham Anglican group, Philip Jones (1972-95) at

---

[257] We should also mention among the briefer ministries that of T. Guy Rogers at St John's (1909-15). See *Sent from Reading* for a longer account of his work.

All Saints, Peter Downham (1979-95) at Greyfriars and Gerald Restall (1972-88) and Brian Shenton (1989-2014) at St Mary the Virgin. Dr Adam Carlill has served St George's. Tilehurst, since 1998.

Other briefer ministries, nevertheless, also made an impact on the town, including those of Allan Bowhill (1984-90) and Dr David Samuel (1991-6) at St Mary's Castle Street and Jonathan Baker (1996-2002) at Holy Trinity.

John Page, continuing the tradition of lengthy ministries at Greyfriars, 1947-68

As previously noted, the last-named is the most recent Reading clergyman to have been elevated to the episcopate, first as 'flying' Bishop of Ebbsfleet in 2011[258] and more recently as Bishop of Fulham. At St Mary's, Castle Street, the Revd Edward Malcolm (2001-) has become the longest-serving incumbent since George Ibberson Tubbs. He has also since 2013 served as the Presiding Bishop of the breakaway Church of England (Continuing) – see below.

Earlier Reading-born Cormac Murphy O'Connor (1932-2017) became Archbishop of Westminster (2000-09) and a Cardinal of the Roman church. The son of a local GP, he attended the former Presentation College in Reading and served as Bishop of Arundel and Brighton from 1977 until his elevation to the archiepiscopate.

The shrinkage of Christendom as a force in the life of the town and the nation has been accompanied by an ongoing debate between conservatives and liberals on a range of matters that can perhaps be summed up in the word 'inclusivity.' Firstly, over the role of women in the church. Should they be allowed to preach and/ or celebrate Holy Communion? Some denominations such as the URC and the Methodists have long admitted women to their ordained ministry but it was not until 1992 that the General Synod of the Church of England voted narrowly to accept women into the priesthood. This decision had consequences for several churches in the town. A number

---

[258] The first bishop of Ebbsfleet from 1994-98 was John Richards (1933-2003), an old boy of Reading School, who had attended St Giles' Church in his youth. Since the more correct but somewhat clumsy title is 'Provincial Episcopal Visitor', it is scarcely surprising that 'flying bishop' is the one that has stuck.

of Anglo-Catholic laymen 'crossed the Tiber' and at St Giles the Vicar, Father Bruce Dutson, also became a Roman Catholic and was re-ordained as a priest of Rome. His predecessor, Tony Boult, had previously joined St James' RC church, where he exercised a lay ministry. Others from the High Church party were content to accept the episcopal ministry of the new breed of 'flying bishops' provided by an Act of Synod to cater for those parishes unable to accept women's ministry.

Perhaps even more dramatic were the events at St Mary's, Castle Street (SMCS), that followed the decision by the incumbent, Dr David Samuel, to renounce his Anglican orders. A meeting of the Chapel Council in December 1993 voted to support him by also leaving the Church of England and this move was supported by all but a handful of the congregation. As a proprietary chapel, SMCS was in a unique position among the town's Anglican churches in being able to separate from the establishment without any penalty in terms of property. Although the Chapel Council had no legal powers to take the action it did, the move was supported by the Chairman of the Trustees and the majority of the other trustees, although some were opposed to what in all sincerity they regarded as a schismatic act. In 1994 the chapel joined with several other breakaway churches in forming a new Anglican body, called the Church of England (Continuing), based on strict adherence to the Anglican formularies, especially the Book of Common Prayer and 39 Articles. In 1995, Dr Samuel was consecrated as its first Presiding Bishop. It could be argued that this exclusivity has restricted the appeal of the CofE (C) to potential members but it has exerted indirect influence through its publications.

One of the concerns of those conservatives, especially evangelicals, opposed to the ordination of women, was that it would open the floodgates to other, potentially more damaging developments, particularly in the area of sexual relationships. As we saw in Chapter 20 this came to a head in Reading in 2003 in the debate over the appointment of a new Area Bishop. The hapless Jeffrey John was replaced by Stephen Cottrell who in his current role as Primate of the Northern Province has been to the fore in supporting recent moves to authorise blessings of same-sex couples in church.

The ordination of women also led inevitably to the consecration of female bishops from 2015 and a further exodus from the Anglo-Catholic parishes took place as a result, especially as the establishment of the Personal Ordinariate of Our Lady of Walsingham by Pope Benedict XVI provided a means by which such converts could retain something of their Anglican heritage. In Reading, the Vicar of Holy Trinity, David Elliott, and a number of his congregation joined the Ordinariate and Father Elliott is now the Reading Group Pastor of the Ordinariate, meeting at St James.

In 2021 the town celebrated, as best it could in the circumstances of COVID lockdowns and restrictions, the ninth centenary of the foundation of its great abbey. Perhaps this is a happier note to end on than a lament for the diminished state of the established church and the traditional free churches in the town. The ruined condition of the abbey and the demolition of many once-loved buildings may also serve to remind us that the Church consists not primarily of 'bricks and mortar' but the living souls of those called by the Holy Spirit into the family of God.

APPENDIX ONE:
Bishops with Jurisdiction over Reading

Date	Name	Episcopal Seat	Remarks[259]
DIOCESAN BISHOPS			
634	Birinus	Dorchester	
650	Agilbert	Dorchester	Later Bishop of Paris, d. 673
663	Wini	Dorchester	
670	Lothere	Dorchester	
676	Hedde	Winchester	
705	Daniel	Winchester	
744	Hunfrith	Winchester	
754	Cyneheard	Winchester	
759	Aethelheard	Winchester	
778	Eagebeald	Winchester	
781	Dudd	Winchester	
785	Cynebeorht	Winchester	
803	Eahlmund	Winchester	
814	Wigthegn	Winchester	
825	Herefirth	Winchester	
833	Eadmund	Winchester	
836	Eadhun	Winchester	
838	Helmstan	Winchester	
852	Swithun	Winchester	Canonized
862	Ealfrith	Winchester	Tr. Canterbury, 872, d. 877

---

[259] Pre-conquest records are sometimes incomplete. Post-conquest a blank entry in this column indicates that the bishop died in office in the same year that his successor was appointed.

872	Tunbeohrt	Winchester	
879	Denewulf	Winchester	
909	Frithustan	Winchester	
931	Oda	Ramsbury	Tr. Canterbury, 942, d. 958
942	Aelfric (1)	Ramsbury	
952	Oswulf	Ramsbury	d. 970
974	Aelfstan	Ramsbury	
981	Wulfgar	Ramsbury	
985	Sigeric	Ramsbury	Tr. Canterbury, 990
990	Aelfric (2)	Ramsbury	Tr. Canterbury, 995
1005	Beohrtweald	Ramsbury	
1045	Herman	Ramsbury	Moved see to Old Sarum, 1075
1078	Osmund	Sarum	d. 1099; canonized
1102	Roger	Sarum	d. 1139
1142	Jocelin de Bohun	Sarum	d. 1184
1189	Hubert Walter	Sarum	Tr. Canterbury, 1193
1194	Herbert le Poor	Sarum	
1217	Richard le Poor	Sarum	Moved see to Salisbury (New Sarum), 1219, tr Durham 1228.
1229	Robert Bingham	Salisbury	d. 1246
1247	William of York	Salisbury	d. 1256
1257	Giles Bridport	Salisbury	d. 1262
1263	Walter de la Wyle	Salisbury	d. 1271

1274	Robert Wickhampton	Salisbury	
1284	Walter Scammell	Salisbury	d. 1286
1287	Henry Brandeston	Salisbury	d. 1288
1289	Walter de la Corner	Salisbury	d. 1291
1292	Nicolas Longspee	Salisbury	
1297	Simon of Ghent	Salisbury	
1315	Roger Mortival	Salisbury	
1330	Robert Wyville	Salisbury	
1375	Robert Erghum	Salisbury	Tr. Wells, 1388
1388	John Waltham	Salisbury	
1395	Richard Mitford	Salisbury	From Chichester
1407	Nicholas Bubwith	Salisbury	From London, tr. Bath and Wells, 1407
1407	Robert Hallum	Salisbury	
1417	John Chandler	Salisbury	
1427	Robert Neville	Salisbury	Tr. Durham, 1438
1438	William Ayscough	Salisbury	Murdered, 1450
1450	Richard Beauchamp	Salisbury	From Hereford, died 1481.
1482	Lionel Woodville	Salisbury	Died, 1484

1485	Thomas Langton	Salisbury	From St. David's. tr. Winchester, 1493.
1494	John Blyth	Salisbury	Died, 1499
1500	Henry Dean	Salisbury	Tr. Canterbury, 1501
1502	Edmund Audley	Salisbury	From Hereford
1524	Lorenzo Campeggio	Salisbury	Also papal legate, deprived 1534
1535	Nicholas Shaxton	Salisbury	Resigned 1539
1539	John Salcot	Salisbury	Died 1557
1560	John Jewel	Salisbury	
1571	Edmund Guest	Salisbury	
1577	John Piers	Salisbury	From Rochester, tr. York, 1589
1591	John Coldwell	Salisbury	Died 1596
1598	Henry Cotton	Salisbury	
1615	Robert Abbot	Salisbury	
1618	Martin Fotherby	Salisbury	
1620	Robert Townson	Salisbury	
1621	John Davenant	Salisbury	
1641	Brian Duppa	Salisbury	From Chichester, tr. Winchester, 1660
1660	Humfrey Henchman	Salisbury	Tr. London, 1663
1663	John Earle	Salisbury	From Winchester.
1665	Alexander Hyde	Salisbury	
1667	Seth Ward	Salisbury	From Exeter

1689	Gilbert Burnet	Salisbury	
1715	William Talbot	Salisbury	From Oxford, tr. Durham, 1721.
1721	Richard Willis	Salisbury	From Gloucester
1723	Benjamin Hoadley	Salisbury	From Hereford, tr. Winchester, 1734
1734	Thomas Sherlock	Salisbury	From Bangor, tr. London, 1748
1748	John Gilbert	Salisbury	From Llandaff, tr. York, 1757.
1757	John Thomas (1)	Salisbury	From Peterborough, tr. Winchester, 1761
1761	Robert Hay Drummond	Salisbury	From St. Asaph, tr. York, 1761.
1761	John Thomas (2)	Salisbury	From Lincoln
1766	John Hume	Salisbury	From Oxford
1782	Shute Barrington	Salisbury	From Llandaff, tr. Durham, 1791
1791	John Douglas	Salisbury	
1807	John Fisher	Salisbury	From Exeter
1825	Thomas Burgess	Salisbury	From St David's, died 1837
1836	Richard Bagot	Oxford	Bishop from 1829, tr. Bath and Wells, 1845
1845	Samuel Wilberforce	Oxford	Tr. Winchester, 1869.
1869	John Fielder Mackarness	Oxford	Res. 1888, died 1889.
1889	William Stubbs	Oxford	From Chester.
1901	Francis Paget	Oxford	

1911	Charles Gore	Oxford	From Birmingham, res. 1919, died 1932.
1919	Hubert Murray Burge	Oxford	From Southwark
1925	Thomas Banks Strong	Oxford	Res. 1937, died 1944
1937	Kenneth Escott Kirk	Oxford	Set up current network of area bishops, died 1954
1955	Harry James Carpenter	Oxford	Res. 1970, died 1993.
1971	Kenneth John Woollcombe	Oxford	Res. 1978, died 2008.
1978	Patrick Campbell Rodger	Oxford	From Manchester, res. 1986, died 2002.
1987	Richard Douglas Harries	Oxford	Res. 2006.
2007	John Lawrence Pritchard	Oxford	From Jarrow, res. 2014.
2016	Steven John Lindsey Croft	Oxford	From Sheffield. Present bishop

SUFFRAGAN/ AREA BISHOPS

1889	James Leslie Randall	Reading	Res. 1908, died 1922
1942	Arthur Groom Parham	Reading	Res. 1954, died 1961
1954	Eric Henry Knell	Reading	Res. 1972, died 1987
1972	Eric Wild	Reading	Res. 1982, died 1991

1982	Ronald Graham Gregory Foley	Reading	Res. 1989, died 2017
1989	John Frank Ewan Bone	Reading	Res. 1996, died 2014
1997	Dominic Walker	Reading	Tr. Monmouth, 2003
2004	Stephen Geoffrey Cottrell	Reading	Tr. Chelmsford, 2010, later to York
2011	Andrew Proud	Reading	From Horn of Africa, res. 2019
2019	Olivia Graham	Reading	Reading and Oxford Diocese's first female Bishop
2025	Mary Gregory	Reading	

PROVINCIAL EPISCOPAL VISITORS (FLYING BISHOPS)[260]

1994	John Richards	Ebbsfleet	Res. 1998, died 2003
1998	Michael Houghton	Ebbsfleet	Died, 1999
1999	Andrew Burnham	Ebbsfleet	Joined Ordinariate
2011	Jonathan Baker	Ebbsfleet	Translated to Fulham
2013	Jonathan Goodall	Ebbsfleet	Joined Roman Church, 2021
2015	Roderick Thomas	Maidstone	Res. 2022
2022	Paul Thomas	Oswestry	Current PEV

---

[260] Ebbsfleet is now the flying bishopric catering for Conservative Evangelicals; I am unaware of any Reading churches coming under its wing.

| 2023 | Robert Munro | Ebbsfleet | Current PEV |

ROMAN CATHOLIC HIERARCHY

1851	Thomas Grant	Southwark	
1871	James Danell	Southwark	Berkshire transferred to new Portsmouth diocese, 1882
1882	John Vertue	Portsmouth	
1900	John Cahill	Portsmouth	
1910	William Cotter	Portsmouth	
1941	John Henry King	Portsmouth	
1965	Derek Worlock	Portsmouth	Subsequently Archbishop of Liverpool
1976	Anthony Emery	Portsmouth	
1988	Crispian Hollis	Portsmouth	
2012	Philip Egan	Portsmouth	

APPENDIX TWO:
Dissenting Places of Worship Registered within Reading 1728–1849

Denomination	Location of Chapel	Registered with	Year	Minister or leading applicant
Quakers	Church Lane, St Giles	B Ad	1728	Abraham Bonifield
Cudworthian	St Mary's Butts	Bp Sal	1752	William Cudworth
Baptist	Hosier's Lane	Bp Sal	1754	Thomas Whitewood
Independent	St Mary's Butts	B Ad	1770	James Simonds
Independent	Castle Street	Bp Sal	1779	William Cockell
Independent/Baptist?	St Mary's parish	Bp Sal	1798	Samuel Litherland
Independent	Earley	Dean Sal	1808	William Norris
Independent [1]	Rose Yard, Minster Street	Bp Sal	1807	Francis Millard
Wesleyan Methodist	London Street	Bp Sal	1813	John Elkens
Wesleyan Methodist	Tilehurst Common	Bp Sal	1816	[G Gellard]
Wesleyan Methodist	Church Street, St Giles	Bp Sal	1817	John Waterhouse
Baptist	St Giles parish	Bp Sal	1818	Edward Burnard
Baptist [2]	St Mary's parish	Bp Sal	1818	Edward Burnard
Strict Baptist	Whitley Hamlet, St Giles'	Bp Sal	1818	Richard Stacey
Ebenezer Independent	Oxford Road	Bp Sal	1819	William Bubier
Wesleyan Methodist	Whitley Hamlet, St Giles' parish	Bp Sal	1819	John Waterhouse
Baptist	St Mary's parish	Bp Sal	1830	J H Hinton

Trinitarian Dissenters [3]	Tilehurst	QS Ab	1835	Robert Rhodes
Independent [4]	Bridge Street	B Ad	1836	William Saunders
Primitive Methodist	London St, St Giles' parish	Bp Oxf	1836	John Ride
Baptist	Kings Road	B Ad	1837	John Howard Hinton
Congregational	Castle Street	QS Read	1838	–
Rational Religionists [5]	n.k.	QS Read	1839	David Vines
Primitive Methodist	Prospect Hill, St Mary's parish	Bp Oxf	1842	John Ride
Christian Brethren [6]	Black Horse, Queen's Road	Bp Oxf	1846	William Henry Dorman
Congregational [7]	London Street	QS Read	1846	William Morton Mather
Congregational [7]	Trinity Chapel, Queen's Road	QS Read	1849	–

Key: B Ad – Berkshire Archdeaconry; Bp Oxf – Bishop of Oxford; Bp Sal – Bishop of Salisbury; Dean Sal – Dean of Salisbury; QS Ab – Abingdon Quarter sessions; QS Read – Reading Borough Quarter Sessions.

[1] Believed to be those who seceded from what became St Mary's Castle Street and other churches, later known as Salem Chapel
[2] Possibly the ancestor to the Providence Strict Baptist Chapel [now Brethren] in Oxford Road.
[3] A daughter church of Broad Street Congregational.
[4] Believed to be the group of seceders from the newly Anglican Episcopal Chapel, that later formed the Castle Street Congregational Chapel, registered 1838 below.
[5] Believed to denote Unitarians.
[6] Often denoted Plymouth Brethren.
[7] Seceders from Broad Street Congregational, initially meeting in New Public Rooms, London St, later forming Trinity Congregational, Queen's Road, 1849 below.

APPENDIX THREE:
Provision of Church Services in Reading in the late 19th Century

Church	Cat	Sunday Services		Midweek Services	Remarks
		Morning	Afternoon(1)/ Evening		
St Mary the Virgin	CE	HC 8 (weekly), 11 (twice monthly) MP, 11 (twice monthly)	EP 3 & 6.30 (weekly)	MP 8, EP 5 daily HC 11 (Thurs)	HC on 5th Sundays when occurring with MP on 4th.
All Saints	CE	HC 8 (twice monthly), 11 (weekly)	EP 3 & 6.30 (weekly)	MP 11 (Wed/Fri) EP 5 (Mon/Tue/Sat HC 8 (Tue)	
St Saviour	CE	HC, 8, MP, 11	EP, 3.15, 6.30	EP, 8 (Tue), HC, 8 (Fri)	Now NC (Pentecostal)
St Laurence	CE	11	6.30	10, 7 (daily exc. Fri, 8)	From Kelly
St Giles	CE	HC, 7.45 (weekly), 12 (last Sun), MP, 11	EP 6.30	EP 7.30 (Fri)	
St John	CE	11	6.30	7 pm (Wed)	From Kelly - now Polish RC church
St Luke	CE	11	6.30	7.30 pm (Fri)	From Kelly

Church	Cat	Sunday Services		Midweek Services	Remarks
		Morning	Afternoon/Evening		
St Mary's, Castle St	CE	HC 8 (2nd Sun), after MP (1st Sun), after EP, 3rd Sun) MP 11	EP 6.30	7.30 pm (Wed)	Now NC (Church of England Continuing)
Holy Trinity	CE	HC 8 (weekly), 12 (1st Sun) MP 11	EP 6.30	HC 7.30 am (Thurs) Litany 12 (Wed/Fri)	
Greyfriars	CE	HC 11 (1st Sun) MP 11 (exc 1st Sun)	HC 6.30 (3rd Sun) EP 3 (weekly), 6.30 (exc 3rd Sun)	EP 7.30 (Wed)	Also Prayer meeting (Sat)
Greyfriars Iron Church	CE	11	6.30	Bible Study 7.45 pm (Tue), Service, 730 pm (Thurs)	Closed 1980
Christ Church, Whitley	CE	HC 7.45 (weekly), 12 (1st & 3rd Sun) MP 11	EP 3 & 7	MP 8 (exc Wed/Fri, 11)	
St Bartholomew, Earley	CE	HC 7.30 (1st, 3rd & 5th) MP 11	EP 3.30 & 6.30	MP 10.30 (Wed & Fri)	
St George, Tilehurst	CE	HC 8 exc 1st Sun), 11 (1st Sun) MP 11	EP 3 & 6.30	Mission Service (Wed eve) EP (Fri)	

Church	Cat	Sunday Services		Midweek Services	Remarks
		Morning	Afternoon①/ Evening		
Reading Union Workhouse	CE	MP 9	HC 3 (4th Sun)	MP 10 (Tue)	Closed
St Stephen	CE	10.30	6.30		From Kelly – replaced along with St John's by new church
St James	RC	HC 9, 11	6.30	HC 8.30 am (daily) 7.30 pm (Thur), 7 pm (Sat)	From Kelly
Presbyterian, London Road	NC	11	6.30	7.30 pm (Wed)	Now St Andrew's URC
Society of Friends	NC	11	6.30	11 (Wed)	
Baptist, Carey Street	NC	11	6.30	7.30 pm (Wed)	
Baptist, Kings Rd	NC	11	6.30	7.00 pm (Wed)	Now Abbey Baptist
Baptist, Wycliffe	NC	11	6.30	7.30 pm (Wed)	
Baptist, Oxford Rd	NC	11	6.30	7.00 pm (Thur)	Now Providence Chapel (Brethren)
Baptist, Zoar	NC	10.30	6.30	7.00 pm (Tue)	Closed

Church	Cat	Sunday Services		Midweek Services	Remarks
		Morning	Afternoon/Evening		
Brethren, Queen's Road	NC	11	6.30		Closed
Congregational, Augustine, Friar St	NC	11	6.30	3.00 pm (Thurs)	Closed
Congregational, Castle St	NC	11	6.30	7.30 pm (Thurs)	Closed
Congregational, Trinity	NC	11	6.30	7.30 pm (Wed)	Closed
Congregational, Broad St	NC	11	6.30	7.30 pm (Wed)	Closed
Primitive Meth., London St	NC	9.30, 12	2.00	7.00 pm (Tue)	Closed
Primitive Meth., Friar St	NC	11.30	6.30		Closed
Unitarian Free	NC	11.15	6.30		Closed
United Methodist, Hosier St	NC	11	6.30	7.00 am (Wed)	Closed
Wesleyan, Queens Rd	NC	11	6.30	7.00 pm (Wed)	

Church	Cat	Sunday Services		Midweek Services	Remarks
		Morning	Afternoon①/ Evening		
Wesleyan, Oxford Rd	NC	11	6.30	7.30 pm (Thurs)	Closed
Wesleyan, Tank Rd	NC	10.30	6.30	7.30 pm (Wed)	Replaced by Whitley Hall (now Hindu temple)

Key: CE – Church of England
      RC – Roman Catholic
      NC - Nonconformist
      HC - Holy Communion
      MP - Mattins or Morning Prayer, sometimes with Litany & Ante-Communion
      EP - Evensong or Evening Prayer

① Some at 3 designated Children's services.

BIBLIOGRAPHY

Arnold, H. Godwin & Gold, Sidney, *Morris of Reading, A Family of Architects*, Ancient Monuments Society, 1989.

Arnold, H. Godwin, *Victorian Architecture in Reading*, Reading, 1976.

Ayres, May, and Sanders, Keith, *As stupid as Oxen*, Reading, 1989.

Bede, the Venerable, tr. J. A. Giles, *Ecclesiastical History of England*, Henry Bohn, 1847.

Betjeman, J. (ed.), *Collins Pocket Guide to English Parish Churches – The South*, Collins, 1968.

Brod, Manfred, *The Case of Reading. Urban Governance in Troubled Times 1640-90*, Upfront, 2006.

Bunyan, John, *Grace Abounding*, Everyman edition, 1976.

Butler, L & Given-Wilson, C, *Mediaeval Monasteries of Great Britain*, Michael Joseph, 1979.

Calamy, Edmund, *An Account of those Worthy Ministers who were Ejected after the Restoration*, London, 1702.

Carus, W., *Memoirs of the Life of the Rev Charles Simeon, M.A.*, Hatchard, 1847.

Cecil, Rev Richard, *Life of the Rev William Bromley Cadogan*, Rivington, 1798.

Cennick, John, ed. Watson, Graeme, *Celestial Anthems*, Culver Press, 2001.

Childs, W M, *The Town of Reading in the Early Part of the Nineteenth Century*, UC Reading, 1910.

Cliffe, David, *Praise in the Heights*, Caversham Heights Methodist Church, 2009.

Clifford, Sue (ed), *Berkshire Schools in the Eighteenth Century*, Berkshire Record Society, 2019.

Consterdine, Rev James, *The Early History of St Mary's Castle Street*, SMCS, 1898.

Dearing, John (ed), *The Reading Book of Days*, History Press, 2013.
Dearing, John, *Beautiful was the Landscape*, SMCS, 2007.
Dearing, John, *John Wesley came to Reading*, SMCS, 2003.
Dearing, John, *Sent from Reading*, J B Dearing, 2021.
Dearing, John, *The Church that would Not Die*, Baron Birch, 1993.
Denny, Barbara, *Kings Bishop, The Lords Spiritual of London*, Alderman Press, 1985.
Dils, Joan and Yates, Margaret, *An Historical Atlas of Berkshire*, Berkshire Record Society, 2012 [Second edition].
Dils, Joan, ed., *Reading St Laurence Churchwardens' Accounts, 1498-1570*, Berkshire Record Society, 2013.
Dils, Joan, *Reading A History*, Carnegie, 2019.
Dils, Joan, *St Giles Parish and People during the Period of the Reformation 1536-70*, address to History of Reading Society, 2023
Ditchfield, Revd. P H, *Ecclesiastical History of Reading*, Blackwell, 1883.
Doak, J, *What about the workers? Life and love at Huntley & Palmers 1847-1976*, Presentation to History of Reading Society, 2023.
Durrant, Peter, and Painter, John, *Reading Abbey and the Abbey Quarter*, Two Rivers Press, 2018.
Florence of Worcester, tr. Thomas Forester, *Chronicle*, Henry Bohn, 1854.
Fox, George, *Journal*, Everyman's Library, 1940.
Foxe, John, *Book of Martyrs*, various editions.
Fulford, Michael, *Silchester Revealed*, Windgather Press, 2021
Gold, Sidney, *Biographical Dictionary of Architects in Reading*, Reading, 1999.
Griffin, Sara, *Encounters with Angels, The Life of John Pordage*, Stuart Press, 1996.

Guilding, J. M. (ed), *Records of the Borough of Reading*, 1431-1654 (4 vols), London: James Parker, 1892-1896

Hadland, Tony, *Thames Valley Papists*, Hadland, 1992.

Harman, Revd. Leslie, *Christianity in Reading*, Crown Press, Reading, 1952.

Harman, Revd. Leslie, *History of St Giles-in-Reading*, St Giles, Reading, 1946.

Haykin, Michael A. G., *Holy Spirit Now Descend, Thomas Davis and the Evangelical Revival in Georgian Berkshire*, Ettrick Press, 2022.

Henig, Martin, *The Heirs of King Verica*, Amberley, 2nd ed., 2010.

Hillaby, Joe and Caroline, *Leominster Minster, Priory and Borough*, Logaston Press, 2006.

Hidden, Norman, *The Later Lollards of West Berkshire*, Berkshire Old and New, No. 7, 1990.

Hole, Rev Charles, *The life of the Reverend and Venerable William Whitmarsh Phelps*, 1871.

Humble, Richard, *The Saxon Kings*, Weidenfeld and Nicolson, 1980.

Hurry, Dr J, *Reading Abbey*, 1901.

Kapic, Kelly M. and Vander Lugt, Wesley, *Pocket Dictionary of Reformed Tradition*, IVP Academic, 2013.

Kemp, Brian (ed), *Reading Abbey Records, a new miscellany*, Berkshire Record Society, 2018.

Kerry, Rev Charles, *The Municipal Church of St Lawrence, Reading*, 1883.

Kightly, Charles, *The Early Lollards, A Survey of Popular Lollard Activity 1382-1428*, U York, 1975 (PhD thesis).

Loane, Marcus L., *Makers of Our Heritage*, Hodder & Stoughton, 1967.

Maltby, Judith, *Prayer Book and People in Elizabethan and Early Stuart England*, CUP, 1998.

Man, John, ed. Sowan, Adam, *The Stranger in Reading,* Two Rivers Press, 2005.

Matthews, Ronald, *English Messiahs: Studies of Six English Religious Pretenders, 1656-1927*, Methuen, 1936.

McKechnie, Rev John, *Happy are They, History of the Parish of St John etc.*, 1973.

Morris, John, and others, *Lives of the English martyrs: declared blessed by Pope Leo XIII, in 1886 and 1895*, Longman Green, 1915.

Moule, Handley Carr Glyn, *Charles Simeon*, Methuen, 1892.

Mullaney, John and Lyndsay, *Reformation, Revolution and Rebirth*, Scallop Shell Press, 2012.

Mullaney, John, *Reading's Abbey Quarter*, Scallop Shell Press, 2014.

Newton, John, ed. Marylynn Rouse, *Diary, 1767, Meeting Friends Old and New*, John Newton Project, 2023.

Oakes, J. and Parsons, M, *Reading School – The First 800 Years*, Oakleaf Publications, 2005.

Over, Luke, *The Parish Church of St Peter, Caversham*, 2nd ed., 2015

Payne, Ernest, *Baptists of Berkshire*, Carey Kingsgate, 1951.

Peyt, M (ed), *The Growth of Reading*. Alan Sutton, 1993.

Philips, Geoffrey, *Thames Crossings, Bridges, Tunnels and Ferries*, David and Charles, 1981.

Proceedings of Wesley Historical Society.

Pugh, Ronald and Margaret (ed), *The Diocese Books of Samuel Wilberforce*, Berkshire and Oxford Record Societies, 2008.

Ralph, H., *Reading and Primitive Methodism*, article in *Handbook of the 96th Annual Primitive Methodist Conference held in Reading in 1915*.

Raynor, Brian, *John Frith, Scholar and Martyr*, Read All Over, 2000.

Redlands Local History Group, *Old Redlands*, Reading, 1990.

Reynolds, Rev John, *The Evangelicals at Oxford 1735-1871*, Blackwell/ Marcham. 1953/ 1975.

Ritson, Joseph, *The Romance of Primitive Methodism*, E. Dalton, 1909.

Sawers, Geoff, *Broad Street Chapel and the Origins of Dissent in Reading*, Two Rivers Press, 1996.

Sellers, Ian, *John Howard Hinton, Theologian*, Baptist Quarterly, 1989.

Seymour, Aaron Crossley Hobart, *Life and Times of Selina, Countess of Huntingdon*, London, 1840 [reprint Tentmaker Publications, 2000].

Sherwood, Mary Martha, ed. F. J. Harvey Darton, *The Life and Times of Mrs Sherwood*, Wells Gardner Darton, 1910 [CUP reprint, 2011].

Slade, Cecil, *The Town of Reading and its Abbey*, Reading, 2001.

Smith, Howard R., *The Wilkinson-Story Controversy in Reading*, Friends History Society Journal, Vol 1 No 2, 1904.

Smyth, Canon C, *Simeon and Church Order: A Study of the Origins of the Evangelical Revival in Cambridge in the Eighteenth Century*, 1940.

Sowan, Adam, *Believing in Reading*, Two Rivers Press, 2012.

Spriggs, Gordon, *History of Greyfriars Church*, Reading, 1963.

Spurrier, Lisa, ed., *Nonconformist Meeting Houses*, Berkshire Record Society, 2005.

Spurrier, Lisa, *The Origins of Wesleyan Methodism in Reading, 1737-1873*, Berkshire Old and New, No. 40, 2023.

Stenton, Frank, *Anglo-Saxon England*, OUP, 1943.

Summers, Malcolm, *History of Greyfriars Church, Reading*, Downs Way, 2013.

Summers, Malcolm, *Reading's Greyfriars*, Downs Way, 2020.

Summers, Malcolm, *Sir Thomas Noon Talfourd*, Downs Way, 2023.

Summers, W H, *History of the Berkshire, South Bucks, and South Oxon Congregational Churches*, Newbury, 1905.

Talbot, Rev William, *Narrative of the Whole of His Proceedings etc.*, Reading, 1772.

Tiller, Kate, ed., *Berkshire Religious Census 1851*, Berkshire Record Society, 2010.

Tiller, Kate, ed., *Church and Chapel in Oxfordshire 1851*, Oxfordshire Record Society, 1987.

Townsend, W., Workman, H. & Eayrs, G., *New History of Methodism*, Hodder & Stoughton, 1909.

Trevor-Roper, Hugh, *William Laud*, Macmillan, 1940.

Tyack, G., Bradley, S. and Pevsner N., *Buildings of England, Berkshire*, Yale, 2010.

Tyerman, Christopher, *Who's Who in Early Mediaeval England*, Shepheard Walwyn, 1886.

Vickers, J. A. (ed.), *A Dictionary of Methodism in Britain and Ireland*, Epworth, 2000.

Wesley, Charles, *The Journal of the Rev Charles Wesley M.A. The Early Journal 1736-1739*, Robert Culley, 1909.

Wesley, John, *Journals*, Epworth and Everyman editions.

Wykes, Alan, *Reading, A* Biography, MacMillan, 1970.

Wykes, Alan, *Reading All Change*, film, 1979.

Christian press including *Church of England Newspaper*, *English Churchman*, *Gospel Magazine*. *Wesleyan Methodist Magazine* and *New Directions*.

WEBSITES

History of Reading Society:
http://historyofreadingsociety.org.uk
John Newton Project: *www.johnnewton.org*

National Association of Teachers of Religious Education (NATRE): *www.natre.org.uk*
Reading Museum: *http://www.readingmuseum.org.uk*
Primitive Methodism: *https://www.myprimitivemethodists.org.uk*
Simeons Trustees: *http://www.simeons.org.uk/simeons-trustees-history*

INDEX

Abbey Gateway School, 169
Aberdeen University, 209, 211, 234
Adam of Lathbury, 13, 23
Addison, W E, 250
Adela, Countess of Blois, 12
Adeliza, Queen, 18-19, 29
Aelfhere of Mercia, 6
Aelfric, Archbishop, 233, 274
Agapemonites, 223-4, 227-8
Aldis, John, 207
Aldworth, Richard, 160
Aldworth, Thomas, 65, 160
Alexander, William, 172
Alfred the Great, King, 232
All Saints, Downshire Square, 202, 238. 253, 255, 268, 283
Ampthill, Craven Road, 228
Anabaptists, 75, 81
Anderson Memorial Baptist Church, Earley, 208
Anderson, William, 207-8
Anscher, Abbot, 13, 18
Argyle Chapel, 260
Ark of the Covenant, Church of, Tottenham, 226, 228
Arles, Council of, 3-4
Arminius, Jacobus, 69
Armorer, Sir William, 79, 82, 86
Arnold, H Godwin, 226, 255
Askin, Thomas, 61
Athelstan, King, 233
Attwell, W C, 153
Augustine Chapel, 211-12, 286
Austen, Jane, 169
Bacon, Phanuel, 92
Bagot, Richard, Bishop of Oxford, 232, 277
Baker, Jonathan, Bishop of Fulham, 187, 268, 279
Baldwin of Exeter, Archbishop of Canterbury, 24

Ball, John, 182, 185, 239
Banwell, George, 142
Baptist Missionary Society, 152, 206
Barberi, Fr Dominic, 176-7
Barkworth, Dr Shadwell, 190-2
Baron, Rev George, 65
Battle Abbey, 27
Bazett family, 154
Becket, Thomas, Archbishop of Canterbury, 20
Bede, the Venerable, 5
Belbin, Peter, 76-7
Bell, Dr Andrew 162
Bell, Richard, 267
Benedict XVI, Pope, 187, 271
Benedictus de Eboraco, 28
Bennett, Joshua, 241
Berkshire Baptist Association, 207
Betjeman, John, 238. 255
Bickerdike, John, 153, 180-1
Binfield Heath Chapel, 1811, 196, 213
Birinus, St, 5-7, 232, 273
Blagrave, Sir John, 70
Blenkin, Frederick, 241
Blisset, Mr, 118
Blood, Col. Thomas, 80
Bluecoat School, 160
Boardman, Rev Mr, 159
Bodley, G F, 263
Bond, Mr, 131
Bone, John, Bishop of Reading, 247, 279
Bonifield, Abraham, 95, 281
Boteler, William, 39
Bottrill, John, 255
Boudry, William, 129
Boult, Fr Anthony, 267, 270
Bowhill, Allan, 268
Bowland, Fr Francis, 175
Bowyer, Lodovick, 68-9
Brent, Sir Nathaniel, 70

Bridge Hall (Brethren), 259-60
Brindley, Canon Brian, 187, 245, 267
Britain, Jonathan, 107, 115-26
British School, 121, 166-7
Broad Street Chapel, 79, 81, 97, 104, 163-4, 194, 200-5, 208-13, 265, 282
Brooke, Hubert, 154, 224, 227
Brown and Albury, 258
Brown, Bishop John, 250
Brown, David, 151
Brown, John Jenkyn, 198
Brownes (Caversham Court), 172-3
Bulmer, Richard, 212
Bunbury, Thomas, 78
Bunting, Jabez, 143
Bunyan, John, 81-5, 99, 102
Burdett, Clement, 61
Burgess, Thomas, Bishop of Salisbury, 237, 277
Burgeys, Lawrence, 31
Burnet, Gilbert, Bishop of Salisbury, 234-5, 277
Burnett, George, 97-8
Burton, Rev William, 65
Butler, Edward, 63, 65
Butterworth, Joseph, MP, 143
Cadogan, Jane, 163
Cadogan, William Bromley, 108-13, 137, 140-1, 147-8, 153, 159-69, 179
Calamy, Edmund, 80, 97
Calcot, 5-6
Calleva Atrebatum (Silchester), 1
Calverley, Henry, 238
Calvin, John & Calvinism, 53, 69, 78, 81, 140-1
Campion, St Edmund, 172
Canute, King, 7-8
Cardinal's Hat (inn), 59

Carey Baptist Church, 207, 259, 267, 285
Carey, William, 151-2
Castle and Falcon Inn, London, 152
Castle Street Congregational Chapel, 153, 164, 212-3, 265
Catholic Relief Acts, 174
Caversham, Lower, 2-3, 259
Caversham Bridge, 19, 33, 36, 264
Caversham Baptist Church, 207, 259
Caversham Heights Methodist Church, 264
Caversham Hill Chapel, 181, 183, 213
Cennick, John, 92, 98, 127-31,133, 145, 190
Cennick, Sally, 100, 128, 120-1
Central Evangelical Church, Reading, 267
Challoner, Bishop Richard, 173
Chapel of the Resurrection, 175
Charles I, King, 67, 69, 173
Charles II, King, 75, 77, 82, 89, 93, 173, 234
Christ Church, Whitley, 168, 202, 244, 253, 284
Christ the King, Reading (RC), 266
Christ Church School, New, Reading, 163, 166, 168, 253
Church Missionary Society (CMS), 152-5, 192
Church's Ministry among Jewish People (CMJ), 152, 156
Clacy, J B, 222
Clarke, Richard Martin, 155-6
Clement III, Pope, 21
Cluny Abbey, 10-12, 17, 21
Coale, Benjamin, 96
Coale, Joseph, 86-7, 89
Coale, Leonard, 96

Colborne, George, 211
Coley Mission Hall, 213
Coley, Reading, 166, 197, 258
Collett, Josiah, 95
Colley Chapel, 28
Compter, Reading, 107, 117-8
Cooper, Lewis, Mayor, 189
Cooper, William, 80
Copenhagen (horse), 157
Corfe Castle, 6
Cottrell, Stephen, Archbishop, 248-9, 271, 279
Cousins, W E, 153
Coventry, Giles, 42
Cowan, Dr, 209-10
Coxe, Leonard, 46. 57-8. 159
Cranmer, Thomas, Archbishop of Canterbury, 52, 54
Croft, Steven, Bishop of Oxford, 242, 278
Cromwell, Thomas, 17, 41, 46
Cudworth, William, 94, 141, 281
Curtis, Thomas, 85, 96
Curwen, Spedding, 212, 239
Cust, Arthur Purey, 238
Daniel, Bishop, 232, 273
Darby, John Nelson, 198
Darter, W S, 156-7, 252
Davenant, John, Bishop of Salisbury, 233, 276
Davis, C A, 207
Davis, Jonathan, 96
Davis, Thomas, 104-5, 109, 142, 205
Deans Farm, 2
Defoe, Daniel, 92
Denewulf, Bishop, 232, 274
Dils, Joan, 62-3
Ditchfield, P H, 186, 189, 257-60
Dixon, William Allen, 252
Domesday Book, 27
Doolittle, Samuel, 97

Dorchester-on-Thames, 5, 232, 243, 273
Douglas, Archibald, 163, 208-9, 2011
Downham, Peter, 268
Dudelsall, Sabaoth, 62
Dudley, Richard, 118, 120
Dudley, Robert, Earl of Leicester, 65
Dutson, Bruce, 270
Dyer, John, 152, 206
Ealfrith, Bishop, 232, 273
East India Company. 151
Edward I, King, 38
Edward the Confessor, King, 9, 16
Edward the Martyr, King, 6, 14, 27
Elfrida, Queen, 6-7
Elias, Abbot, 13, 22, 31
Elim Pentecostal Church, 258, 266
Elizabeth I, Queen, 48, 171-2
Elliott, David, 187, 201
Englefield, Sir Francis, 62, 171
English Martyrs Church, Reading (RC), 48, 264
Eton College, 78-9, 145
Everett, Thomas, 209
Eynon, John, 47, 49, 62
Eyre, John, 112, 153
Eyre, Joseph, 150, 180
Fairbairn, Gordon, 267
Faringdon, Abbot Hugh, 42-3, 45, 47-8, 57
Fifth Monarchists, 81-2
Finch's Buildings, 174-5
Fisher, John, Bishop of Salisbury, 162, 277
Fletcher of Madeley, John, 137, 140-1
Fletcher, Selena and Sophy, 155
Foley, Graham, Bishop of Reading, 246, 279

Ford, Simon, 73
Forster, William, MP, 165
Fosbery, Thomas, 136, 239
Fowler, Christopher, 74-5, 78-80, 84
Fox, Francis, 161
Fox, George, 88-9, 95-6, 99
Foxe, John, 51, 54-5, 58
Francis of Assisi, 35
French, Bishop Thomas Valpy, 153-4
Friar Street (New Street), 31, 37, 41, 163, 211, 216
Frith, John, 54-6
Fulford, Prof. Mike, 1
Gardiner, Captain Allen, 156
Garrett, Thomas, 53-4
Gauntlett, Henry, 181
George III, King, 117, 184
Giddings, Dr Philip, 248
Gilbert, curate, 28
Gillmor, F J C, 267
Glorious Revolution (1688), 91-2, 235
Goddarde, Katherine, 38
Goward, Charles, 211
Goodhart, Charles J, 149, 156, 182, 197, 222, 224, 239
Gordon, Samuel Clarke, 211-2
Gore, Charles, Bishop of Oxford, 241, 278
Gorham, George C, 178
Gosbrook Road Methodist Church, Caversham, 260
Graham, Olivia, Bishop of Reading, 249, 279
Grainger, Cecil, 182, 186, 239, 251, 254
Grange URC. Southcote, 265
Grant, Charles, 151
Great Exhibition of 1851, 193
Green, William, 180-1

Greyfriars Church, Reading, 32, 35-42, 155, 166, 182, 186, 188-92, 248, 251-3, 266-8
Greyfriars, Wardens, 38, 41-2
Griffiths, Venerable David, 250
Grosseteste, Robert, Bishop of Lincoln, 24-5
Grovelands Baptist Church, 207, 259-60
Halhead, Miles, 85
Hallum, Cardinal Robert, Bishop of Salisbury, 233, 275
Hallward, John, 108-9
Hampton, Master, 60
Harries, Lord Richard, Bishop of Oxford, 242, 248, 278
Hedde, Bishop, 232, 273
Henig, Martin, 5
Henry de Essex, 19
Henry I, 9, 12, 15, 18, 25, 29
Henry II, 15, 19-20, 24
Henry III, 33, 36
Henry VI, 44
Henry VIII, 13, 41, 43, 51, 57, 237
Heraclius, Patriarch of Jerusalem 24
Herbert, Edward, 71-2
Herman, Bishop, 233, 274
Hervey, James, 115
Hill, Bishop Mike, 250
Hill, Rowland, 110, 181
Hinton, John H, 206, 281-2
Hoare and Wheeler, 263
Holloway, John, 206
Holy Trinity, Cambridge, 112, 145
Holy Trinity, Reading, 184-8, 192, 245, 267-9, 271, 284
Honey, C. Robertson, 258
Honorius I (Pope), 5
Horton, Thomas, 212
Hosier's Lane Chapel, 104, 152, 206, 281

Howard, Francis, 257
Hubberthorn, Richard, 89
Hugh de Boves, Abbot,
Archbp. of Rouen, 13, 17-19
Hugh of Anjou, Abbot, 13, 20
Hulme, George, 184-5, 197
Hume, John, Bishop of
Salisbury, 234, 236-7, 277
Huntingdon, Selina Hastings,
Countess of, 104, 107, 109-10,
115, 137, 179-80
Huntley and Palmer, 216-7, 258
Inkpot Chapel, 142-3
Innocent II, Pope, 18
Innocent III, Pope, 22
Innocent IV, Pope, 25
Irvingites, 223, 227
Ives, Jeremiah, 82
James II, 91, 173-4, 234
James the Apostle, Saint, 15-16
Jane Seymour, Queen, 46
Jemmatt, Samuel, Mayor, 77
Jewel, John, Bishop of
Salisbury, 64, 234, 276
John, King, 16, 22, 24
John, Very Rev Jeffrey
Jones, Evan, 104
Juice, Thomas, 80-1, 97
Julian the Apostate, 3
Katherine Parr, Queen, 52
Kay, Arnold Innes, 155
Kempe, Charles Eamer, 256-7
Kendrick, John, 71
Kent, Thomas, 64
Kenton, Mary, 82
Keswick Letter, 154, 227
Key, Mark, 84
Kinchin, Chas. 98. 100, 127-8
King's Arms, Reading, 174
King's College, Cambridge,
140, 145
King's Road Baptist Chapel,
206-7, 266
Kingsbury, Canon Richard, 267

Kirk, Kenneth Escott, Bishop
of Oxford, 242-3, 278
Knell, Eric, Bishop of Reading,
144-5, 278
Knollys, Sir Francis, 65
La Tournelle, Mrs, 169-70
Lamboll, George, 88
Lamboll, William, 96
Lancaster, Joseph, 161-2
Langton, Stephen, Archbishop
of Canterbury, 24
Lathbury, John, 39
Laud, William, Archbishop of
Canterbury, 67-73, 98, 144, 234
Leakey, Harry, 154-5
Leakey, Louis, 155
Left Leggs, The, 211
Legg, Ven. Richard Wickham,
243
Legg, William, 202, 209-11, 213
Leland, John, 33, 39-41
Leominster Priory, 13-14, 23
Les Andelys, 16
Leverech, Peter, 30-1
Leveva, Abbess, 27
Lewes Priory, 11, 17-18, 20, 36
Life Spring Church, 267
Livingstone, David, 155
Lollards, 44-5, 51, 62
London Missionary Society
(LMS), 112, 151, 208
London Street Primitive
Methodist Chapel, 215-6, 260,
265, 286
London, Dr John, 41, 46
Longuet, Fr Jean-Baptiste, 175
Luther, Martin, 23, 57
Macalister, Mrs, 164
Mackarness, John F, Bishop of
Oxford, 252, 255, 258, 277
Mackenzie, Bishop Charles
Frederick, 155
Malcolm, Edward, 91, 269
Malmesbury, William of, 10, 12

Mangan, WC & J H, 264
Marsh, William. 112, 159,161, 163
Mary I, Queen, 53, 62
Matilda, Empress, 15, 19
May, Isle of, 23
McKechnie, John, 252, 267
Morgan, Selwyn, 267
Morris, Frank, 226, 229
Morris, Joseph, 31, 24, 221-30
Morris, Thomas, 221
Morris, Violet, 221, 229-30
Morris, William Rickards, 264
Mossop, Daniel, 211
Murphy O'Connor, Cardinal Cormac, 269
National Schools, 162, 167
Neale Joseph, 161
New Testament Church of God, 267
Newman, John Henry, 177-8
Newton, John, 110, 115, 137, 180
Nicholas de Whiteley, 28
Nicholls, John, 160
Noon, Thomas, 104, 163, 208
North, Leslie, 125
Notley Abbey, Bucks, 33
Nottidge, Ms, 225
Nowers, Edward, 131
Oda, Archbishop, 233, 274
Ordinariate, 187, 271, 179
Osmund, St, Bishop of Salisbury, 233, 274
Our Lady and St Anne, Caversham (RC), 34, 264
Our Lady of Peace, Earley (RC), 266
Over, Luke, 4
Owen, Robert, 209-10
Owen, Ven Walter, 155
Oxford Road Methodist Churches, 216, 260, 266
Page, John K, 190, 267-8

Page, William, 70
Palmer, Julins, 51, 58-61, 64, 159
Parham, Arthur Groom, Bishop of Reading, 243, 278
Passionist Order, 177
Paul VI, Pope, 48
Payne, Canon William, 241, 252
Peckham, John, Archbishop of Canterbury
Penn, William, 90, 99
Perkins, Francis, 172
Peter, Prior, 11
Phelps, Ven William, 184-92, 198, 241
Philip II Augustus, King of France, 22
Pordage, John, 73-5, 78
Prideaux, John, 78
Prince, Henry James, 224-8
Pritchard, John, Bishop of Oxford, 242, 278
Propagation of the Gospel, Society for the (SPG), 239
Proprietary chapels, 147, 179-80, 185-8, 251, 270
Proud, Andrew, Bishop of Reading, 249, 279
Providence Chapel, 259, 282, 285
Pugin, Augustus Welby, 176, 187, 251
Quaker meeting-houses, Church St &Sims Court, 90
Queen's Road Wesleyan Methodist, 214, 286
Raikes, Robert, 159
Rance, John, 82
Randall, James, Bishop of Reading, 242-3. 278
Randall, Ven James, 189, 242
Rankin, Thomas, 139
Ravenscroft, Frederick, 264-5
Reading Museum, 2-3, 9, 16

Reading School, 46, 57, 64, 67, 69, 71-2, 153-4, 158-9, 215, 269
Recusants, 171, 173
Redman, James, 154
Restall, Gerald, 268
Resurrection, Community of the, 241
Richard II, Abbot, 13, 23
Richards, Bishop John, 269, 279
Richards, Silvester, 94, 132, 141
Richards, William, 92
Rigby, Richard, 105
Ring, Dr Thomas, 148, 180
Risby, Richard, 57
Robert de Sigello, Bishop of London, 19
Robert of Burgate, Abbot, 13, 23
Robert, Friar, 40
Roberts, Daniel, 82, 84
Roberts, James, 84
Roger, Abbot, 13, 20
Rogers, Travers Guy, 267
Romaine, William, 110, 115, 137
Romanis, William, 238
Ross, John, 153
Ross, Thomas, 211
Rugge, John, 47-8
Rundle, John C, 190, 267
Russell, Ven. Norman, 249
Ryland, John, 152
Sacred Heart Church, Reading (RC), 266
Salem Chapel, 181, 195, 201, 205, 215-6, 282
Salthouse, Thomas, 85
Salvation Army, 213, 226-7
Samuel, Dr David, 268, 270
Sandall, Arthur, 120
Schefford, Peter, 38, 41-2
Scholefield, Professor James, 149

Scott, Joseph, 142
Sewell, Herbert, 211
Shenton, Brian, 268
Sherbourne, Prior John, 53-4
Sherman, James, 153, 180-3, 206, 208, 212-3
Sherwood, Martha, 169-70
Shoar, James, 142
Shoemaker, Christopher, 45, 51
Sigeric, Archbishop, 233, 274
Silchester, 1
Simeon Trustees, 149-50
Simeon, Edward, 145, 149, 161
Simeon, Charles, 98, 112, 115, 140, 144-57, 159-61
Simeon, John, MP, 145, 157
Simeon, Richard (father), 145, 147
Simeon, Richard (son), 145
Simmonds, Thomas, 154
Simon, Abbot, 13, 22-3
Slade, Dr Cecil, 7, 10, 30
Smith, John, 67
Smith, Mrs Anne, 141-2
Smyth-Pigott, Hugh, 227-8
Soane, Sir John, 145
Soole, Seymour H, 190-1
South American Missionary Society, 156
Spaxton, Somerset, 224-5, 229-30
Spurr, S W, 198
St Agnes, Silver St &Whitley, 223, 263-5
St Andrew's Presbyterian Church, London Road, 260, 266, 285
St Andrew's, Caversham Heights, 264
St Anne on the Bridge, 32-3
St Aubyn, James Piers, 252, 254-5
St Bartholomew's, Earley, 258, 263, 284

St Edmund's Chapel, 31
St George's, Tilehurst, 259, 268
St Giles, Reading, 29-31, 47-9, 62, 65, 89, 92, 106-13, 115, 118, 137, 147, 159, 153, 155, 160, 164-5, 179-87, 194-5, 198, 200-1, 216, 223, 236, 239, 245-6, 251-5, 258, 263-70, 281-3
St James' Church, Reading (RC), 164-5, 175-6, 195, 199, 201, 204, 270-1, 285
St James, hand of, 15-17, 47
St John & St Stephen, Reading, 150, 155, 164, 182, 194, 200, 241, 251-2, 254, 265-7, 283-5
St John's School, Newtown, 163, 166
St John's, Lr Caversham, 259
St Laurence, Reading, 30-1, 33, 57, 62-5, 71, 73, 92, 99, 112, 129, 145, 161, 163, 182, 185, 191, 202, 233, 239, 283
St Luke's, Reading, 254-9, 283
St Mark's, Kensington Road, 256, 263
St Mary and All Saints School, 163, 166
St Mary's, Castle St, vii, 40, 83, 112, 128, 147, 149, 154-6, 164-6, 179-84, 188, 190, 192, 209, 212, 218, 222, 227, 237, 240, 245, 251, 269-70, 282
St Mary's, Reading, 6-7, 27-9, 74, 78-9, 161, 164, 166, 179, 186, 192, 194, 197, 239, 243-4, 246-7, 258, 281-2
St Michael, Tilehurst, 31, 202
St Paul's Presbyterian Church, York Road, Reading, 260, 264
St Paul's, Lower Whitley, Reading, 263
St Peter's (RC), Marlow, 17
St Peter's, Caversham, 31-3, 173, 195, 202, 268

St Peter's, Earley, 195, 202
St Saviour's, Reading, 258, 266, 283
St William of York, Reading (RC), 263
Stallwood, Spencer S, 223, 263
Stamper, Thomas, 209
Stanshawe, John, 39
Starky, Samuel, 224, 227
Stennett, Edward, 83
Stephen, Jonathan, 67
Stewart, George, 212
Story, John, 95
Stubbs, William, Bishop of Oxford, 241, 277
Sturges, Charles, 169
Sturgion, John, 81
Summers, Malcolm, vii, 38, 202, 212, 252, 264
Sunday Schools, 164
Sutton, Audley, 192
Sutton, Martin Hope, 192
Sutton, Richard, 192
Swithun, Bishop, 232, 273
Talbot, Mrs Sarah, 109-10, 147
Talbot, Ven Edward, 236
Talbot, Rev William, 106, 109-10, 115-26, 137, 236
Talbot, William, Bishop of Salisbury, 235-6, 277
Talfourd, Thomas, MP, 105
Thorne, George, Mayor, 79
Thorne. Abbots John I & II, 43-4
Tilehurst Independent Chapel, 196, 201, 212
Toker's Green Chapel, 212
Torrent, Samuel, 92
Tovi, standard-bearer (Tofig), 8
Trench, Francis, 182, 239, 241, 251-2
Trinity College, Cambridge, 149

Trinity Congregational Church, 165, 211, 213, 282
Tubbs, George, 182, 239-41, 269
Turner, Daniel, 103
Ufton Court, 172-3
Universities' Mission to Central Africa (UMCA), 155
Vachell, Thomas, 172
Valpy, Dr Richard, 57. 153. 158-9, 161-2, 169
Venn, Henry, 110, 115
Victoria Hall, 255
Wait, Daniel, 124
Walker, Dominic, Bishop of Reading, 247-8, 279
Walter, Hubert, Bishop of Salisbury, 233, 274
Waltham Abbey, 8
Ward, Seth, Bishop of Salisbury, 235, 276
Waterhouse, Alfred, 218-9, 258
Waterhouse, John, 142-3, 214, 281
Watkins, Abraham, 181
Welham, Mark, 83
Wesley, Charles, 69, 103, 124, 138-9, 214
Wesley, John, 69, 94, 98-101, 109, 127-44, 148, 187, 214
West, Frederick, 197
Wheble, James, 176
White, Sir Thomas, 67
White, William, 253
Whitefield, George, 54, 69, 101, 104, 128-9, 139, 214
Whitewood, Thomas, 104, 106, 281
Whitley Methodist Hall, 263, 266, 287
Wilberforce, Mr, 108
Wilberforce, Samuel, Bishop of Oxford, 186, 189, 197, 201-3, 238-41, 247, 251, 277

Wild, Eric, Bishop of Reading, 244-7, 253, 278
Wilkinson, John, 95-6
William de Lincoln, 38
William de Okam, 39
William Goldore, 31
William I, Abbot, 12, 20
William I, King, 9
William III, King, 91, 235
William Longespee, Eral of Salisbury, 22
William, Prince (d. 1120), 9
William, Prince (d. 1156), 19
Wilmot, Kezia, 101
Windebank, Sir Francis, 67
Wood, John, 212
Woodford, J R, Bishop of Ely, 189-90
Woodman, W H, 189, 252
Woodyer, Henry, 252-3
Wycliffe Baptist Church, 207, 259, 285
Wycliffe, John, 44
Yates, Samuel W, 238
Yorke, Bishop James, 106
Young, W B, 159
Zoar Strict Baptist Chapel, 259-60, 285

Printed in Dunstable, United Kingdom